THE Quest

FOR FAMILY

THE Quest FOR FAMILY

JESSICA CLANCY
A Human Interest Story

ENDORSEMENTS

In a society where Satan is increasingly attacking and devaluing the family unit, this book shows the journey and pursuit to overcome generational chaos while constructing a family that is based on the Word of God, displays the character of Christ, and is led by the counsel and power of the Holy Spirit.

Robert L. Williams, D. Min.
President of MMM, Inc.
Author of Not on my Watch: Practical Principles for
Planting, Pastoring, and Preaching the Word of God

Not only do the author and I share the same parallel experiences with our European travels but we also have the same appreciation for hard work and perseverance. We accomplished the unattainable when no one else believed in us. I am honored that the Newman Castle will represent the author's lifelong fantasy of achieving the family she never had.

Mike Newman. Creator and Owner of Newman's
Castle and Bakery. https://newmanscastle. com/

Jessica Clancy has a remarkable story. She was frequently abandoned, berated, and even abused by an immature mother and by two out of three stepdads. She went through so much pain! But she did not give up. She did not become bitter. She did not become a victim. She persevered by God's grace.

In this book, Jessica looks back on her life and tells her story. She is a wonderful storyteller. At times, you will not want to put the book down. The story is poignant and powerful. There is honesty and humility. Your heart will go out to her. But you will be so encouraged by the grace of God in her life, and the grace of God poured out through her life to others.

Amazing story, amazing grace.

Jeff Wells
Senior Pastor at WoodsEdge Community Church
and Author of Love Revealing the Heart of God
Love Jesus / Journey Together / Bring Hope

When I first met Jessica almost ten years ago, I knew she needed to write a book and share her story.

Her story shows the hard work and steps she took to heal from such traumas as abandonment, rejection, and attachment issues.

Her story shows how God was always with her, how God transformed and healed her just as He can transform and heal others if you just believe.

In her story, she used my "no send forgiveness letter" as a tool to aid in healing and releasing the pain in lieu of obtaining God's blessings in her own life.

While reading her story, it was as if we were sitting, talking, and drinking coffee as she recited her innermost personal secrets.

I highly recommend this book.

Rosalinda Orta MA, NCC, LPC-S
Kingdom Dwelling Christian Counseling
I give permission for her to use no send forgiveness letter.

Author Jessica Clancy allows the past to remind her that everything is going to be alright.

As Jessica shares her story of God holding her through the darkness of her childhood, it is clear God held her soul and brought her through. As a result, He is allowing her testimony and accomplishments to be used to help others who may have wondered the same thing in their desperation: Will I make it? Can I make it? Just as God uses the song "Be Alright" to minister to others in dark places, this book may speak to others in comparison.

It Is a perfect reminder of God growing the author's faith and our faith through all the chaos to see how his plan works out everything for his good in the end

> *Sean Cook/ Co-writer /Producer: "Be Alright"*
> *Instagram: _Seancook*
> *And*
> *Nina Cook, Vocal Coach*
> *Instrumental Guitar Teacher*
> *Instagram: nina_vocals*

Jessica,

I had the honor of reading your rough draft in the making as you shared with me your secrets. This sentence alone is worth your book: "I pray God will use my life experience to minister to your soul to redeem your life." This happened for me. THANK YOU

> *Charlene*
> *Retired Nurse, 26 years of service*

"Jessica shares a tremendous story of God's redemption from a very broken, abuse-filled upbringing. Anyone suffering from abuse at any stage in life would be encouraged and strengthened by reading this incredible story. God bless you and your family."

Fred Sabins, Lay Counselor (Faith Bible Church)

Truth be told and God willing, if you've lived long enough and have had the good fortune of experiencing life in all its fullness… the "good," the "bad," and everything in between, you too would have quite a story to tell.

Such is the case with Jessica, who was born into what many would consider a dysfunctional environment. She had to fight and endure many hardships in her young life only to experience rejection after rejection in pursuit of the loving home many of us take for granted.

From child abuse and sexual molestation at the hands of people who should have taken care of her to traveling almost the entire continent of Europe, she managed to overcome all these adversities to become the loving wife, mother, and professional that only God's love and perseverance could deliver.

Her story is filled with twists and turns that only through His grace and mercy could she have ever overcome all these obstacles and become the champion that God has ordained for her life since the beginning of time.

Jerome Durán
Team Leader: Transformed Living
Community Home Group
WoodsEdge Church, Spring, TX

A beautiful story about what only God can do and his work of redemption in a broken world. He is steadfast.

"As for you, you were dead in your transgressions and sins, in which you used to live when you followed the ways of this world…but God, being rich in mercy, because of his great love with which He loved us, even when we were dead in our trespasses, made us alive together with Christ-by grace we have been saved…." Ephesians 2:1-5 NIV

This is a portrait of beauty that overshadows the brokenness of people and relationships and a full display of God's process of healing wounds that were opened by those who trespassed against her from her childhood. Seeing Jessica now, my sister in Christ and friend, is like seeing a glimpse of God's glory, mercy, and goodness. I know He was there in every moment, loving and walking with her through it all, but with the same love, yearning for those who caused her harm and wanting them to turn to him.

Sara Ortiz, sister in Christ and Community Group Shepherd.

Es una bella historia acerca de lo que solo Dios puede hacer, su trabajo de redención en medio de un mundo roto, Él es constante.

En otro tiempo ustedes estaban muertos n sus transgresiones y pecados, en los cuales andaban conforme a los poderes de este mundo… Pero Dios, que es rico en misericordia, por su gran amor a nosotros, nos dio vida con Cristo, aun cuando estábamos muertos en pecados, nos dio vida juntamente con Cristo- por gracia ustedes han sido salvados! Efesios 2:1-5 NIV

Este libro es un retrato de la belleza opacando al quebrantamiento en las personas y las relaciones, y una demostración cargada del proceso de Dios para sanar heridas que fueron abiertas por aquellos que pecaron en contra de ella desde su niñez. Cuando veo a Jessica ahora, mi hermana en Cristo y amiga, veo un destello de la gloria, piedad y bondad de Dios. Yo sé que Él estaba ahí en cada momento, amándola y caminando con ella a través de todo; pero con el mismo amor, anhelando por aquellos que le hicieron daño y deseando que regresaran a Él.

Sara Ortiz, hermana en Cristo y líder de estudio bíblico.

The Quest for Family is the real-life testimony of Jessica Clancy's ultimate journey through the foster/adoption world. Not one to shy away from hard work, she has demonstrated that personal sacrifice together with community can make a world of difference for orphans. There is no contribution too big or too small!

A Quite Extraordinary Story!

Can't put it down at times.

Marlena Cantu
Foster/Adopt Home Developer
Child Placing Agency

In my career as a chiropractor over the last 20 years, a few of my patients have shared some amazing stories related to the healing of spinal conditions like scoliosis that Jessica was diagnosed with. I have too many patients, however, who suffer their entire life with scoliosis, so the reading of that part of her story (of miraculous healing) was a wonderful testament for me and a reminder that divine healing is real. Reading this book also takes me back to my undergraduate days when I was a psychology major and working with high-risk kids through the University of Houston's "Victims Resource Institute." The institute worked diligently to help high-risk kids that were victims of physical and mental abuse and other hardships often associated with drug and alcohol dependency. Too many of these children and teens I worked with were unable to overcome their negative life experiences and circumstances. Thankfully there were children that were resilient and were able to overcome seemly insurmountable obstacles, much like Jessica Clancy.

From the study of psychology, strong relationships are the foundation of children's resilience. Without these foundations, too many people are lost. But to quote the late Wayne Dyer "With God, all things are possible." In Jessica Clancy's case, her relationship with God was truly her saving grace.

A Truly Inspiring Story!

Timothy D. Runnels, D.C.
NORTH HOUSTON SPINE & SPORTS MEDICINE
5643 Treaschwig Rd.
Spring, Texas 77373
Ph: (281) 443.1287 Fax: (281) 443.1288

I met Jessica on Fiverr and started creating her chapter summaries as we worked together.

I'm really overwhelmed. This is a lifetime experience for me. I have digitalized your life like a movie and can experience that only because of you. I'm grateful for that.

You are really a true inspiration.

Suman Dutta
Graphic Artist, Animator, and Musician
Kolkata, India

DEDICATION

To my husband, Adam. I would never have been able to live out God's vision for our lives without your support, which includes writing this book and sharing my story. Thank you for enveloping me in your God-like heart as we endeavor to help others. I can't wait to partner with you as we discover God's next step for us!

To my kids, who spent hours listening to me think out loud. You helped me process my story and brainstorm ideas for the book. Your support, especially during our long road trips, helped me write a book that, hopefully, will touch many people.

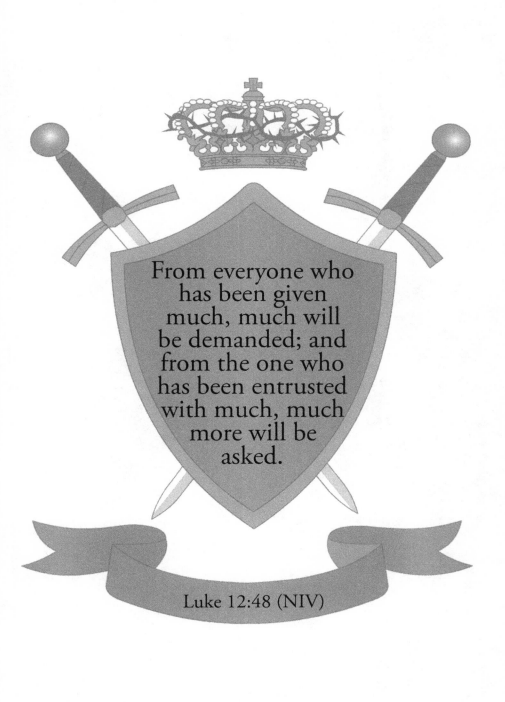

From everyone who has been given much, much will be demanded; and from the one who has been entrusted with much, much more will be asked.

Luke 12:48 (NIV)

PROLOGUE

*M*ost every little girl dreams of being a princess, of having someone love and treasure her. This story is about a little girl who walked through the dark ages of her childhood. She was subject to the will of others.

Escaping into the vastness of unknown territory, her arduous journey through self-actualization and enlightenment helped heal the wounds.

As she began to experience spiritual renewal, she searched for the family she never had. She learned how to fill the void. In the end, she found acceptance through the kind people who surrounded her.

This story shows how God can transform a person's life. God helped the girl to find love and acceptance and build the home she wanted. Little by little, she saw progress.

Perhaps you are on a quest. Perhaps you desire a family. The Quest for Family can take you on a road to redemption and healing. It can teach you that light defeats darkness and that perseverance fosters hope.

CONTENTS

Part One:

GETTING PAST THE PAST

Chapter 1
THE BRUSHSTROKES
TO A MASTERPIECE

*J*essica Clancy is a first-time author. Her book, *The Quest for Family*, describes her long— often painful, yet encouraging— journey to find the family she never had growing up.

She has worn many hats throughout her life: daughter, granddaughter, world traveler, wife, daughter-in-law, mother, foster mom, dietitian, hairdresser, mentor, church member, facilitator of marriage classes and Bible studies, camping club enthusiast, friend, and confidant. Her story highlights God's faithfulness in every circumstance and shows that He stretches us in ways that honor Him and bless others.

Jessica and her husband, Adam, recently celebrated 15 years of marriage. They have two beautiful children, one biological and one adopted. They strive to teach their kids about the world, with its fascinating people and cultures, as they travel and learn about history. They stress the importance of family, tradition, and faith, three topics dear to Jessica's heart.

Jessica and Adam helped facilitate a marriage class at their church, called ReEngage. They led a corresponding small group that showed couples how to strengthen their relationships. They also co-led a study on Peter Scazzero's book, *Emotionally Healthy Relationships*, which teaches people how to communicate and resolve conflict in a positive, productive way.

The couple was part of an expedited pilot program that helped families like themselves attend classes and receive a foster license as they opened their home to several child placements. When time permits, they volunteer with various children's programs, including sponsored foster programs. They also teach Sunday School classes for kids.

Jessica is a registered dietitian employed with a large, internationally recognized dialysis company. She finds great satisfaction in helping patients live longer, healthier lives as they enjoy their families and transition through a life-changing diagnosis of end-stage renal disease and becoming dialysis dependent.

She helped create and promote a "Bee Happy at Home" t-shirt campaign for patients. She teaches patients the importance of dialysis from home and helps them recover much-needed time with their families. Her efforts resulted in recognition for her clinic and the region, reminding people that home dialysis is a viable option for many individuals. She promotes teamwork and celebrates family values at home and elsewhere.

Jessica's experience as a dietitian includes working with families and women. She teaches them how to promote good health habits, avoid illness, and manage serious conditions like diabetes, gestational diabetes, kidney disease, hypertension, and obesity. She has worked at the world-renowned Medical Center Trauma Hospital in Houston, Texas, and at various county outpatient clinic settings.

Jessica graduated Magna Cum Laude with a Master of Arts degree from the Academy of Nutrition and Dietetics (AND). She is a certified and registered dietitian who completed a rigorous 1200-hour internship program.

Jessica obtained a cosmetology license in high school and started working professionally at the age of 17; She put herself through college working as a cosmetologist at a Fortune 500 company and salon located in Houston, Texas. During her 18 years as a hairdresser, she completed more than a million dollars in lifetime total sales when haircuts averaged $18-$50. Jessica maintained a 70 percent "clientele request" despite her fluctuating college schedule. As a cosmetologist, Jessica learned how to set goals and persevere. She completed the workshop "Seven Habits of

Highly Effective People," which helped her learn coping skills to combat anxiety and manage her time wisely.

Eventually, Jessica earned a Bachelor of Science degree from the University of Houston. She also studied Business at Sam Houston University and received grants to live with a family in Puebla, Mexico. There, she studied international business.

At one point, Jessica was accepted into the British Universities of North America Club (BUNAC). She traveled to 17 countries and lived with several families and hostels over a six-month period. She worked in London at Selfridges on Oxford Street.

Jessica continues to look for opportunities to help people and believes in giving back whenever she can. She has volunteered at fundraising activities, such as the "MS150 Bike Ride to Austin," the "Kidney Walk," and the "Love Fosters Hope" walk to support foster kids. She became a registered organ donor after witnessing a live kidney transplant and heart surgery. She donates blood as a tribute to those who previously gave her life-saving blood. Jessica and her family sponsor two children through Compassion and Hope for India.

Life didn't come easily for Jessica, which is why she is grateful and motivated to bless others. God used events in her life to create a masterpiece, with skilled brushstrokes that attest to His love and wisdom. Today, she sees how each stroke contributed to a beautiful picture that includes a family and a heart of grace, despite the obstacles and setbacks she suffered. This is her story of faith, strength, perseverance, and forgiveness. It is a story of hope and a childhood dream of finding love. It is a story of choices and a journey toward love and acceptance.

This book is not intended to tell you which religion you should embrace or which belief is superior. It is meant to be a reflection of Jessica's faith, which brought her through trials, questions, and healing.

This book is not intended to tell you how your family should look. It is intended to serve as an example of hope based on Jessica's values and the desires of her heart.

She hopes to help people understand that not everyone finds family in the traditional way, and through perseverance, hard work, and acceptance, anything is possible.[1]

<hr />

1   According to statista.com, there are 83.9 million families in the U.S., with an average of three children in each. In 2020, the marriage rate was 5.1 per 1,000 people, which decreased from 9.8 marriages per 1,000 people in 1990. As of 2019, there were 750,000 divorces, with 2.9 divorces per 1,000 people. There are more divorces between the lowest and highest economic levels. We don't know the struggles people and kids endure. We don't know why someone's marriage is failing. Jessica says, "I want to challenge and encourage people. Our families, whether traditional or nontraditional, are the future of this country. Our attitudes and decisions impact all of us. Find ways to serve. Mentor others. See the needs around you and offer a helping hand. Our families and world will be a better place by lightning someone's load."

Chapter 2
LET'S MEET!

HUMBLE BEGINNINGS
SHAPED MY LIFE

*O*was a child, sitting on the platform of a stone-cold, three-tiered cement block stair step, facing the open, blue sky. *Will someone rescue me?* I wondered as I stared off into the billowing, white clouds. I had just completed my ballet class and was sent on my way to wait for my mom or someone else to pick me up and take me home. What seemed like hours passed as the day turned to dusk. I wondered if anyone would come.

In many respects, that moment shaped my thinking. Throughout my life, I have battled feelings of fear, abandonment, and insecurity. Maybe you, too, have struggled with fear and anxiety. There is hope. I'm proof of that truth.

CAN YOU RELATE?

No matter how you have been hurt, know that God has a purpose and a plan; he will not waste your pain. If you stay faithful and believe, He will rescue you. He will take the old experiences with their bad memories and replace them with something new and good. Your sorrows can be your song to help others overcome.

Let me introduce myself. I am a lady from the South; I am Texas born and raised. Even though I was born in Texas, I have traveled and lived in many places. I was born in Dallas, and Texas has been my home for most of my life.

I am like you. I suspect that you can relate to one aspect of my life's journey. We are no different; we have our own struggles to bear.

I have known for many years that I have been called to tell my story. During my first career as a hairdresser, I would share parts of my life with my clients to either guide them on their path or explain who I was. People would always ask, "How did you endure so many hard things? How did you turn out to be normal?"

Many of those people also mentored and influenced me. They have reminded me to share my story and help others. Later, an elder in the church prophesied that I would write a book about my life, and many others have either confirmed or suggested the same, reminding me of this plan God had for my life.

THERE'S PURPOSE
IN THE PAIN

My struggles, pain, sorrow, loneliness, near-death accidents, travels, and "ah ha" moments have pointed to God's light and grace. Repeatedly, I have seen God's outstretched hand reaching out in the storm, bringing me to safety. He taught me how to cope with tumultuous events. He helped me grow. He showed me how to repair the wounded places, allowing me to move forward.

I have learned to overcome my menial beginnings and rise above dysfunction. I have become an educated, successful individual who contributes to society and helps others.

I hope my story can touch you where you are at this moment. I pray that it will speak to your heart and let you know you are not alone. I trust that you will know that God loves you very deeply—and so do I.

God has brought me through incredible pain so I can speak to your heart and wrap you in his love so you can feel His warm almighty touch. He wants you to know that you are not alone.

It's ok to cry; I did as I composed this story. I cried oh so many times! Never let anyone tell you that you cannot cry, as it can be healing and cleansing as we process how we feel about things that happen to us. God holds our tears, and one day we will know that none of them were ever shed in vain. They are like snowflakes, each carrying their own shape, symbolic of our pain.

FINDING HOPE
AND HEALING

Find strength, knowing that God created beauty out of nothingness. He created you for an almighty purpose! Seek God and ask Him what your purpose is. I promise He will show you.

Ok, let me get past these introductions so we can get into the story. I will describe my hardships and explain what I learned. I will share the light in the midst of darkness and credit the people that brought me through the trials. I believe in miracles. I believe in prophecies, special words from God that provide guidance and encouragement. I want you to know how to have hope and find miracles in your own life. I pray that God will use my life's experiences to minister to your soul to redeem your life. Know that God has brought you here for a reason!

I have changed the names to protect the identity of each person and help me share my story the way I remember it.

My life has been full of obstacles and miracles, as I have overcome difficulties. God saved me. As you read my story, think about God's work in your life. How has He saved you? As you read about my miracles, ask God to remind you of your own miracles. Consider the times when life could have been so much worse, but God lifted you up and protected you in the storm.

As you read my story, I pray that God encourages you and helps you to endure. I know that looking back can be challenging, but God can speak to you in those moments. Sometimes God protects us by allowing pain to keep us from much worse things that could have a longer, more detrimental impact on our life. Oh, the joy when we get to heaven and see all the events that occurred, realizing how God protected us, using every experience to prove his love.

I have a great memory and can recall events that were deeply rooted in my heart and soul. My mother was a great "picture taker," and so am I. I can still vividly see the pictures, images, and memories as I walk through my timeline, which only confirmed that my story needed to be shared to help others.

I used to write letters, which are being used as a template for part of my story. Despite various traumas and setbacks, I have always used my memories to push forward in life. I have tried to document events as well as I could.

Chapter 3
MY LIFE WASN'T
SUPPOSED TO HAPPEN

FORMED IN MY
MOTHER'S WOMB

*M*y mother's name, Jo, means "adventure loving, free or freedom." She was a bit of a free spirit, as she would call herself. She did not like to follow the rules and was very selfish; to this day, that has not always helped her succeed in life but has only hurt her. Some of her negative character traits may have been, in part, due to her childhood and upbringing. My mother's mom, my grandmother, did the best she could, losing her mom at a young age herself. She tried her best to care for my mother even after fleeing from her husband and leaving her daughter behind, reconnecting years later after remarrying.

Anyway, my mom had a choice. We all do, and those choices pave our future and affect our dreams and desires.

I was conceived when my mom went out to party one night late in November or December 1971. She crashed a Polish wedding party because she did not know anyone there. She met my biological dad that night and had a one-night fling with him, telling him she could not have children. Clearly, she was wrong.

My mom once told me she knew she would get pregnant that night; she wanted a child of her own, someone to love her for who she was.

"CHANCE" ENCOUNTERS

My biological dad's name is "Warrick," which means "strong leader." My grandma's name is GG, and she met my dad when he came to pick up my mother for their second date. This moment was important because my grandmother had a profound impact on my dad— 35 years later! With God, there are no "chance encounters." He sees the end from the beginning, and He is working everything together for His glory.

My mom's pregnancy was plagued by a serious case of illness, possibly the flu. She had a high temperature, threw up, and experienced a loss of fluid; eventually, she went to the doctor. He said he was surprised she had not spontaneously aborted the baby. My mom told me this story several times, suggesting that she really wanted to have a child. She had been a heavy smoker, but she chose to quit during her pregnancy. It was a gift of selflessness for me.

In the womb, I was rocked gently as I started to connect with my mother. We do know from research that the connection between mother and child begins early, as babies learn to kick, drink, and grow. Some babies die; their spirit rises to be with the one God, the Creator who gave them life and numbered their days. I had been given life. But what was my destiny?

MARRIAGE AND DECEIT

During the era when my mom was carrying me, ladies were meant to be married. It was uncommon to be pregnant and unmarried, and many people told my mom to have an abortion. She was considered a disgrace to society, and people shunned her until she got married.

My mom insisted that she wanted me. When she knew she was beyond the first trimester, she told my dad she was pregnant. He reminded her that she said she couldn't get pregnant. He had moved on and was now engaged; in fact, his fiancé was at his side when my mom made that call. He was in complete denial. He had been married before, but he had never fathered a child.

Knowing my parents, I imagine that they had a loud dispute on the phone and then went their separate ways, as if the problem of one innocent little being would just disappear. Eventually, my mom married when she was still pregnant with me.

I will call this man "Clancy," as this is my maiden name and the name I choose to use as an author. He was a normal, loving, and kind man and was considered upright in society. He had a job and a son from a previous marriage. Even though my mom was pregnant by another man, he chose to love her, and he showed her empathy, grace, and acceptance. He was proud to take her and the baby she carried as his own. His only son cradled me when I was a baby and looked after me. He demonstrated brotherly love and protection. It was good for my mom to have someone really love her, someone who could offer her a secure future. But she threw it all away.

One Christmas, at a party at their house, my mom had an affair with one of Clancy's work associates, and Clancy caught them! As kind as he was, Clancy tried to forgive my mom. He tried to write it off as a bad decision, possibly linked to the elements of the party that evening. But my mom eventually packed her bags, bundled me up, and hit the road with this strange man, who became my second father.

RUNNING FRIVOLOUSLY

*H*er escape was not warranted, and not welcomed, as my mom imposed on her younger sister, who was living in Colorado.

We arrived at an odd time of the night as my mom demanded she let us stay. I was less than two years old at the time. This was my introduction to an aunt who later shared this story, a guarded aunt who attempted to shelter my safety.

My aunt knew my mom was married, and not to the person who stood beside her on the doorstep. They had arrived at an obscene hour of the night after driving many hours from Magnolia, outside of Houston. It's as if I could hear my aunt saying, "Jo, go back home. What are you doing?" Sigh. My mom was a rule breaker.

I later found out that my mom had used a form of birth control that caused permanent damage to her female reproductive system. She had to have a hysterectomy. Although I wanted siblings, she was no longer able to bear children. She had not loved Clancy, and she quickly transitioned into another relationship, which became abusive. Life became increasingly difficult.

Looking back, I believe that God had a plan, and things unfolded for a purpose. However, that didn't free me from terrible loneliness and a constant yearning for siblings.[2]

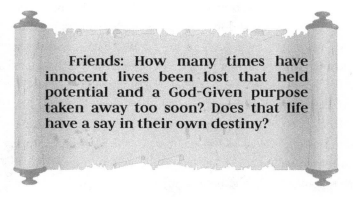

Friends: How many times have innocent lives been lost that held potential and a God-Given purpose taken away too soon? Does that life have a say in their own destiny?

---

2   If this chapter touched you and you would like more information to help on your own *Quest*, see page 313, **Housing, Food, Family Support,** page 314, **Pregnancy Prevention,** and page 315, **Unwanted Pregnancy and Adoption.**

Chapter 4
THE MEAN MAN

TRYING TO ESCAPE
THE MADNESS

*M*y mom's second husband was from Germany. She had met him when he was working in Houston, and later, his company transferred him to Germany, then Bermuda. My mom married him in part for the thrilling prospect of travel, I believe.

I remember a little green racecar I peddled at the park and eating ice cream cones that melted and oozed, dripping on the pavement below. I had a trundle bed with a little ladder I climbed to reach my bed. A little music box chimed lullabies as I drifted to sleep each night. I remember going to annual fundraisers where ladies made, sold, and wore red silk poppies to honor soldiers who fought in WWI.

Some of these memories continue to resonate in my head as an adult. Although it seems that I had a normal childhood, there was a hidden, dark side.

TRAPPED AND ABUSED

My second stepdad physically abused my mom. He was very violent. As I cowered under the table or ironing board, I watched as he hit my mother. When the arguing, wrestling, and beatings ended, my mom would run away. I never knew when she would return, and she never took me with her.

We lived in Bermuda at the time, and I remember standing at my window, watching her flee down the stairs. She would race outside with the moon glistening over the ocean, then jump into her car and disappear into the darkness of night. I would cry, feeling scared, alone, and abandoned, trapped in the house with a monster I called "dad."

I never knew where she was going, and I worried that she might never come back. I spent many nights crying myself to sleep. Where was my mother going all those nights? She was frantic, and in her desperation, she never thought to look back. She was trying to escape the violence, and I understand that. But she didn't think to take her fragile little girl with her.

Years later, my mom talked about those terrible days. She described her terror. She felt helpless and had been so depressed that she considered suicide. Once, as she sat along the shore, she gazed past the ocean and into the vast darkness. She felt utterly helpless. Then she heard a voice whispering in her head: "All you have to do is go into the water and go under. That's it. It will all be over. Keep going further into the water and keep going under. Everything will be ok." As she looked across the horizon, someone motioned, urging her to step toward the ocean. The kiss of death awaited. But then my mother saw a brilliant light. She saw another man with arms stretched out, and He was walking on the water. He said, "Your life doesn't have to end. It doesn't have to be like that." A sudden sense of calm replaced the fear, and the menacing voice in her head faded. Only peace and love remained.

My mother believed Jesus had appeared that night and saved her life. She walked away from the beach and returned to me. Had she not come back, I shudder to think what would have become of me. I was living on a foreign island with a monstrous man.

Most parents take care of their children. They bathe and feed them and protect them from harm. They comfort them when they are hurt or afraid. My mom left me with a terrible person, and he sexually abused me. He made me take baths with him. He abused me with baby nasal aspirators as I lay on the bathroom floor. Sometimes I think he hurt my mom so that she would leave, giving him time and opportunity to hurt my little toddler body.

FLICKERS OF HOPE

*W*e lived in Germany for a while, and I remember running around on the slick, wooden floors. I once slipped and busted my chin, requiring stitches. The experience was traumatic, and as a result, I developed a fear of needles.

Occasionally, my mom made cassette tapes to send to our relatives in Texas. She recorded conversations with me. She sent the tapes to my grandma, GG, to let her know how she was doing. Years later, I found one of those orange cassette tapes, and I listened, remembering the day. People were singing children's songs. Then I heard my mom asking me to walk outside. I heard the screen door open and close as the pitter-patter of my tiny feet echoed while I ran after her to fetch the mail. As we came back inside, my mom's recorded words repeated "Mean Man" over and over, telling her mother about the danger hidden between the lyrics of kids singing, as if in morse code. How frightful it must have been for my grandma, living thousands of miles away in Texas, to hear this recorded message she later received in the mail! How powerless she must have felt to help us or to express her concern!

Finding that tape triggered my memories of the abuse my mom and I suffered. I heard my childlike voice and my mom's soft but stern reply. The tears welled in my eyes as I heard the warnings about "Mean Man." Little did I know that some of those memories would resurface later as we worked through foster care with other children and the effect it had on me when our own biological son experienced personal trauma.

A WORD OF WARNING

*F*riends, please be careful when you leave your children with someone. Trust your own motherly instinct. If you are hesitant, don't walk away. Meet the babysitter's family, friends, and coworkers. If the person attends church, talk to members of the congregation. Find all you can about the person who is going to watch your children. Do a background check.

Even if you are asking a boyfriend to watch the kids, do your homework. Don't allow "love" to distract you. Listen to what he says but check his words against his actions and what you hear from other people. Learn the signs of abuse and neglect, then keep your eyes open. A monstrous person can verbally, physically, emotionally, and sexually hurt your babies when no one is looking. A monster can destroy your life.

Too many children are exposed to obscenities and die at the hands of so-called "friends." Children usually trust adults, and they do not know how to defend themselves. When an abuser tells a child to do something, the youngster does not know how to differentiate between what is normal and what is deviant.

After a couple of years of horrific abuse, my mom was able to divorce the monster. She and I both escaped with deep scars.[3]

> **Friends: Don't be a victim. Loss, guilt, and survivor's remorse can over-shadow your life long after the abuse ends. Get help, and most importantly, love yourself and your child like no one else can.**

---

3   If this chapter touched you and you would like more information to help on your own *Quest*, see page 312, **Family Support** and page 314, **National Domestic Violence Hotline.**

Chapter 5
MOMMY AND ME:
ALL IS WELL

GETTING TO KNOW THE
WOMAN I CALLED "MOM"

My mother eventually left the Mean Man, and we moved several times to places like Maine, Bermuda, Texas, and Kansas. It was a shock to leave sunny Bermuda and travel to the extreme cold of Maine. My mom did not have a college degree, and she was unskilled, which meant she had to take any job she could find. She was a waitress, a telephone operator, and a nursing assistant, among other things. As a single mother, she did whatever it took to pay the bills. That also meant leaving me with babysitters, my grandparents, or my aunt.

My mother never knew if she would receive child support, so she watched her pennies. I remember sleeping on the floor in a small apartment. We drank water out of disposable, triangular paper cups, which sat precariously in a moldy plastic holder. We ate hot dogs with chips or canned pork and beans. Sometimes we ate Spam and eggs. I often ate sliced bananas sprinkled in milk as a poor man's cereal.

My mom's parents divorced when she was a teenager, and both eventually remarried. My grandmother, GG, moved to Texas, while my grandfather stayed in Kansas. Long before I was born, he had built a house from the ground up. He and his second wife lived there when my mom and I were moving around. He invited us to stay in the basement.

A HERITAGE THAT MATTERED

My ancestors came from Bohemia, in what is now the western part of the Czech Republic. They had been given land in the Midwest, so they worked as farmers.

My great-grandfather and grandfather were self-taught carpenters. They had an eye for precision and built many homes around town, establishing a rich family legacy in the Midwest.

BAKING AND BONDING

I have fond memories of staying with my aunt, who lived in a trailer next to my grandparents' house. She frequently watched me while my mom went to work. I also loved sitting at my grandma's island, eating cinnamon Bundt cake or saltine crackers, and talking. My mom's stepmother made every effort to bond with me. I felt that she really understood me, like she could peer directly into the windows of my heart.

My mom would bake traditional pumpkin pie, fruit kolaches, and cinnamon rolls. Sometimes she took the leftover pie crust and put it in a pie dish, sprinkled it with cinnamon sugar, and baked it until it was crispy, flaky, and sweet.

I slept next to my mom, snuggling close to stay warm at night. I don't remember ever being this close to my mother. These were days of peace and safety. There were no strange, mean men in those days.

We rode horses on my grandparents' property, and this was my first introduction to the large and powerful, yet docile, animal. My grandfather tenderly guarded me when I was riding. My mother had fallen off a horse, which left her with lifelong back pain.

I remember getting into my mother's make-up and discovering scissors there. I painted my great-grandfather's walls, then found my way to the bathroom, where I cut my hair. I chopped my bangs, which contrasted with my longer, slightly wavy golden hair. My great-grandfather was not happy about my "decorating" skills, but I survived. We didn't stay at the house much longer after that incident.

As far as I was concerned, this had been a happy, heavenly time, mainly because I could share so many sweet moments with my mom.

BACK TO BERMUDA

*W*e eventually moved back to Bermuda and rented a room with another man. The rent there was high, and many people who owned homes rented out rooms, garages, and second-floor flats to help offset the cost of living on the island.

Mom said there were no snakes, poisonous spiders, or dangerous critters. The island was surrounded by relatively shallow waters and sandbars. We seldom saw sharks and never heard about shark attacks. In my eyes, Bermuda was a paradise with no snakes or sharks—nothing to fear!

Bermuda was beautiful too. The locals had limestone homes, and rainwater drained through the roofs and ran onto the ground, where it collected in underground cisterns, allowing people to use the water in their homes. I learned to preserve water; I never left the water running when I brushed my teeth or washed the dishes. We only flushed the toilet for "number two," not "number one."

As far as I can recall, everyone of every class, color, and income treated the island with respect. I never saw anyone drop their trash and leave it behind. People recycled everything. No one used plastic water bottles. Islanders sold drinks in glass bottles, then recycled the bottles over and over. People treated their goods with care, repairing what was broken and recycling what they could.

Another amazing feature is that, even though Bermuda is located in the Atlantic Ocean off the coast of North Carolina, the homes, buildings, and monuments do not display much wear and tear, especially since they experience tropical storms, hurricanes, and flooding. Either homes in Bermuda were built to last or they were repaired quickly.

Since Bermuda is a British colony, everyone speaks with a proper British accent. I remember asking a person with golden brown skin about his nationality, and he answered in the most beautiful accent, "Bermudian, of course!"

I loved to hike down the shore and wade in little troughs of water. The tides swept the water to the beach, leaving many colorful fish behind. I threw them pieces of bread and watched them swarm around my legs and feet. The flashing, brilliant blues and greens cast a spectacular ray of light onto the sand as fish flopped and jumped in the tide pools. The water was so clear the fish seemed to be suspended in the water, magically dancing to the pulsing water drifting in and out.

LIVING THE ISLAND DREAM

Somehow, my mother had been able to scrape enough money to move us to Bermuda. Our first stay there had been challenging, but this time was different. My mother thought about the transition. She asked my grandmother in Texas to watch me while she traveled to the island and found a suitable home and a job as a telephone operator. Then she enrolled me in school, even though I was young. I entered kindergarten at the age of four, turning five the next month, in September.

I learned resilience and independence during that time. For instance,

I remember coming home to an empty home, knowing that mom would be gone for a while. I scrounged around and found a delicious package of honey buns. I tore off the cellophane and slid the pastries into the microwave. As the icing melted, I inhaled the aroma of cinnamon. I held the honey bun like a prize, carefully peeling away each layer of bread as I savored the sticky-sweet sponge in the middle. Those were happy times. I learned to treasure the small things: the sight of tide pools and sparkling fish, the clopping sound of a horse's hooves on the city's streets, the feel of my mother's body sleeping next to me, and the taste of warm pastries. It was an island paradise indeed.[4]

> **Friends:** The traditions of our ancestors may be shared or rediscovered, recreated, and practiced while knitting our souls together in family unity and a sense of belongingness. If you don't know your traditions, create and share your own.

---

4   If this chapter touched you and you would like more information to help on your own *Quest*, see page 312, **Food Assistance** and page 313, **Housing, Food, Family Support.**

Chapter 6
THE SNAKE/CHARMER
IN BERMUDA

ESCAPE INTO PARADISE

The third time was not the charm for me, to say the least. My mother worked as a telephone operator in Bermuda and met her third and final husband, a man named Brute. She had met him during one of her shifts as she directed calls. He was one of the calls she had intercepted, which resulted in their first date.

I remember the moment I met Brute. He walked into the kitchen and took a seat at the table—where our landlord was also sitting. I always thought it was kind of weird that the guy who owned the house was also in the kitchen that day. He seemed somehow protective of us, like he was drawn to my mother and me. He didn't say anything when he met Brute, though, probably because he needed to keep his tenants happy. I have wondered many times what life would have been like had my mother made different choices. Here she was, though, with Brute, being carried away once again.

Brute was tall, dark, and handsome. He was a strong man, and I was struck by his polished, white Navy uniform. He seemed jovial, cracking jokes and letting me climb on his neck and back. As far as I could tell, he seemed fun and nice. My mom locked her eyes on Brute, and I could tell that she was smitten.

Before long, we were living with him. Somehow, this time felt familiar, and I worried about our safety. I wondered if my mom had learned anything from her last relationship.

TAKING THE BAIT

Brute would take my mom and me fishing. We went to the black, lava-like cliffs in Bermuda. They climbed about, casting their lines to make a catch. They strung their fish and left them in the ocean until they were ready to head home to clean and cook their dinner. I wandered around, finding little ponds and puddles with fish in them. As I played with my Barbies, I imagined them swimming in their own private pools. As the tide ebbed and flowed, the ponds and puddles transformed. Sometimes there were fish; other times, the pools were empty. I remember walking the cliff edge, looking down at my mom and Brute as they fished below. I saw brilliant blue parrot fish swimming in the water, like neon lights flashing through a world of their own.

Mom and Brute often took bread to attract the fish, and I watched swarming fish fighting over the sweet, soggy pieces of bread. It was easy to fish from the sidelines on those days. It almost felt like cheating. The unsuspecting fish didn't see our hands snatching them from the water. Isn't life sometimes like that? It grabs you when you least expect it. Sometimes it lures you in, and before you know it, you have been snagged— hook, line, and sinker. Life can feel like an abyss that sucks you down into the murky darkness. In those moments, you have to keep your eyes open, looking up and fighting to survive. Trust me, I have had many of those moments, and it was important to come up for air and assess my situation.

NO STAIRWAY TO
HEAVEN FOR ME

*B*rute had a few "bad habits." When my mom met him, Brute lived on the naval base, but after a while, they decided to live together. We moved to the downstairs part of a rental house, and it was there that I first noticed that Brute had a problem. I would find a tray parked on a stool in the bathroom, with square, white papers and small bags of crumbled-up, dried grass. The tray was always loaded and ready to go. I never touched it. It just looked as if it were part of my mom's new decor.

The house was dark and musty. The curtains were always drawn tight, and if anyone came to the door, my mom and Brute would jump up, run around frantically, and start spraying smelly stuff everywhere, as if it covered up the smell of burnt grass and musk. A continual cloud of cigarette smoke hovered in the air, suspended like magic.

I watched my mom and Brute carefully pack grass into the papers, then roll them tight and lick the seal as if kissing each joint. They would light up and inhale deeply as they rocked out to *Stairway to Heaven*. When the tray was empty, we rode in the car at all hours of the night. I was told to lie down; under no circumstance was I to look up or get up. In those dark nights, Brute became Snake.

He would come running back to the car, elated and declaring that he got "it," whatever "it" was. Looking back, I realize they were taking me on drug runs. We managed to escape various perils, but each drug deal could have ended with violence. I was a blond-haired, blue-eyed five-year-old hiding in the back seat while Snake made another big score. I had to get up the next day and go to school bearing this terrible secret.

Eventually, I saw Snake's temper. Sometimes he got so angry that he picked up my frail body and threw me against the wall. My mom stood by and watched. She said that my body crumpled like a sack of potatoes. Snake hurt me many times. I will never forget it.

KITE FLYING

*B*ermuda was known for its Kite Flying Day, which occurred every year on Good Friday. The event was the brainchild of a teacher who wanted to teach his students about Jesus' victory over death and his ascension into heaven. The teacher built a kite with a cross, symbolizing the resurrection. To this day, the locals and tourists gather to fly their handmade kites to commemorate Good Friday.

I was fortunate that a neighbor boy helped me make my own kite. I chose light shades of purple and pink to adorn the little strips of balsa wood. The colors highlighted the cross-shaped frame, which held the triangular tissues. The kite was a prized possession. It was proof that I was invited to attend the festival, where I could fly my own kite and, more importantly, a reminder that someone cared enough about me to help me. My neighbor provided the materials and expected nothing in return.

I set the kite carefully on the couch in my room and admired this simple reminder of love. My stepdad came into the room and, in his fury, hurled me across the room, where I landed on my kite, smashing it to bits and leaving me crushed, sobbing over my lost treasure. What did I do to deserve this? I don't know why Snake projected his own guilt, fear, and anger onto me. I don't know if he blamed me for his broken ego. I don't know if he was jealous because I turned to a neighbor, to a kind boy who had shared my joy. Snake had terrible issues, and he was, in many ways, tormented. The pain that people inflict on us isn't always about us; often, it's related to the other person's struggles and their unfinished work. As scary and painful as that time was, I know now that Jesus was there. He saw me. He was in my story the whole time.

TREES OF LIFE

Bermuda was my playground, mainly because I was either locked in my room or locked out of the house. Once outside, I ran up the hills and found other kids to play with. I climbed loquat trees and picked the fruit, eating them straight off the branches. How satisfying the fruit was! I peeled back the skin, slurped the juice, and ate the sweet flesh. It quenched my thirst and hunger when I was banned from my house.

In many ways, the tree symbolized life. If you didn't see other kids climbing trees and eating fruit, then you could find them huddled on the ground, squaring up for a game of marbles. We thrived in the shade of the loquat trees.

UNEXPECTED TREASURES

We paired up and played with marbles or brightly colored glass beads, trying to knock our opponent's marbles out of the circle. The kid with the last marble got to keep all the marbles. It was a fun game and a way to get to know other kids. Evidence of our marble wars was everywhere. We'd find marbles half buried in the dirt, peeking out in the dust and glistening in the sun, refracting light as rays bounced off the colored glass. Sometimes kids pushed their marbles into little holes in the posts that lined the street or wedged them in crevices in the trees.

Occasionally, neighbors invited me into their homes and showed me how to bake cookies. When we finished decorating the last cookie, they encouraged me to claim some of the cookies as my "reward," which I gladly took home and saved for later. I treasure those moments because I see glimpses of a happy childhood, despite all the trauma I suffered. I am grateful for the kindness of neighbors who opened their homes and hearts to me.

A NEW AWARENESS

*O*found many friends and once had a couple of girlfriends, but sometimes the playtime turned mean. At a friend's house, the girls started mocking me, saying, "Honky, Honky, you don't belong here!" I didn't understand what was going on. I just knew that they were laughing at me. I ran all the way home and told my mom what they said. I pointed to my golden brown hand and said, "I am not a honky. I am brown." During the long summers, I spent hours outside playing in the waters and soaking up the sun, leaving my skin a golden color. But I wasn't brown, not like my friends. From that moment on, I was aware that my skin was different. I was white and a minority in Bermuda.

That experience shaped me, and ever since that time, I have made it a point to accept people's cultural differences and learn about their heritage.

FINDING STRENGTH
AND COMFORT

*O*nake's violent temper continued to dominate my world. Sometimes he would grab me by my ears and lift me up on my toes as I pleaded for him to leave me alone. I became more isolated, retreating to my room, which was my only place of solace. I nursed my loneliness by doing math problems from my textbook. I colored papers while creating artwork to present to my mom, competing for her love and hoping she would love me because of their beauty.

Snake grounded me, ordering me to my room and threatening me if I left my room, no matter what. He would send me to bed when the sun was still shining just so he didn't have to deal with me.

My only source of consolation was listening to my radio. As the music of the 70s wafted through my room, I dreamed of love, imagining how wonderful it would be to have someone to hold me dearly in his arms. My only goal in life was to survive. I wanted to see womanhood, and I hoped someday my kisses would light a fire for a man who truly loved me. I found happiness in upbeat tunes and despised the dark music my parents listened to. Songs became my prayers and dreams for a better future.

As a lonely child, I focused on my schoolwork, which distracted me from the pain and terror at home. Over time, I developed good study habits and mental discipline, which carried me through college, aided in my career, and propelled me into adulthood. I have enjoyed success in part because of those hard, lonely days.

My other source of comfort was sucking my thumb. I slept with a baby blanket every night and carried it everywhere, stopping only when I started elementary school. Snake despised my thumb-sucking. I don't know why he cared since he never gave me that much thought. The more I sought comfort, the more I snuggled with my blanket and sucked my thumb. My thumb was my distraction from the chaos around me. Many times, Snake stood over me and stared at me as I drifted off to sleep. If he saw me sucking my thumb, he put pepper on my thumb, hoping that would make me stop. Unfortunately, it didn't work, and eventually, he poured pepper down my throat when I was sleeping. It was a miracle I didn't die.

He made me wear BAND-AIDS on all my fingers to school to shame me. If I came home without them, he would beat me and throw me around like a rag doll. I was too scared to enter the house. Once, I sat on the sidewalk, waiting outside for several hours until my mom got home. I don't recall if her presence lessened the blow, but I do remember sitting on the curb for a long time, anxious and afraid of what would happen once I stepped inside without the BAND-AIDS.

A FORGOTTEN CHILD

I was full of life and enjoyed expressing myself through music. I loved to sing. I would sing anywhere, even at dinner. I don't know why I sang during dinner; maybe it was because I didn't have anything to talk about. Snake, however, didn't enjoy my singing. He would pick up the long, serrated bread knife and threaten me with it.

My mother always wanted to be in dance, and when she signed up for a belly dancing class, she signed me up for ballet classes. I don't remember ever completing any rehearsals or performing in any dances, but I do remember how to stand on my toes and point them and line up with the bar. To this day, I practice standing on my toes to lengthen and strengthen my calf muscles as a reminder of what could have been.

After one class, I was dismissed to wait for my mom. I waited and waited for what seemed like hours. The silence surrounded me as I sat on the concrete steps. All the teachers and students left. It was just me and the sunset when my mom finally appeared. I remember the anxiety I felt, wondering if she would ever come. Did she remember me?

SEEDS OF BITTERNESS

*O*resented Snake for taking my mom from me. She had disappeared in a cloud of enchanted smoke as the charmer led her further into darkness, oblivious to the damage she was causing her little girl. I felt betrayed. She was cultivating habits that would last a lifetime and haunt us both.

My mom was 28 years old when she met Brute; he was 22. He was immature and had a very dark past, including heroin addiction and imprisonment. He had impregnated a minor before beginning the relationship with my mom, often talking about how he got a young girl pregnant and her dad chasing him once he found out. Brute never met his child. I hoped he would cherish me as a daughter, but he didn't.

It would be years before I found freedom from bitterness through faith in Jesus. I would find healing and hope. The Snake/Charmer did a lot of damage, but he didn't destroy me. I became resilient instead. I became empathetic instead.[5]

> **Friends: Are you a victim of wounds bestowed upon you by others? Have you been set free of these wounds, and are you living in the freedom this healing brings?**

---

5   If this chapter touched you and you would like more information to help on your own *Quest*, see page 313, **KSBJ Contemporary Christian Music, Streaming, Prayer** and page 314, **National Domestic Violence Hotline.**

Chapter 7
MARCHING ONWARD
TO ZION, ILLINOIS

ANOTHER FRESH START

The Navy transferred Brute to a small town located just outside of Chicago, and I have some very fond memories of this transition. As you may imagine, a move from Bermuda to Zion, Illinois, was a shock.

For starters, I enjoyed small-town life. We lived in a house that was divided into three separate sections. My parents rented the main floor, a family with a baby lived on the floor above us, and the homeowner lived in the basement.

I don't remember having many interactions with my stepdad during this time. Mainly, I remember my mom talking to him on the phone since he was stationed at sea for quarterly stints.

On weekdays, I walked alone to a nearby school. I was entering second grade with a world of experience about some of life's seedier elements; nevertheless, I had hope. I was literally the new kid on the block, and I formed friendships with kids who seemed curious about me and where I came from. I adjusted to the changes, including a new model of education that interested and challenged me. By the time I settled in, though, it was time to move again. I don't think we lived in Zion for more than six to nine months.

A NEIGHBOR WHO CARED

Although we didn't stay in Zion for long, it was a life-changing experience. I got to know our neighbors, and I offered to hold the baby as the mom vacuumed, cleaned, and tended to the laundry. I had longed for a sibling, especially since I was such a lonely, vulnerable child, so caring for the baby helped fill that void. I was also able to watch a loving mother in action. I learned what *normalcy* looked like. My neighbor was very kind and grateful for my presence, which freed her to work more efficiently. I watched in awe and dreamed of what it would be like to have a tender, loving mom.

My mother got upset with me and often yelled, and I would escape. Two doors separated each floor, and carefully closing the door behind me, I would climb the stairs and sit on the top step, wishing I had a normal family like my neighbors had. I cried in the silence and imagined a better life. Looking back, I am grateful that I had such kind neighbors. Their example shaped my dreams and allowed me to retreat from the chaos into another realm for a few moments. I feel certain that those encounters with my neighbor helped shape my view of motherhood, helping me to embrace parenthood with love and hope.

CRAFTING HOPE

My teachers and peers accepted me, and I appreciated their kindness. I joined a local Girl Scouts troop, which I loved. I especially enjoyed crafts, which allowed me to express my creative side. For instance, I made a hanging bird feeder from newspaper, covered with something sticky, like peanut butter, then rolled in seeds. I remember hanging the feeder in our backyard and watching the birds enjoy the seeds. I felt a sense of peace and awe.

EXHILARATING ANGELS

Obviously, I hadn't had much exposure to snow while we were in Bermuda, so the frigid Illinois winters were a surprise. The snow was cold and exhilarating! One time a neighbor showed me how to make snow angels on the front lawn. It was fun to lie on the ground and stretch my arms as far as I could, then wave them back and forth. I peppered the yard with little angels. I don't think I even understood what angels were at that time, but it was fun making them.

BOOKS AND APPLES

One good thing my mom did early on was read to me. Like working math problems and making pictures, reading was an escape. A Book Mobile visited Zion Elementary School every week, and I was able to get scores of books from this traveling library. I looked forward to the new adventures that books held.

I could even buy candied apples on Book Mobile Day. Outside, the apples were bright red, like sticky gems; inside, the apple was sweet and crunchy. I don't know if candied apples were my favorite childhood treat, but I was always excited to see them because it signaled Book Mobile Day.

A VISIT FROM TEXAS

My grandmother (GG) and her husband lived in Houston, Texas, where he worked for Cameron, a manufacturer and servicer of oil and gas. He had traveled to Chicago on business, which meant that we got to see him. My stepdad was between deployments, so we all boarded a train and journeyed to Chicago, 43 miles away. I remember that day vividly.

I was excited to see the "big city." We arrived early and walked down the sidewalks to my grandfather's hotel. The buildings stretched above me, and I craned my neck to see the giants scraping the heavens with their tiptops. We visited with my grandfather all day, and he took us to his room, which seemed to float in the sky.

Eventually, darkness descended, covering the city like a blanket. His room overlooked the deep blue of the pool below. I could see for miles as I stared across the Chicago skyline. Twinkling lights illuminated the city. I had never seen such magnificence, and I was completely smitten. The city, with its grand adventure, had captured my heart!

My grandfather had brought gifts, and I giggled in delight. One of my favorites was the Avon bubble bath that my aunt had sent from Texas. She used to sell Avon, and she chose a special scent for me, which my grandfather delivered to my eager hands. GG had left her first husband, so this man was not biologically related to me. Still, he was kind and he loved me. As far as I was concerned, he was my grandfather. Our visit to Chicago was a blessing, and it made life in Zion a little sweeter.

THE BABYSITTERS' TRUTH

One night, my mom went to work, and she asked a couple to babysit me. I don't remember much about the man and his wife, but my encounter with them impacted me deeply. I will be eternally thankful for these two people who gave me a truly great gift.

They asked me if I wanted to live forever, never to suffer. I was interested but perplexed. Although I was a child, I knew enough to know that people die, so what did it mean to live forever? I began to ask questions, and little by little, each one of those questions was answered. They showed me a little book with pictures in it, then began to read some stories to me. I loved books, and I loved whenever someone read to me.

They showed me pictures of Jesus and said that He came from heaven to earth and did many wonderful things, healing the sick and raising the dead. Jesus was the Son of God, and his Father had sent Him to earth to free us from the destructive power of sin so that we could live forever with him. Jesus died on a cross, and God brought Him back to life. He defeated sin and death. No matter how bad we have been, God forgave us because of Jesus' sacrifice.

My parents had made me feel that I was unworthy; I was a bad *person* because I did wrong *things*. The babysitters said something different: God *loved* me. God saw my sin and loved me anyway. He would never leave me. He would always be with me, no matter what.

Looking back, I know that God was working at that moment. I don't know how my mom found these babysitters; only God knows. I don't know how they could see into my soul and speak to the loneliness and sadness I had buried deep within. I didn't understand how Jesus would always be with me if I couldn't see him, but I had always wanted a sibling or friend who would never leave me. So I chose to believe what they said about Jesus. That night, I prayed, asking Jesus to come into my heart. I asked Him to be with me and change me. I believed that He would never leave me or forsake me; He would be with me forever.

My life absolutely changed that night. I met Jesus as my Provider, Comforter, Companion, Protector, and Advisor. If I hadn't met Jesus that night, I don't know if I would be alive today. I began talking to him. I didn't understand what it meant to "pray without ceasing" (1 Thes. 5:17-19). I didn't really understand prayer, but I knew I could talk to him.

You can read more about Jesus in the Bible, in the New Testament Gospels (Matthew, Mark, Luke, and John). *The Chosen,* a television series written by Dallas Jenkins, nicely portrays Jesus in his meager, humble descent to earth as God turned spirit to flesh, who sacrificed his son for our atonement. This series brings Jesus' biography to life through the four Gospels. Jesus can provide you the same comfort, love, peace, and everlasting life that you read about in John 3:16: *"For God so loved the world that He gave his one and only Son, that whoever believes in Him shall not perish but have eternal life"* (NIV).

This was my cherished secret. My mom and stepdad did not go to church or talk about spiritual things, but this new life, with its promise and hope, was safe. It was between Jesus and me. It was my own little secret.[6]

Friends: My secret saved me. The same secret can save you!

6   If this chapter touched you and you would like more information to help on your own *Quest*, see page 315, **WoodsEdge-stream church, prayer.**

Chapter 8
THE EAST COAST, DRUGS, AND DECEPTION

SOMETHING'S NOT RIGHT

*W*e moved from Zion, Illinois, to Moyock, North Carolina, when the Navy transferred my stepdad. We lived close to Virginia Beach, which had one of the biggest naval bases in the world. He was deployed on several occasions, until he declined to renew his term of employment with them. I was in second grade by that time, and it became another big transition.

Our move to North Carolina had a most profound impact on me, largely because I lived there for a relatively long time, from age 7 to 12. My mom had had three spouses, and none of them had been my biological dad. I lived in at least nine homes, five states, two countries, and one island—twice. In North Carolina, I experienced more stability and was able to establish friends. I attended the same school and maintained proper school attendance. I got to know my teachers. I fell into a routine that seemed almost mundane. My life seemed normal on the outside, but behind closed doors, life was anything but normal.

THE TRAILER PARK

My parents secured a trailer of their own, and we moved into a trailer park. I was often asked to ride my bike to the office to deliver the monthly rent check. We lived in the back of the park; it was just over a mile from our front door to the front of the park. Thick woods, separated by a little creek, encircled the trailer park. I could see the woods from the back of our trailer.

I worried that my stepdad was losing his grip because his behavior seemed so erratic. He smoked marijuana regularly and had a history of dabbling in hard drugs. My grandma and aunts believed that his previous abuse of heroin had caused brain damage. I began to resent him more and more each day. My parents would walk around the trailer naked. I don't mean that they were wearing underwear; I mean literally buck naked. They would sit on the couch naked, smiling and smoking their joints. I felt repulsed, embarrassed, and ashamed. My stepdad cracked jokes about it, saying, "Hey, you can walk around naked too!" He would always try to persuade me to join them, and I felt afraid and humiliated. I tried to hide in my room or escape outside. I knew this was not normal behavior.

One night, I made my stepdad extremely angry. I can't exactly remember what I did to set him off. Maybe I didn't want to eat something for dinner, or I didn't want to clean the kitchen. Maybe I didn't flush the toilet. As a little girl, I didn't always understand the rules, and I crossed the line more than once. He was so angry with me that he picked me up and threw me off our little wooden deck. If you are familiar with trailers, you would know that those patios are elevated a few feet off the ground, so it wasn't a nice landing. He had no remorse. I flew through the air like a rag doll with my yellow nightie sailing in the wind. I crumpled on the ground below, horrified that the neighborhood could see such a spectacle. I kept wondering, "Where is my mom? Can't anyone save me?" In my desperation, I cried out to God. He was all I had.

LISTENING IN THE
DARKNESS

*M*y room was located at the front of the trailer, facing the street. Many times, my stepdad would come into my room and turn out the lights, then open the window and tell me to be quiet. He would strain to listen in the stillness. Usually, we could hear a group of teenagers or young adults laughing or talking loudly. One could see the embers of their shared cigarettes burning in the darkness.

I don't know why my stepdad crept into my room to listen to strangers. What I do know is the midnight drug runs were a thing of the past, but the continuous haze of burnt, munched-up grass cigarettes remained a constant. I always thought it was uncomfortable and weird. My stepdad was spying on people who were walking down the street with their own cigarettes.

CHORES, CHORES,
AND MORE CHORES

*M*y parents assigned me specific chores. My grandma once told me that when I was little and could hardly reach the top of the mattress, my mom made me make my bed daily—"or else." So, I complied.

I cleaned the kitchen every night, washing nearly every dish we owned; my mother used a *lot* of dishes, utensils, pots, and pans when she cooked. It felt like she was trying to see how dirty the kitchen could be. I cleaned as they watched TV. I would stand on a stool, stretch out over the sink, and grab the faucet. The hot, soapy water burned my soft skin. The sink water got so dirty that I had to change it out several times. My stepdad inspected the dishes to see how well I was cleaning, and if he found a morsel of food or dirt, I had to start over. I would place the dishes on dish towels to dry. Later, I hung up the damp towels and put everything away. I resented the chore, and to this day, I hate washing dishes and wiping off countertops.

Weekly chores included cleaning bathrooms, dusting, and putting up mountains of laundry. I felt like a prisoner when most kids were outside playing. Being so young and having little concept of time, I didn't realize that there was freedom once I got the chores done. On occasion, I finished early. My parents would tell me to go outside, then lock me out of the house. But away from their rules, I was liberated. I could run off to play.

The bathtub—in fact, the entire bathroom—was always a chore in itself. The porcelain was stained with dark brown resin. Armed with Comet and sponges, I knelt as I scrubbed my Saturdays away. My stepdad inspected the bathroom, and if it wasn't to his liking, he made me start over, sometimes cleaning until the sun set.

My mom was a serious clutter bug. She saved everything: papers, mailers, trinkets, and who knows what else. Routinely, I had to clean the counters, which meant dealing with piles of stuff. Papers and other items littered every counter and shelf, and they all collected dust. There was no internet or electronic mail back then, so we couldn't opt out of advertisements and flyers. All our bills came in envelopes. I tried to arrange the letters and papers by size, then neatly stacked them to the side. I condensed piles to create more space. My mom joked about my organizational skills and then told me to organize her junk drawer.

My parents expected me to clean their room too. My stepdad had explicit magazines on his side of the bed, and I saw pictures of men and women doing the unthinkable. He left them out as if they were his prized possessions. I was repulsed, but I also felt curious. *Were those people in love? Is that what love is supposed to look like?* I wondered. Love became a fantasy. My mother had given her heart to many men. She took belly dancing lessons and dressed provocatively. Her behavior seemed to mirror what I saw in the magazines. Clearly, I needed an intervention.

THE CHURCH

Each week, a Baptist church in town sent its bus through our trailer park. One day, I asked if I could go to church, and surprisingly, my parents said yes. Looking back, I think my parents saw my time at church as a break. It freed them from their parental duties, and instead, they could sit around and smoke pot.

I am not sure how the church even allowed a young kid like myself to show up without an adult. I went back to the trailer park and saw where we lived. I could not find a Baptist church nearby, so it must have been quite the journey. Still, I looked forward to the weekly event. I got to go to kids' classes and work on crafts. I heard stories about Jesus. The teachers gave me fruit-flavored beverages to drink with a crispy vanilla, chocolate, or strawberry cookie. It was a real treat.

We sang, and some of the songs resonate in my heart today. I vividly remember this song: *"Jesus loves me. This I know, for the Bible tells me so."* The lyrics assured me that, no matter how bad I thought I was, Jesus loved me. He would provide me with daily comfort, despite my circumstances. The second song I remember is this one: *"Jesus loves the little children of the world. Red and yellow, black and white, they are all precious in his sight."* This song still stirs my soul. As a child, I traveled to many places, and I understood that all of us are God's children. People may have different skin colors, places of origin, and cultures, but they are all the same in one fundamental way: They are loved by God. They were created in His likeness.

One day, there was an episode on the bus and I got in trouble. I was probably being too rowdy; maybe I didn't sit down. I just remember the lady saying, "Act your age, not shoe size." She hurt my feelings, and her statement didn't make sense. My shoe size was 12, and I was seven years old. When I told my parents about the incident, my weekly trip to church ended.

FOOD IS THE ENEMY

My mom stayed home for a while when we moved to North Carolina, while my stepdad continued to work with the Navy. He would ship out to sea, then come home. Typically, weeks passed before the next deployment. During his absence, my mom sometimes made cookies or something sweet, and I came home to the lovely aroma of freshly baked treats. I loved her chocolate chip cookies. She used a Betty Crocker cookbook to create homemade cinnamon rolls, chocolate cake rolls, fried doughnuts, and homemade bread. She also made Czech fruit kolaches from an old family recipe.

She usually prepared meals, or we ate leftovers, often because she would batch cook in the Crock Pot. She made salads and made sure that we always had a vegetable with our meals.

I was expected to eat everything on my plate, no matter how big the helping was. I remember contests to see how many pancakes I could eat in one sitting. It wasn't fun, and I don't particularly like pancakes to this day.

You wouldn't know it, but my mom had an eating disorder. She had such a poor sense of her body image that she fell into a destructive pattern of starving herself and bingeing. I watched her skip meals, then devour two or three whole avocados at once. She tried several diets, like the "cabbage soup" diet or an Ezekiel bread fast. Later, when she became a Christian, she called her self-imposed starvation "fasting." Bingeing, then, was "breaking the fast." Every time her weight started to climb, she starved herself. Over time, she added exercise. She weighed herself every day.

This vicious cycle of skipping meals and bingeing started when I was young, and it had a lasting impact on me. I once asked her if I was fat and if I needed to be on a diet. She said, "Diets aren't for kids." Still, I started to look at myself in a full-length mirror. My own body image wasn't very healthy either. I felt that my mom expected me to look a certain way, so I would sneak into her bathroom and weigh myself. I learned to watch the numbers.

I started skipping meals, only to be ravenous later. I then ate whatever

I could find at home, sometimes scarfing down entire packages. I had no sense of "portion control" or "healthy eating." I grabbed cookies from the cookie jar. I spooned out cake frosting from containers in the back corner of the fridge. I ate "marshmallow fluff," along with pickles, saltines, chips, and crackers. I mirrored my mom's eating habits. The pantry seemed to call me, but I didn't know why. I didn't understand cravings.

WAKE-UP CALLS

*O*woke myself up in the mornings with an alarm and got ready for school. I woke up regardless of whether I slept through the night or not.

I also medicated myself. Many nights I woke up with throbbing pain in my legs and body, pain that only grew in intensity. The pain was so intense that many nights I simply curled up and cried. The abuse taught me to tolerate pain, so pain that drove me to tears was worse. I felt helpless, and when I woke my mom and asked for help, she just told me to go back to bed.

Eventually, she bought me baby aspirin and put it in my cabinet over the bathroom sink. She instructed me to take aspirin every time I woke up and felt the pain. The aspirin helped, but it only masked the pain; we didn't treat the cause. It is not recommended for kids to take aspirin, as recent research indicates this can lead to Reyes syndrome or swelling in the liver and brain. Some doctors thought I was experiencing growing pains, but later, naval doctors determined that I had Scoliosis. I suspect that the pain I was feeling was from the bones in my legs lengthening and growing out of alignment.

I don't know if I even knew how to tell time, but when the alarm went off, I knew it was time to get up and get ready for school. My mom and stepdad would sleep in, and I would slip out, telling them a quick goodbye.

I carried my schoolbooks in my arms for approximately a mile to catch the bus. I didn't own a backpack, and I struggled to keep the books level as they slid back and forth like the keys to an accordion. Trying to walk and balance the movement seemed like a failing venture as I found myself continuously picking up books that dropped to the ground. I walked to the bus stop every day, whether it was raining, snowing, or blazing hot. Still, the daily trek was worth it. I loved school, and I couldn't wait to get there.

BUGGED

*S*ince I was only a child and the only one who cleaned the house, I doubt that the house was ever adequately clean. I remember growing up with roaches, spiders, and mice. I constantly worried that snakes would slither into the trailer.

My mom had a heart for animals, more than for kids, it seemed, so we had various dogs and cats, all of which stayed inside the trailer. It was a daily occurrence to pull out a plastic tub to put food in and see a German roach scurry past or see the remnants of eggs that once housed baby roaches. Many nights, I heard the cat chasing something. It was frightful and disgusting to see the cat flinging a mouse around, playing with it before devouring it. I would lay silently, listening to the sound of crunching bones. I guess my parents thought the animals would control the "critters," but the extra filth they generated was disturbing.

TRAVELING TO
OHIO—AND BACK

*M*y stepdad's family lived in Ohio. At least once a year, we made the 466-mile journey there to see his relatives. My parents packed up the station wagon, and off we went. We usually spent Thanksgiving with the family in Ohio.

The first time I met my stepdad's parents was at my parents' wedding.

My grandparents had arranged for a simple ceremony to take place on the front lawn. I was the flower girl, but it was not a pleasant experience. I had to smile and pretend I supported this union. Following the wedding, my parents had a big party at the community hall. It seemed like the whole town had been invited.

The bartender served up plenty of drinks, and I watched people stagger around the room. Nobody paid much attention to me. I have a vivid memory of listening to a guy bragging that he had eaten dog food. YUCK!

My stepdad's family was established in the community, and from what I could tell, they were prosperous. They had a wooden, two-story house with a long front porch that faced one of the town's main streets. My stepdad's father was the mayor.

My stepdad had a couple of other brothers. One brother was married and had kids; he had a solid career. The younger brother still lived at home, and I usually hung out with him during our visits. He took me hiking out on their property, and I watched him shoot targets and hunt rabbits. Sometimes my grandma gave me a dollar, and either she or my uncle would take me down the hill to the candy store. This was especially nice because my parents rarely bought me candy.

I could never understand what happened to my stepdad. He had turned out so differently! He came from a stable, well-rounded family. His parents were loving, and his siblings were responsible individuals. Why had he made such poor choices with his life? Why was he so hateful toward me? Years later, I got to ask him about it.

I remember the long trips to Ohio. We often drove late at night, sometimes over icy or snow-covered roads. We hugged mountain ledges, and I hoped we would make it safely to our destination as I peered into a bottomless ravine.

The plus side of having a station wagon back then was that I got to make a bed in the back. I piled blankets on the seat and slept most of the way. Many times, I would wake up just as my parents pulled into a rest area so they could take a nap before completing their journey.

TRAVELING THROUGH
THE TRAILER PARK

Traveling wasn't limited to cross-country trips, though. I also traveled through the trailer park. On days when I was locked out of the house, I explored the area near my home. My parents told me to check in periodically, and I would ride my bike through the trailer park, stopping at the park's "circle," a central area that featured a pool, field, park, mailbox room, country store, and office.

CARE PACKAGES

Sometimes my stepdad's parents sent care packages. Inside, I found fun treats. They usually tucked a dollar in the box too, with strict instructions that my parents should allow me to use the money to buy my own candy.

I usually got these care packages for my birthday and during holidays, so a few times every year, I had the luxury of going to the community store and buying one hundred pennies' worth of candy. I filled my little brown bag and surrendered my only dollar. I could barely see over the counter, but I felt like I was ten feet tall. I loved Swedish Fish, Red Hots, and Lemonhead candies. I loved Tootsie Roll Pops and chewing gum. Back home, I ate the whole bag in one sitting.

Although the candy didn't last, the feelings of love lingered. I knew that, for a moment, someone was thinking about me. Someone cared.

TRAVELING MATES

I would ride my bike, seeking anyone to play with. Sometimes I just rode to a classmate's house. One friend's mom worked nightly as a nurse. Another friend's dad worked in the military like my stepdad did. There were several military families living in the park. I've been told that it was cheaper to live in North Carolina than in Virginia. The taxes were lower, and the commute across the state border was short.

A number of retired couples also lived in the trailer park. They were always willing to listen to me, and I often passed the time chatting while sitting on their couch as they rocked in their chairs. I am not sure they even heard my stories, but somehow, they just smiled and kept nodding at me.

Other times, my friends and I explored deserted trailers. Some had been abandoned; others had been damaged from a fire. Fires were common in the park, and once someone's trailer burned, it was often deserted; kids used them as hangouts.

Many times, though, I rode my bike alone. Older boys in the community called out, "You sure are pretty. Why don't you come find me when you get a little older?" I didn't know what they meant, but I enjoyed the attention.

Looking back, I know that I was starving for love, and any attention, whether it was from classmates, old people, or strangers, made my life feel a little less lonely.[7]

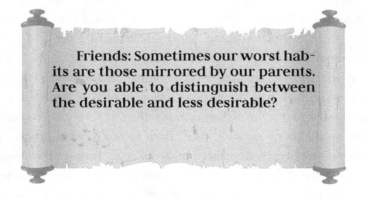

Friends: Sometimes our worst habits are those mirrored by our parents. Are you able to distinguish between the desirable and less desirable?

7   If this chapter touched you and you would like more information to help on your own *Quest*, see page 314, **National Domestic Violence Hotline.**

Chapter 9
EIGHT FOR EIGHT: A
SUMMER TO REMEMBER

*M*y grandparents in Texas, Grandma GG and Frank, had a daughter named Delilah when they remarried. My aunt Delilah was only three years older than I was, and there was a two-year difference by grade level. My aunt was my pen pal and I looked up to her. She was like the sister I always wanted and never had. We wrote letters to each other, and my grandmother sent me her clothes when she outgrew them. She was in baton twirling, ballet, and dance, so I got her old costumes to dress up in and dream that I could someday be like her. She sent me the latest clothing trends of shirts, dresses, shorts, jeans, and tops. I would look forward to these care packages, as my mom never bought me the new styles of clothes or anything new, for that matter. My parents would always say they didn't have money. Looking back, I am sure they didn't have money since they spent it on drugs and themselves. If anything was in fashion, I would request a special item, for example, a Michael Jackson jacket at Christmas time from my grandparents afar. Since my parents seldom bought me clothes, I was always made fun of at school, and when kids came to school each new fall and each new year, they would be adorning their newest garb. My newest garb was wearing an ugly burnt orange dress I tried to hide under my bed that my mom bought at some resale shop. I have the picture to prove it to this day. What kid wears burnt orange?

RV TRAVELS THROUGH
THE LENS OF AN
EIGHT-YEAR-OLD

The summer I turned eight, my grandparents in Texas bought me an airplane ticket from North Carolina to Texas to come stay the summer with them. My grandparents owned a driving RV, which had a full-sized bed over the cab and bunk beds in the back across from the bathroom. My aunt and I got to choose which bunk bed to sleep in. She, of course, chose the top. Being older and the fact it was her parents' RV took precedence. I had the time of my life as we traveled across many states: Texas, Colorado, New Mexico, Utah, Arizona, California, and Oregon, making memories of a lifetime. As we approached each state line, my grandparents would pull over and have my aunt and me stand by the state sign and snap a quick polaroid for us to remember the adventure forever. They would hand each of us our own picture and we would shake it and blow on it to watch the picture dry and form before our very own eyes.

MY REST LIES IN
GREEN MEADOWS AND
MAJESTIC MOUNTAINS

Our voyage across the United States was a long but short three-week trip. My grandparents had the trip well planned out and used maps during that time in 1980 to meticulously plan every detail. My grandma tracked the miles and mileage and helped grandpa through every twist and turn, highway, exit, gas station, and even all the KOA campsites we would set up and camp at each night. Oh, how I loved the KOAs they chose. They all usually had a pool and sometimes even putt-putt or mini-golf. After driving what seemed like hours each day, my aunt and I would quickly change into our swimsuits and go run to the swimming pool, jumping off the diving board and diving for weighted pool sticks at the pool's bottom. Grandma would get dinner ready, and since I was with my older aunt at the pool, we had alleged freedom. Grandma had peace of mind also since she knew I could swim. She had already paid for me to learn how to swim in previous swim classes, and now we had earned the liberty to swim and explore the campsite. Grandpa got a break from the kids to set up our electricity, water, toiletry, and hookups, while Grandma got dinner ready and didn't have to compete with stepping on our little toes or dancing around us during her preparation time. During this road trip, we drove into the highest mountains of Colorado. The RV had a top bunk with a window view facing the street and driving direction of the vehicle. My aunt and I would lie up there and navigate the trip visually. Coming up into the mountains and driving with only miles of sloping mountain sides lined with trees beneath us was exhilarating. The sky was so blue, and we were literally on top of the world. We were either driving on a cliff's edge or side by side, looking at the mountain and potential rockslides along our coach. The colors and layers of rock all changed as the stones and land formation had evolved and weathered over the many years of time. I remember driving down into the capital city, Denver, nestled between the two mountain ranges as if the mountains were holding the city in their hands, and its covering was a puffy blue and white bonnet. When we arrived in Denver, Colorado, we stayed at my great aunt's home or with my grandma's sister. I don't remember staying long, but I do remember my great-aunt growing rhubarb in their backyard. I didn't know what rhubarb was, but it was very enticing. It had a long stem, and the root or bulb of the plant was a nicely colored purplish red. My great aunt had used the root to make rhubarb pie. The pie was sweet and had a little tinge of bitterness to it. Its tender doughy crust and the sugary jelly consistency made it an interesting and delectable treat, opening up my taste buds to a new adventure I wanted more of.

ANCIENT ANCESTORS –
TRAVELING BACK IN TIME

*A*fter a few days' visit, we said our goodbyes and headed onward, and so the voyage continued. When we finished visiting family, we headed to see Mesa Verde in Colorado. Mesa Verde is the cliff dwellings of the Anasazi pueblo people in the 13th century A.D., or over 700 years ago, located in the Southwest corner of Colorado. These entire villages were built into the cliffs, rocks, and mesa of the rugged terrain. This place forever changed me. Oh, how I wanted to be a Native American and live off the land. Climbing and hiking into the cliffs was the most magnificent thing to do, imagining our Native American ancestors of the old way before America was established, building their homes in these rock crevices, farming the lands above. Risking life carrying children up and down ladders to get to the mesa tops for harvesting and finding food with hundreds of feet of elevation beneath them. One little slip of a parent with child or child without parent would be devastating, as rocks would plummet beneath them. I was amazed at how these Natives could access this cliff and terrain, scrimmaging back and forth without the loss of life. It's a mystery how they were able to work and serve, making crops, hunting the bison, growing families, making baskets, clothes, creating fire and using water welling up from the ground as if magically appearing was more than my little brain could envision. Walking through how daily life was for these individuals and the kids of my age living in this village was so vivid.

REST AREAS AND
LOSS OF FOOTING

*A*s we drove from destination to destination, my grandparents would pull over in little rest stop areas to have a lunch break and give my grandfather some time to stretch his legs. We would make a little snack lunch consisting of sandwiches, chips, and possibly some fruit. We would eat under the wrestling of the trees blowing softly in the wind. You could hear the pitter-patter and swooshing of the creek nearby and the birds singing in the air as they flew overhead, watching for a morsel of bread to be dropped. Afterward, we would take a little hike across the stream and continue along its bank on the opposite side, exploring nature. As we crossed back across the riverbed and I made that leap from rock to slippery rock, my red-and-pink-striped flip-flop dropped onto the water. I stood frozen in time, watching the ripples of the waters whisk it away. I started bawling as my brand-new flip-flops sailed down and over the rocks as they wafted merrily down down away from me, never to be seen again. I knew I would probably never get another pair of flip-flops, and these were my very own new pair. I treasured them so much, knowing there would be no replacement. My grandparents shook me and hollered to catch my attention and pull me back into reality, as we needed to cross the river and return to our trip endeavors once again.

SUNNY STATE OF SUNFLOWERS, PIZZA, AND GRAPE JUICE

*O*ur next stop was the sunny state of California. My grandfather's parents lived in a quaint neighborhood in the suburbs. Once we got settled in and made our acquaintances, we got a tour of the house and garden. Growing in the backyard along the fence line were the tallest and largest flowers I had ever seen. They towered over me, and as I peered up at them, it was as if they were smiling at me. My great-grandfather called them sunflowers, brilliantly yellow and as happy as could be. I met my older cousins, and one of them loved to play the guitar. He sang and strummed songs of good cheer. That same cousin took my aunt and me to Chuck E. Cheese, a pizza place for kids. It had a lot of life-sized video games and carnival-type games. He gave us each some coins to take our chances in conquering the highest score or just trying to make our game last longer than the coin redeemed. We had a great time and came back at the end of the night more enthusiastic and full of energy than when we left. As we left their house and drove across the countryside of California, one could see the many grape vines growing, waiting to be harvested into wine. California, one of the biggest producers of grapes and winemaking, draws many tourists year-round with its temperate climate. My grandparents chose a fairly common winery to tour and learn about growing grapes and the process of winemaking. Even as a child, I thought it was a very interesting process. We walked through the storage rooms with the wooden barrels that stood taller than my grandparents, and, well, that was a lot of juice! My grandparents tasted wine, and we minors tasted grape juice, which was just as good as any wine for me.

FOREST GIANTS

While heading north to our utmost destination, Oregon, we passed through San Francisco and headed north to explore the ancient Redwood National and State Park. My grandparents pulled into the parking lot as we all exited the vehicle and set out to confirm these trees were, in fact, some of the oldest, tallest, and largest unique to this area alone. As we set out on a dirty well-laden trail, a park representative gave us a brief history of the park and the trees and gave us their blessing to proceed through the park. Around and under the trees we hiked. Suddenly, we found the path was covered by a fallen decaying tree whose body was decomposing back into the ground. Lichen, ferns, and mini ecosystems of plants and insects lay attached to the broken pieces of bark and the trunk of the fallen tree as if sucking its last breath of life. Symbolizing the cycle of life and death, the fallen tree returned to the dust from which it came only to regenerate in its new life form and grow again with a new beginning. Over this tree, we traversed and suddenly found we had lost the trail. Which way should we go? We set out walking for what seemed another hour or so as the sunray beams started fading, and my grandparents admitted we were lost. As we walked through any open areas of brush, the trees suddenly lost their magnificence, as our main focus was only finding the vehicle and mankind again. But wait, what was that sound? Swooshing of vehicles and the well-accustomed sound of the highway and traffic traversing in the distance. We followed the sounds of humanity and let our ears lead us back to the correct path. Suddenly the highway appeared as we pondered whether left or right would be the correct turn to take. And in that moment, all the blanketed trees in the eve of dust looked exactly the same. My grandparents determined which turn to take, of course. I wasn't sold at that time, but I followed. As our hike neared the end, the sky opened up, and before us stood, as if a mirage in the desert, the park sign, and the concrete entrance of the parking lot welcomed our tired feet and eased our anxious minds, for we were at our vehicle at last. No sight of a big tree could appease our eyes better than the sought-out park entrance at this point, especially with the dusk of night upon us!

HIGHWAY TO 101, SEA LIONS, GOOD HEALTH, AND HAPPINESS

Oregon was our final destination and goal, the furthest North we would have traveled in order to see my aunt and grandma's youngest daughter. We stayed with my aunt and cousins for the longest of days assigned to the trip. Oregon was a beautiful place, and my aunt lived relatively close to the coast. One of our afternoons was spent driving to the coastline. The highway is divided by the ocean on one hand and the rocky terrain on the other side. Highway 101's coastline is one of the most renowned for its beauty and windy hairpin turns. Our destination was the sea lion caves—one of the largest colonies of sea lions in North

America, if not in the world. We traveled down an elevator to the den of thousands of lions resting on the rugged rock families and babies, all squawking and wining as if they were welcoming us into their den and then jumping into the water, as if to say, *look what I can do*. My aunt lived in a small town that had a kefir factory. Kefir is a very thick probiotic rich fruit-flavored yogurt drink. It was one of the first probiotic drinks of its time. Oregon was a very natural and healthy-driven culture where people ate and drank things good for them no matter the taste. It was fun visiting the factory and learning about this yummy and healthful drink. We even got the shirt to prove it! Not only did people who lived in Oregon eat and drink healthy, but they loved music, dancing, and festivals. People were dancing in the streets, moms feeding their babies, guitars strumming their strings, and people singing. It was a very lively time.

GRAND LAKES, CANYONS, AND CAVES

Once we left to head back south, we visited Crater Lake, Oregon. Crater Lake, one of the largest lakes in North America, has a depth greater than 1900 feet. It formed when the volcano above it collapsed, and now the lake's perimeters are surrounded by trees with several beautiful lookout points. The lake is also noted for its pristine and clear blue water, the color it reflects, in part, due to its depth.

My grandma did her research and trip planning well, as she found the National or State parks in each state that we would hike and explore. Each historical site, monument, or natural wonder gave all of us a reprieve from the meager RV cabin we resided in day and night. One of our quick trips just south of Crater Lake was to the Lava Beds National Monument, which allowed us to touch and walk on the lava rocks. We stooped over and picked up the porous black disproportionate rocks and held them in our hands, imagining the heat and flow of live red-hot magma. This eruption, which occurred millions of years ago, as it flowed like a river leveling everything in its path and leaving it lifeless and barren, was the very land we were standing on in awe.

As we headed back south through California and turned to head back in the direction of my grandparents' home in Texas, our next destination was Arizona, The Grand Canyon. The Grand Canyon visit, in all of its magnificence, was short-lived, as time was limited, and we were just passing through the area. It seemed like miles driving across the remote and vast deserted lands until, just like that, it appeared. My grandparents found a lookout point where we were able to get out of the vehicle and embrace its beauty and vastness. As we stood at the edges of the canyon, we saw the layers of rock from brown, red, pink, gray, and all the shades of the earth, with the rays of the sun highlighting its cloak of many colors. The Canyon's depth and grandeur were enticing to explore and hike, but the time afforded us was all the eyes could do to embrace it, locking in these visual memories for decades to come. I always vowed to come back and explore in greater detail, as the Canyon called my name.

One of our last stops as we headed in the direction of Texas was the Carlsbad Caverns in New Mexico. We explored this sunken cave, and that is when I learned about stalactite, minerals collected from time hanging down from the cave's ceilings or stalagmites, which are minerals growing upward from the cave's bottom, as if blossoming out of the ground crevices much like a flower in bloom. At the end of our tour, we got to take a group picture, and there stood my family, my grandparents, aunt, and me right in the middle. My grandparents allowed me to keep a copy of the picture, which still fires my memory to this day.

REFLECTION: REDEFINING NORMALCY

*D*riving across the vastness of the United States, including all the states we got to explore, made me sad to have to return to what lay in wait. I knew this dream was about to end and my pinch would bring me back to the reality of returning to my home in North Carolina. The drive through the grandiose plains of Texas as we neared closer and closer to my grandparents' home in Houston brought me down from the elation of the trip as my former life of reality set in. But the drive across Texas alone in length and time seemed as long as the trip itself, with the flat landscaping that seemed to stretch for miles. Watching the iron horses going up and down, pumping oil from the ground, served as a countdown to our final endpoint home. The summer adventure came to an end, and I found myself back on the plane by myself, looking out into the blue fluffy clouds and horizon, pondering what it would be like coming home, dreading the next chapter of my life.

> Friends: There is a peace that comes from being alone with God, exploring the wonders of His creation. Take time to revel in his beauty.

Chapter 10
RELIGIOUS CONVERSION

I'M NOT MY OWN: LOST
IN THE CONVERSION

*S*omehow my mom had gotten a job at The 700 Club, a ministry of the Christian Broadcasting Network (CBN) in Virginia Beach, Virginia, while my stepdad was still working in the Navy. This was a nearly impossible feat for my mom to accomplish, considering the abuse and deception that lay behind closed doors. I don't know how my mom managed to get a job there. She later testified that during that time, she would do drugs with Brute and then pray God would deliver him. which finally came to fruition.

I don't know what was worse, the physical and emotional abuse under the influence of drugs or the physical and emotional abuse under the influence of religious legality, legalization, and my parents' misinterpretation of the Bible. The 700 Club was a Christian television show that originated in 1966, directed and presented by Pat Robertson, and aired on live television. It would show Christian viewpoints from the Bible and relate them to current events in the news and share people's testimonies and how God saved them. They requested that people share their own miracles or stories with them to share worldwide what God had done in their lives. The Christian network and staff would pray together on the set before starting a day's work. The show was commonly played daily in the home, and I was very hopeful to see how so many other people could overcome so many hardships and tragedies and find hope in God and their Savior, Jesus, like I did. This confirmed and fueled my belief in Jesus and his mighty working power in other people's lives.

My latchkey days had returned, as both parents would be at work on many days when I got home from school. Shortly after my mom started working at the Network, we started to attend a Pentecostal church in Chesapeake, Virginia, just across the border. My stepdad stopped abusing drugs and then transitioned into wanting to be a registered minister. He started studying religious books and workbooks to take the test and start his own church. I thought his personal goals were nonsense, as I enjoyed going back to church and loved the experience of developing my own relationships with God and Jesus. I didn't want my stepdad to be the minister I would have to take spiritual heed and guidance from. Like so many things I found refuge in, I wanted to share going to church with my friends, so my parents traded in the station wagon and bought a van. We loaded up the local kids and took them to Cedar Road Assembly of God Pentecostal Church in Chesapeake, Virginia, just across the Virginia border. My relationship with Jesus and the Church was different than the relationship I was afforded through my parents. I had heartfelt, constant communication about so many things, experiences, and emotions with my Lord and Savior. I talked to Him about all things, especially when I was outside in his creation. I could feel his presence with the sun shining on my face or watching the birds singing and flying carelessly in the air.

WALKING THROUGH
THE LIGHT AND DARK

*O*ur church attendance increased to Sunday, both a.m. and p.m., Wednesday night, all night prayer services, and prayer chair rocking rock-a-thons. The abuse transitioned from sexual priming and physical abuse and neglect from being locked out of the house to physical abuse and Christian legalism and being locked in the home. My parents started to do prayer walks through the trailer park, taking pictures and saying a demonic presence was reigning over the community, but they were praying over it in the name of Jesus. It was very common to turn on the 700 Club and see people's testimonies of their personal experiences with the occult, Satan, and charming others or being a victim of being charmed through witchcraft. I remembered reading about the Winston-Salem witch hunt in 1692, with witches being burned at the stake for fear of practicing black magic. Now during the 1980s, people were starting to openly practice this form of magic and talk about their own experiences and how they were delivered from the dark side. They would speak of witchcraft happening in the woods behind us and the evil in the community. Our church would preach the living scriptures and practice the power of Jesus through the blood of the lamb, and although we were living in a world of evil and darkness, we could be free and not afraid. But of course, all of this was a very horrifying thing for such a little girl to have to learn about and see how my parents felt it was their mission to save our trailer park from the supposed evil that lay in the heavens claiming this territory.

MANIPULATION OF THE
LIGHT AND DARK

*D*uring this time, our church played the *Left Behind* movie series, showing the book of Revelation and how those who were not saved nor forgiven would perish when Jesus came back for his second coming. My parents often would use the end times teaching of Revelation and the Bible to justify that I was a sinner and that if I didn't act right, I would go to hell and perish when Jesus came back. Not only was the movie terrifying but also the way my parents used it as ammunition to further control me. Many times, my parents had me fearing my own salvation and questioning my own relationship with God. However, since I was exposed to these types of things, I knew Jesus and spiritual things on a deeper level, and my mind had no limitations on the type of physical and spiritual miracles He could perform in my lifetime and had performed many thousand years prior in the Bible stories I read. I would say the sinner's prayer often and always ask God to forgive me and find me worthy. It was as if God was giving me eyes to see Him work in the spiritual realm and believe.

The physical and emotional abuse turned a quick corner as my stepdad started to read the Bible and use what was said literally to justify his anger and behavior. He would spank me and say things like "spare the rod, spoil the child." The spankings would be out of anger and not controlled. He would use a belt, his hand, or anything he could grab in a quick fit of anger. Sometimes marks were left in hidden places.

I have learned that the Bible is full of parables, stories, and prophecies to come. When reading the Bible, one should always consider the context, history, and culture at the time scriptures are written to understand the hidden meanings. For example, "spare the rod, spoil the child" may have symbolized the leading of animals, cows, and oxen with a steering rod and yoke when they would plow and farm the land. So, as you can imagine, sparing the rod was symbolic of allowing your children to act and roam aimlessly. But on the contrary, parents are called to lead their children by example, as the cows are being led by the plows and rods, and reinforce good behavior into the direction of their lives, role-modeling how they should carry themselves and behave. Farming was a main source of survival during biblical times. Most people were farmers or had animals to produce milk and cultivate their land. So many common people would understand this analogy.

During another one of his times of fury and frustration, he wanted me to learn how to tell time and banished me to my bed with a clock until I figured it out. I don't know how long it took for me to finally catch on to time, but eventually, I was free to leave my bed and room. Other times, he banned me to bed until I read the Bible and gave him a full report. I would cry and highlight pages through my tears as if I was reading them so I could show him my completed studies. It made me start to resent the Bible and the scriptures he used to validate his abuse and poor behavior toward me. It took a very long time into adulthood for me to want to voyage into reading the Bible again on my own.

THE HEALING LIGHT AND
WARMTH OF JESUS

*O*was receiving medical treatment through the Navy doctors, who found I had scoliosis after an X-ray. Scoliosis is an abnormal curvature of the lower spine, and no one really knows what causes it. It caused my shoulders and the core of my body to be crooked, with one shoulder higher than the other. If the curvature got worse or too bad as I grew, the doctors said I would need surgery and have to wear a brace to support my spine. During one of our all-night prayer services, my mom asked the church to pray for me. I remember just being a little girl in fifth or sixth grade going before the congregation as the elders stood around me. They placed some holy oil on my forehead and started to pray. Holy oil is usually derived from olive oil from olive trees, as olive trees were common in Israel and during biblical times and considered to be sacred.

The elders of the church would pray over the oil in advance, asking for God's mercy and power to help heal others in the name of Jesus. Just a dab of the oil would be applied to the patron's body, usually on their forehead or any area of concern that may need healing from pain, etc. The Bible speaks of this practice in James 5:14: "If any among you may be sick, ask the elders to pray for you, anointing you in oil in the name of the Lord." I stretched out my arms to heaven, asking God and Jesus in my spirit to heal my back. I was young and didn't quite understand the lifelong implications of having this crooked spine condition. I did know I was terrified of potentially needing back surgery, wearing a brace, and being unable to swim and play like a normal little girl. I pleaded with God to heal me. I remember having a warm feeling come over my body and my legs collapsing beneath me. Not being able to bear my body weight, I slumped down on the ground. I could hear the background noise of people praising, singing, clapping, dancing, and rejoicing as I came to, looking up at the minister who was standing over me, helping me to my feet, saying that I was healed. My mom, curious as she was, took me back to the naval doctors and requested a follow-up X-ray. They had many X-rays on file, and the new X-ray was compared to my previous medical history. I saw the image on a well-lit whiteboard in which he was tracing each vertebra, trying to track the previously recorded curvature. He could not find it! The doctor was in awe as my mom told him the story about how our church prayed for me. He admitted the curvature was gone, and he even contested it was a Medical Miracle. My mom then took me to see a chiropractor. She had frequented a chiropractor for treatment of her previous back injury and used them to help relieve occasional pain. When we went for our initial chiropractic visit, the chiropractor identified my shoulders were crooked and out of alignment. He requested a copy of my X-rays and medical records before working on me to confirm that, in fact, my back was straight, as he didn't want to cause any further damage to my spine. I followed up with the chiropractor, who performed several stretching and lengthening adjustments over time, which then caused my shoulders and body alignment to be straight and in position with my now straight spine. If it had not been for the residual crooked shoulders and body alignment, it would have been harder to believe that this was truly a miracle, but as you see, God didn't heal me in that instance. He healed my body over time. He healed me through steps and exercises, thus showing me how great his power was. He heals many of us today in stages, causing us to be dependent on him, growing our faith over time, earning our trust, and making us depend on him. He heals us through our portion, doing the work we need as we lean on Him to seek his miracles in his time. Nothing is short of a miracle and a testimony in his time. Even the chiropractor gave us his second opinion on the matter after many sessions with him. It was a medical miracle.

BE CAREFUL WHAT YOU WISH FOR

*D*uring this time of spiritual growth as a young child, God taught me a very valuable lesson that I have since carried with me. We had dinner with our neighbors on the weekends. Their two girls were my classmates, and after we started playing together, our parents started getting together for dinner. One night, I noticed the girls drinking soda, which I was not allowed to do. We never had it in our home. When I did get soda, it was a root beer or orange soda in an occasional kid's meal from a fast-food restaurant. That night, I had jealousy in my eyes as I watched the girls drink their soda without limitation, enjoying the carbonation and rich sugar flavor that I longed to taste. Glaring at them, I thought, *I hope they pee in the bed*! I kept watching and wishing with every drink they took. Little did I know God was about to teach me a lesson.

Ironically, when I stayed that night at their house, I had the urge to go to the bathroom in the middle of the night. I slept in one of the girls' rooms, and the sisters stayed together in one of their own rooms to accommodate me. When I woke up in the morning, I felt very cold and very wet. As I got up and looked around, I realized I was the one who had, in fact, wet the bed—not just a little bit and not just on myself, but on the whole entire mattress and sheets! I wet the bed despite my bathroom break in the middle of the night.

My friend's mom stripped the sheets and took the mattress outside, and I was assigned the duty of spraying down and cleaning it for the whole world to see! I'd never been so embarrassed in my entire life. As I was cleaning the mattress, it was as if I could hear God's voice inside saying, "Never wish in jealousy or in anger anything bad on anyone, for as you can see, it will only come back to you." I learned my lesson, and to this day, I seek to help others, not wish harm or desire what others have in a vengeful, jealous way.

HOME HAIRCUTS AND
A FUTURE VISION

My mom always wanted to cut hair and become a hairdresser. She even had the old 1970s cosmetology workbook in preparation for taking the licensing exam. My mom always cut my hair and referenced her book for partings, techniques, perms, pin curls, and roller styles. She believed in her skills so much she would perm her own hair, perm my stepdad's hair, and create her own techniques for cutting our hair. She would always remind me that she wanted to be a hairdresser, as if this gave her the credentials and expertise to do so.

My hair was relatively straight or slightly wavy in my younger years, but as I approached puberty, it got frizzy and uncontrollable—at a time when it mattered most. The kids bullying and making fun of me was only magnified by the scrappy recycled wardrobe I wore to school. In 7th grade, I knew in my heart I wanted to cut hair to help others so they would not be bullied, mocked, and made fun of. I knew I would have to take care of myself when I got older. Since there was no college fund or parents who sought out grants or support for college, I knew trade school would be my only option. Neither of my parents were educated, nor did they understand the importance of college. And they didn't know how to apply for assistance.

I studied my cosmetology book between breaks and told my classmates that I would cut hair one day. The kids all took one look at this scrappy, disheveled little girl and mocked my beaming vision of becoming a hairdresser. They taunted me, saying repeatedly, "Cosmenot, Cosmenot, you will never cut hair!" One little boy sitting in front of me on the school bus turned around, grabbed my hair, and wrestled with me, saying, "Why don't you get a real haircut!"

I never gave up. Despite the loud chanting and catcalling, inside, I knew without a doubt I would one day cut hair. Even though I lived in North Carolina at the time and never saw a beauty school, I still knew I would cut hair. I knew that was my purpose, and if that was my purpose, God would find a way to make it happen. Little did I know a few years later, I would move to Texas to live with my Grandma GG, where I would attend the local high school, take Cosmetology for free, and get my license upon completion of the class. I always believed in the vision, despite feelings of hopelessness and a picture of a seemingly bleak future my parents laid out before me.

UNEMPLOYMENT AND THREATS OF HOMELESSNESS

My mom stated she was fired from The 700 club, and my step-dad resigned from the Navy and sought mechanic jobs. He eventually found himself unemployed with my mom. They had a build-up of poorly managed finances and debts. They had multiple credit cards and piles of mail/unpaid bills, which I would shuffle around when doing the household chores. Shortly after they lost their jobs, the phone began to ring and the mail became more frequent. My mom started to throw the letters away instead of stockpiling them.

One day, my parents told me they had not been paying the bills and that we would be living on the street. They said, "Think about what bags you want to pack and keep, as that will be all you have. We will live in a tent." I was told they had no money, and the bank was coming to get our trailer. As far as I knew, one day I would come home and the trailer would either be locked or completely gone, and we would be left standing on the curb with nothing. Such a scary and vivid memory is left in my mind of homelessness. This terrified me as a little girl, and all I could imagine was losing my home, my bed, and the only part of my world that was secure. Those months of trauma have not ceased to haunt me. Whenever I have a job or financial change, anxiety wells over me as I ponder the what haves and could be's of the past and/or future to come. This could be why as an adult, I overcame my challenges to finish college and climb the ladder of success in my career. I have this inner desire not just to survive but to succeed. Due to my anxiety-gripping fear of failing, I always push forward to overcome.

STARTING A CHURCH
AND A SECRET

*D*uring this time of unemployment, my parents were trying to start their own church at the community center located in the park. We had said goodbye to the Pentecostal church and no longer attended their services. I was crushed. I loved going to church and felt committed to the church, my friends, and the stability of practicing my faith there. I dreaded having to follow my stepdad's supposed spiritual leadership.

They would have Vacation Bible School in the summer for kids and hold services on Sundays at the community center or at their homes. My parents had established relationships with another military family who had a daughter my age and an older son. The wife helped lead the kids' programs and facilitate the church services. My mom led and arranged the songs to be sung at the services. My stepdad created an office in one of the rooms in the trailer and did his supposed sermon studies there. My parents expected me to be a role model and present them and the church in the best light in the community in which they were trying to grow.

One Sunday morning when I wouldn't sing, my mom told my dad to take me home for an attitude adjustment. My mom was leading the song service, clapping her hands, acting joyous, and kept motioning for me to clap, sing, and act happy. All I could think about was how much I resented them for taking the one thing I wanted away from me, my church. How could I sing and be happy when my spirit was defeated?

She stopped the song service, and my dad took me home. He had me drop my pants and bend over the couch, and then he gave me 50 licks with a belt. Mind you, I was approaching my teen years and was no longer a little girl. Then he took me back to church and once again expected me to sing. He told someone in church that was what it took to break my spirit. Shortly afterward, he pulled me into his dark, musty office with plywood paneling walls and had me sit in front of him. He said some teachers at school might ask me how things are at home, but I could not say anything. Everything was a family secret he said, as he chuckled dryly, and I could not share the family secrets.

I remember being called out of class and being asked questions, as my stepdad had warned. The teacher asked me to bend over in the hall and pull up my shirt as they looked at my back. I thought they were checking my now-straight spine to see that my scoliosis was gone. Why wouldn't everyone want to see my miracle? Now, as an adult, I realize they were looking for the marks those 50-plus lashes afforded me. How convenient that the lashes and marks were hidden by my underwear.

RUNNING AWAY
WITH A SECRET

I later found out someone had reported my parents to the officials for the abuse, and we abruptly moved to Kansas. I was told my grandparents, my mom's dad, William, and stepmom, Olive, were helping us find a house. My parents were going to start a church in the Midwest because they needed Jesus. What a better place to go. I was happy. I could see my grandparents again, whom I had only seen once since we had left my great-grandfather's basement many years ago. We packed up everything we could and loaded them in U-Haul trailers, which we pulled behind station wagons and vans.

Now the strange thing about this move was the military family my family was trying to start a church with, well, they parted ways. But they didn't part ways in the way you would commonly think. The wife and daughter moved with us, and the husband and son went in another direction. She left her husband to follow my sick family, as she was smitten by the potential of God needing her to start a church in Kansas! It was like my stepdad had some kind of lure or curse over her. He was a snake charmer for sure.[8]

> **Friends: Don't be someone else's religion. It's your relationship with Jesus, not what someone else wants you to be or do. It's not about the religion but about the relationship.**

---

8   If this chapter touched you and you would like more information to help on your own *Quest*, see page 312, **Bullying** and page 313, **Healing Adjustments Chiropractor.**

Chapter 11
SUNSHINE IN THE SORROWS

DISTRACTIONS
OF THE MIND

*B*efore we move on to what happens in Kansas, I would like to share what it was like living in North Carolina. It was a great place to live—a place of great intrigue and so much history. There were so many things to learn about, and just imagine walking on the same barren land as our first British settlers did when they first arrived by boat.

BIRD SANCTUARY

*E*ach year during elementary school, we went on field trips, usually exploring the things we were studying. One of my favorite projects was studying ornithology. We got to pick a favorite bird known to coexist in the area, draw an image of it, and study its characteristics. Then we visited a local bird sanctuary and park reservation. We studied birds that were all known inhabitants of the area, such as cardinals, crows, woodpeckers, warblers, sparrows, mockingbirds, doves, bluebirds, goldfinches, and hummingbirds. So off we went to the Currituck bird sanctuary with our binoculars and brown bag lunch in tow. Our goal was to spot as many birds as we had studied. We were true bird watchers for a day. We learned about the National Wildlife refuge and the land that made up the marshy protected terrain that was home to not only the birds but so many other critters. It was their world and home, and we were their house guests for the day.

ANCESTORS FORMED OUR FREEDOMS

*S*ome of my most treasured field trips were learning about our early ancestors, who founded this great country that we call America. The freedoms we have today, such as the right to work, buy a house, practice our faith, have a family, start a business, and the ability to vote, were because of our founding fathers. It amazes me that in the 21st century, many people don't practice the freedoms our forefathers fought for.

We went to the first of the 13 colonies, the Lost Colony of Roanoke, established in 1585. It was the first established English settlement in North America by Sir Walter Raleigh. There wasn't much to see other than the small shadow of a town on an inlet of water and the outside amphitheater that makes the settlement come to life, carrying on the stories of the past. The lost colony, as its name suggests, leaves behind a mysterious past. Even though this was the first settlement of the English on American soil, the ancestors who came to this great country leave behind a mystery as they disappeared, leaving no record of the lives they were trying to create. One of the greatest legacies of this colony was the first-born English person Virginia Dare, which the town prides itself on to this day.

The following year, we took an all-day field trip to Jamestown and Williamsburg, located in Virginia. Jamestown was established in 1607 as the first permanent English settlement in America. You can visit it today and see the enclosed fort encased with small huts or homelike structures that families inhabited, their church, and the kitchens they would cook out of. The first settlers were promised the opportunity to make their fortune in the new lands across the ocean. Little did they know when they arrived, it was late in the season, and a harsh winter brought a lack of food for the settlers. Later the settlers found resources and money in crops they grew, such as tobacco, which became their cash king. Talk about poor timing. Many settlers lay in wait for food and supplies from England, while most died. Some remaining settlers created relationships with the Native Americans, the Powhatan tribes, and depended on them for food and survival until relations became strained and they fought against each other.

STANDING IN THE GAP FOR OTHERS

*D*uring this war, Pocahontas' brothers captured Captain John Smith of the colony. Pocahontas stepped in on behalf of her father, the leader of the tribe, and pleaded for his life and freedom. She then bridged the relationships between the settlers and the tribe, although their differences and the settlers' desperation for food and survival continued to strain this union. Pocahontas was later taken by the settlers and held for ransom for the release of other English prisoners by her dad, the tribal leader. To her dismay, her dad did not uphold his end of the bargain, and she remained with the English settlers, marrying John Rolfe, learning the English language and Christianity, and being renamed Rebecca.

I can't help but parallel Pocahontas' relationship with the settlers to Esther in the Bible. Esther was a Jew who lived among the Persians. The king chose her as his wife, and she became the queen. She took risks to defend the Jews by providing food and standing on their behalf to prevent the king from calling an order to kill them. Both women, coming from different backgrounds, languages, and cultures, had the courage to defend others different from themselves. Funny how history repeats itself. If only we can learn from these stories of unity despite our cultural differences and stand in the gap for others.

ESTABLISHING A COLONY, ESTABLISHING A FAMILY COMMUNITY

*W*e went to Williamsburg, which was established in 1699 and is the capital of the Virginia colony. It was relocated from the original Jamestown colony. By this time, the settlers were becoming more established and not just surviving but thriving. They no longer had to wait for the English to bring them the resources they needed but the resources they desired. This city grew much into what became the basis of America's economic, political, religious, and societal structure that we embrace today. We learned about how precious our right to vote is. Back then, the only people who could vote were white males who were Christians and had land and/or were wealthy. The way we have evolved to give everyone this privilege to have a say in the development of our country was eye-opening.

We got to see how wax was made and dipped to create candles. With the invention of candles, families were able to gather and have dinner, politicians could study and write things with quills and ink bottles, moms could spin cotton, make thread, and possibly even make material and sew their clothes. Candles were a wonderful invention that helped our nation progress. As we strolled through the streets of colonial Williamsburg, we saw ladies making candy coins on wax paper and the blacksmith sharpening and heating iron to make muskets, artillery, armor, and other weaponry. It was important for Williamsburg to always be armed and ready for any potential invaders. An unexpected invasion could mean life or death for the colony.

Every passerby walking or working was dressed in colonial outfits for that era, including the wigs. Wigs were a fashion statement for men, or they just used them to cover up their patchy baldness and show their aristocracy, class, and position in the colony. Since history and fashion repeat themselves, maybe wigs will be on the forefront for men again during our time? The colony really exemplified how simple life was and the importance of family and the community. Their survival in life made them interwoven and dependent on each other. The survival of the colony depended on their teamwork and the completion of daily chores and routines as they took care of themselves and each other.

THE FLIGHT THAT BRIDGED CULTURE AND COMMUNITIES

The Wright brothers' flight changed everything, bridging country to country across vast waters. We got to see the Wright brothers' memorial and the models of the first planes in flight. Orville and Wilbur created and flew the first-ever plane in 1903. What a joyous celebration that was! This changed the whole trajectory of America and the world for generations to come. It impacted how we gave and received supplies. Planes were made to be used in times of war locally and abroad and made the world appear small.

Previous forms of transportation, especially from country to country, were by ship, which took months to traverse. People would die during transit by boats, and much-needed supplies would be consumed out of necessity due to the long journey. Planes shortened the time lost in traveling. Planes today allow us to travel for leisure and fun and allow us to see distant family members or distant lands, unearthing the world's magnitude from the heavens above. Traveling by plane was only for the noble and affluent; however, just about anyone can travel today. Funny how we may take planes and the luxury of traveling for granted, stealing others' freedom by selfishly refusing to conform to basic safety guidelines. I remember the days when kids traveled for free and got their own wings, a pin symbolic of the flight.

But one may say, "I can't afford to travel." First, be smart with your money and budget. If you are a wise planner, you can get a credit card that gives you credit in miles as you pay for gas, food, clothes, bills, and daily living. Eventually, those dollars spent will buy you a free plane ticket. Buyer beware. Make sure you pay the balance off every month, or else you will be paying for tickets in interest!

As we left the Wright brothers' memorial, we drove along the Cape Hatteras coastline parallel to the Atlantic Beach, with the beach to our right and the sand dunes to our left. Looking up, you could see the brightly colored life-sized kites soaring high above the dunes and ocean, just as the Wright Brothers flew so many years prior. These kites, sailing so peacefully through the sky, were being directed and turned by just a bar in hand. I made a pact that someday as an adult, I would fly my own kite. I never knew where life would take me or how I would pay for it, but I knew I would fly too!

We turned in to the parking lot of our last destination for the year's trip, the sand dunes. As all of us kids scuttled off the bus, we must have looked like a pack of ants all scurrying after that last sweet piece of apple dropped to the ground as we all charged up the biggest sand pile ever. The reward of the magnificent view of the vast ocean and the wind blowing through our hair left us all speechless, which is hard to achieve with kids. It sounded like you had a shell up to your ear as the swooshing sounds of the waves hitting the shore lingered on the sandy mountain tops. It was awe-provoking and amazing. My mind turned back to how it must have been when the new settlers first saw this land and shore, calling it America.

A BUSLOAD OF KIDS
JOURNEY TO FLORIDA

One of the last and final field trips I got to take while living on the east coast was to Florida. I don't know how my parents conjured up the money for me to attend, but I do remember my mom telling my dad all the reasons why I should go. Maybe there was some kind of grant, or maybe his parents helped provide the money. Either way, I loaded the bus that night with a highlighted road map tracing our path to Florida. We rode the overnight bus to Cape Canaveral and toured the space city of NASA, tracking the history of flight across land and sea to flights going out into the unknown. My respect and appreciation go out to the brave souls who followed their passions for a dream bigger than the norm, willing to sacrifice against all odds for our gain. Exhausted from driving all night, we headed to the hotel after the tour.

It's hard to imagine how teachers managed to corral a busload of kids into Disney World and Epcot. I can't imagine that happening in today's world. I am sure a few kids would be misplaced or disappear in the crowd. What brave teachers we had! My favorite ride was space mountain and the futuristic implications of tomorrow as we rode on an escalator afterward, seeing images of electronic phones and TVs, all of which have come true.

Finally, we had our dinner at the medieval castle, cheering the blue team versus the red team as horses ran and hoisted past each other. We would all stomp and clank our heavy pewter cups on the tables or plates, cheering our team on in the competition. What a great time we had.

GIFTED AND TALENTED

I have always loved school and learning. I looked forward to the field trips each year, as they made the stories of the history we learned about in the classroom come alive. I loved school so much that my friends and I played school. I had a very good memory and got my homework and schoolwork done before the other students, so I thought what better way to help my friends learn more than to create projects for them to do after they completed their assignments? It was fun teaching others, and I guess my friends liked being my students.

I would often get in trouble in class for talking. My teacher saw my academic strengths and referred me for gifted and talented testing. My test scores were very high, and in my last few years in elementary school, I was able to be dismissed to the G. T. trailer. My time in the trailer was spent on activities such as problem-solving and using the process of elimination techniques to solve mysteries. We used computers to study different languages. I remember studying French and learning the colors bleu and rouge. Ha, if only I had practiced Spanish, but who would have known I'd live out my adult years in the south? It was so much fun learning, and when I wasn't doing my extras in school, you could find me far, far away in suspense, curled up in a corner of the classroom reading my latest book from the library.

During my fifth-grade year, I was assigned to study a list of words. Since I loved school and learning, I took heart to conquer the list and have it memorized. I worked diligently until the big day, the spelling bee. The kids were lined up in two rows as the teachers went down each row, asking us to repeat back each word letter by letter. To my dismay, I was one of two kids left standing. I remember clearly that day the word was beautiful. My opponent missed a letter, and it was my chance to spell it correctly. So with all I had to muster, I spelled B-E-A-U-T-I-F-U-L and waited in anticipation. Since I had spelled it correctly, I was handed my prize of red hots in a plastic tube with a plastic heart topper on it. The spelling bee has been a national competition since the first spelling bee in 1908. Well, nothing came of my big win, but as an adult, I now know I should have competed at the next level, another opportunity lost in time. That word always lingered in my mind. I was beautiful no matter what the kids said, as they laughed and scoffed at me. I was beautiful and felt as if God was telling me Himself.

Friends: You are beautiful! Don't let anyone tell you otherwise. Find the beauty in yourself and in your life. Don't use others' perceptions to define your own beauty. Pray to see yourself and others the way God sees you.

Chapter 12
WHAT DOES KANSAS HOLD?

FROM PRAIRIE PLAINS
TO CITY LIGHTS

*O*was able to complete my seventh-grade junior high class in North Carolina before our abrupt move to Kansas. Looking back, I think the move was prompted in part by my parents being reported to officials for the abuse I had endured. My stepdad bragged to trailer park residents who attended his church meetings that it took 50 licks with a belt to break my spirit when I wouldn't sing in church. Also, neither of my parents had a job, and they expected the church to make them money. So they packed up what they could fit in a car with a U-Haul trailer and a U-Haul truck, and off we drove to Kansas with my mom, stepdad, and our neighbor's wife Grace and daughter Bethany.

MUSIC FOR THE SOUL

*I*t was a strange move, but I was told it was to start a new church in the Midwest. All five of us lived with my grandparents, William and Olive, for a month until a home was rented in town. Our stay in town was very short-lived, and I made the most of our move to Kansas during this time. I could walk to school and walk around town or go to the store. I had an escape outside of the home and a distraction. I had started practicing the flute in fifth grade after someone in the church gave my mom the instrument. It was my extracurricular activity in school through my ninth-grade year, so I could stay after school for lessons and walk home afterward. Playing the flute was music for my soul and an escape.

STEAMY DAYS AT
THE COUNTY FAIR

*A*nother great thing about living in town was that it was easy to go to the fair every day of the week in August. The county fair was an annual event, and people traversed from all areas of Kansas for the midget car races, carnival rides, games, concerts, animal auctions by the FFA students, and the Czech kolache and baked goods contest and sale. It was not only the highlight of the community but an annual event that preserved the livelihood of the town brought families and community together, and left behind much joy. Bethany and I walked up and down the many aisles of carnival games and booths and watched people on the rides as their joyous screams circulated through the air. Many times, I would stop and talk to the people who traveled and worked the show, commonly called Carnies. It would always start with small talk about trying to conjure up bystanders to spend money playing their games. Well, of course, we didn't have money to play games, but the discussions often led to dreamy words and compliments, which would draw me in. I remember many of them staring deeply into my eyes and commenting on how pretty and blue they were, like the ocean. I sought out any attention I could get and longed to get words of shallow affection from them. Oh, how I loved going to the fair!

LOSS OF INNOCENCE

Since I was the new kid on the block, one boy took a liking to me. He was very kind and helped me get acquainted with the students, school, and community. His family was also new to the town, and he felt he hadn't quite found his place with the other students either. He helped me transition into a new school setting. I met his family and sister, and he visited my house several times. In fact, he was planning to visit me after school for my birthday on 9/11. I knew he was late as I watched the clock, and my mom kept asking when I wanted her to cut the cake. He was the water and supply boy for the football team and attended practice after school. I knew he would come over afterward.

I waited and waited, but he never came. I remember distinctly hearing ambulances in the background but dismissed any thoughts quickly from my mind. After what seemed like hours of rejection, I called his family.

His sister answered the phone. "Hello?"

I sensed a deep and solitary expression in her voice as a dark sensation loomed over the phone. In a timid and soft voice, I asked to speak to my friend.

She paused for what felt like a lifetime and said, "He is no longer with us."

I said, "What? What do you mean? He was supposed to come for my birthday! I just saw him at school today."

"I know," she said and stated he had passed away at school on the field today.

Later, we found out he had been inhaling a substance in the gym locker room deep in the basement for the last few days. It was a dare by a bully, and my friend just wanted to be accepted and liked. That day as he brought supplies to the bully on the field, he collapsed, never to take another breath of life again. That bully stole his life that day. Once young and naive, now that bully (or bullies) has to live out his earthly existence plagued by his conscience, painted by the blood of an innocent loss of life. Don't be a bully, and don't be a victim of bullying. Get help. Don't let others force you into being a bully. Be the big, strong one and stand up for the right thing.

I dropped to the ground in disbelief, not because of my birthday but because of the loss of an innocent life, someone so pure in heart and so kind, who only fought for others to be liked and accepted—a life of a future unknown and a purpose left undone. But his life was not left unrecognized, for he was my hero because of the impact he made in my life for just a short time. I knew I was loved and accepted. I slumped to the ground, tears streaming down in disbelief for myself, his family, and the impact he could have had on the world. Heaven gained a precious soul that day, and he was greeted warmly in the love and acceptance he had always sought.

COUNTRY CONTROL AND
FARMHOUSE PRISONER

My parents then moved to a home in the country to keep us girls out of trouble. It didn't take long for the townspeople to see that we were "two oppressed young girls," as my grandma later told me, and my parents were shunned by the town. In fact, the whole church project fizzled out very quickly, as the close-knit community saw my parents' true colors.

This house in the country was six miles from the city. It was a large house set high up on a hill, with rolling hills and creeks to traverse once you exited the highway. When it rained, the low-lying creeks would flood, and it was as if you were taking your chances to brave the waters to get to the other side. It was an old farmhouse, with the master bedroom downstairs, where Grace, the neighbor mom, resided, and four other bedrooms upstairs. My parents' bedroom was to the right of the stairs, and my friend's bedroom sat across from my parents'. I wanted to be as far away from them as possible; therefore, my bedroom was down the hall next to the bathroom.

The shape of the house was square, and the rooms were in all four corners upstairs. The wooden doors that covered the room entrances left a gaping hole underneath that light and air could freely pass through. Each door had its own ancient keyholes that paired with a skeleton or an antique key. There were lots of windows, well-lit with lights at night, and it had a very open feeling. The bathroom window upstairs had a small sheer curtain that barely covered the bottom third of the window, the two halves barely stretching across to meet in the middle. I don't remember any curtains or blinds on the other windows; however, my parents' room always seemed without light.

But on the dark side, the house was like a scorpion nightmare and was known in town as the scorpion house. It was as if it was built on an endless nest of invaders. You wouldn't dare walk barefoot at night, as they would commonly come out at that time. If you were lucky and sat still on the floor long enough, they would venture out at any time of day, and one could be encircled by two to three at will. I would lay awake many restless nights, wondering if they would come into my bed and sting me.

THE UNLIKELIEST OF
FARM ANIMALS

We had horses, a goat, and some dogs. I had never had a goat before, and she was a really neat animal to have. She really did eat most anything she could get a hold of, like the books say. I always remember her sweet, beady eyes and chewing chops every time I saw her. She would follow me around and rub up on me as if she was a dog, butting me and pushing me with her head to get more attention. She would even pull the laundry off the clothesline, and after a chew or two, it would be found strewn across the landscape.

Well, maybe that was the final chewing straw that broke the camel's back, or it just showed the ill intent in my parents' character. One day, my stepdad said he was going to kill the goat and feed her to us! After his continued verbal assault, I ran outside barefoot in the icy cold dew and held my goat tightly so he could not do her harm. As I stood barefoot and cold, the standoff began between myself, the goat, and my stepdad. Bitterly cold and infuriated, I refused to come in until my mom finally convinced me he wouldn't kill her. Later the goat disappeared, and I banned myself from eating meat from that point on.

One Saturday, they asked if I wanted to go kill chickens. I looked at them in disbelief, wondering if I had even heard them correctly.

I said, "Kill chickens?"

He said yes, as my mom and he laughed and said they were going to go chop off the heads of chickens with someone they knew in town. I couldn't believe my parents would ask a young teenager to do something so revolting. I said no way. I didn't want to carry that image in my mind of chopping off these poor creatures' heads just to watch them running amuck as entertainment afterward. Besides, not going would give me some peace away from them. Don't get me wrong—these things happen out of necessity for our food supply. But it seemed they were making a spectacle about it. It was a form of visual torture and manipulation, another way to control me and a display of their character.

So off they went—my stepdad, mom, Grace, and Bethany. I stayed behind, sitting on my bedroom floor listening to my Amy Grant tapes and weeping, asking God to save me from these conditions. As I sat there, I saw something move out of the corner of my eye. I looked up and saw two scorpions inches from my feet. It was like a standoff. What were they going to do as I sat there motionless and watched them scurry on?

Several years later, I asked my grandma what had happened to the old farmhouse. She said that years after we moved out, the house was torn down and no longer stands on that plot of land. I can only assume the scorpions took over the residence in vengeance with no one living there, making the home inhabitable.

DUST BUSTER TROUBLE

One day I was upstairs and my mom started yelling at me from downstairs, "Can you get the dust buster?" I came from my room to the stairs and asked my mom where it was. I knew if I didn't answer her request, trouble would soon follow. She told me it was upstairs in the spare room. I went and looked but did not see the dust buster, so I told her it wasn't there. Her voice got more firm, and she assured me it was in the spare bedroom, in the closet. I looked in the closet and came back to the top of the stairs and said it wasn't there.

Well, this angered my mom tremendously as she stormed up the stairs and rushed to the spare bedroom. She went into the closet, pulled out a box, and moved aside some items it was buried under. She held it up as if it was her trophy and repeatedly said, "How dare you call me a liar." In her rage, she grabbed a coat hanger and started beating me with it. All I could think was how in the heck would a 13-year-old even know to look in a box for a buried dust buster. The damage was done as I retreated to my room to find solace in my Amy Grant songs, and she retreated back downstairs.

DOGS VERSUS COYOTES

When we moved, our dogs from North Carolina came with us. They had lived relatively protected lives inside our previous trailer and gated yard. When we moved to the country, my parents would leave them outside. The dogs would run like a pack and would remain gone for periods at a time. The length of time they would be gone between their adventures would stretch longer and longer between stints. My parents showed little concern for them—they just casually said the dogs were missing. I was so afraid for the dogs. They were my only friends who provided comfort and consolation. They were my loyal and unforgiving pals. When they didn't come home at night, I would ponder every time I heard the coyotes cry whether they had gotten my friend. After a few days, our dogs returned, but one was missing, never to return—the leader of the pack, the mama bear cocker spaniel. My parents had bred her for years, and she produced puppies and cash for them. She was the older and wiser but frail one, and she was the one they got. I cried myself to sleep again that night. I look back and think about how careless my parents' thoughts and intentions were toward my precious pals, who provided such unforgiving love. Why didn't they offer our senior pets and the babies more protection and guidance after all their years of loyalty?

PRIMING

*M*y stepdad's ill intentions, sexual appetite, and prowess only seemed to intensify and become more evident as I casually pretended to dismiss his advances. I always felt aware of his underlying thoughts as he gazed at me. His mannerisms always left me feeling creeped out, unsafe, and guarded. Many times I awoke, startled to find him standing at the foot of my bed, hovering over me and staring as I slept.

During this time of my life, puberty was fast approaching for both of us girls. My stepdad would laughingly make crude jokes about skid marks in our underwear that I found rather embarrassing—not to mention the jokes about females and the changes they go through. Each night as I took a shower, he'd say he was outside taking care of the animals. I often saw him passing by outside and veering as far away from the window as I could while showering and preparing for the night.

One evening as I was preparing for a shower and sitting on the toilet, I had a sick feeling in my stomach, a feeling of being watched. I had this feeling many times, but this time, it came to fruition as my eyes met with his on the other side of that keyhole. Our eyes locked for what seemed an eternity. He was watching me! The light was void, not passing through underneath the door as I heard him scurry to get up. I had so many mixed feelings as my stomach turned inside out, and I wanted to throw up. My body started to shake. There was no escape from this creature.

But that moment didn't serve as a wake-up call for him. Instead, he seemed to take it as an invitation to make himself more available. One morning as I always did, I went to say goodbye. My mother was in the bathroom and called me in as she stood there naked, dry bathing and cleaning herself with a washcloth. I kissed her goodbye as usual. I was then expected to tell my stepdad goodbye and say I loved him. I resented their "I love you's." I learned early on "I love you" without action is just mere words, and their actions never made me feel loved or safe.

I went to their room door, hoping to say a quick goodbye to my stepdad, protected by the barrier between us. But he responded, "hold on," as I stood there and waited. Finally, he asked me to come into the room. He was sitting against the headboard at a 90-degree angle, legs stretched out, and a thin white sheet pulled up, barely covering his lower abdomen. The sheet was elevated and formed a tent by his appendage as he sat there smiling sheepishly. I leaned over quickly and kissed his very wet, slimy lips as expected. I repeated the chant and turned and ran away, unable to escape fast enough. What did he want from me? I only shuddered to think of his intent for me and literally ran down the long stretch of a driveway to greet the bus and make my escape.

FINDING REFUGE IN
AMY GRANT'S LYRICS

One of my classmates befriended me and allowed me to confide these dark secrets of isolation, pain, and moments of priming. She gave me a copy of Amy Grant's tapes. She was a popular Christian artist at that time. Radio stations didn't play the popular genre of Christian music we enjoy today. Her songs became my music of choice, and refuge songs like "Father's Eyes," "El Shaddai," "All I Ever Have to Be," and "That's What Love Is" were some of my favorites. I would close my eyes and envision prayers in my head as if talking to God through the music. It was like God had used Amy to write these stories about my life, meeting me in spirit every time I heard the words. I would envision how my mom made me feel as if she didn't see her dream of the little girl she wanted in me. Since kids made fun of me, it reminded me of the people who scoffed at my appearance. Instead, I would pray that people could see God's eyes in mine, and when others looked at my appearance, they could see God, not me, as He reminded me I was his child.

The lyrics to "Father's Eyes" mirrored my life and how I felt at that time. I would often sit in my bedroom on the floor, listening to my cassette player and weeping. I prayed, "Give me your eyes to see things as you do, to see myself the way you see me, not the way others see me. Give me your eyes to be like you." I asked God to accept me and thanked Him for reminding me I was made in His image and that I was loved just for being me. There was nothing I had to do or earn. I found comfort in these words during those dark, guarded, and lonely days isolated in the country.

MY WITNESS

*O*would often ponder about the time when we lived with my grandparents in Kansas for the first month. I always lived in fear of being abused, being hit, and doing something wrong for no apparent reason, and even wondering if I was good enough to go to heaven. My grandmother confirmed that it wasn't my fault and my feelings were real. Someone really understood me and saw my pain and lived through it with me for the first time. The days of talking to my grandmother and seeing my grandparents were numbered, as the six-mile distance in the country prevented the highly sought-out visits I longed for, making up for lost time from my early childhood years.

When I did get to visit my grandma, I would sit at her bar in the kitchen or main area of the house my grandpa built. I recanted my struggles and feelings and trying to process my home life and relationship with my parents. My grandma would tell me stories about how when I was a baby, my mom would leave me in the crib, and no one could pick me up, no matter how hard I cried, until my mom got herself ready and had her hot tea. My grandmother said at some point, I just stopped crying, trying to pacify my hunger by sucking my thumb and waiting in silence.

She also recited stories about how angry my grandpa would get at my stepdad when I was told I couldn't have ice cream, and he would eat a big bowl in front of me. My stepdad acted as if he was king of the house, withholding precious commodities at will. No one in the family liked Brute much either. Grandma and my aunts recalled times of seeing him grab me by my hair in his fits of anger in my younger years. That probably explained why I never saw my grandparents much due to the distance in miles and the preservation of the family secrets, as my stepdad would say often.

BREAD WINNER
AND BETRAYAL

*M*y grandma told me later she saw Grace giving her monetary checks to my stepdad, as she was paying her portion to take care of the house we were renting. Not only was she passing off her checks to my parents, but she got a job in town, as it appeared she was the only one who was financially inept. When the idea of church failed, she was probably starting to distrust her own judgment and belief system of following God's plan and leaving her own husband to live in the middle of nowhere.

Her daughter and I had been friends, but we both had different personalities. I was very loud-spoken and always trying to verbally process the reality of our living situation, while she was very withdrawn and timid, internalizing and withholding her emotions. I can only imagine how both of them felt as if waking up in a dream, being plucked from their comfortable beds and sane situation with family intact to residing in an old farmhouse on top of the hill in the Midwest with scorpions crawling about.

My friend would stare out blankly as if in a state of shock. *What just happened? Please pinch me and wake me up from this nightmare"* must have been the thoughts going through her head. Our friendship deteriorated as we continued living together. I can imagine the anger they must have both felt for my parents, resenting how their whole lives were turned upside down. But, of course, who would blame them if, in fact, they harbored these feelings?

SAVIOR TO HER SISTER

My mom was always in close communication with her mom, my grandma GG in Texas. My mom was GG's oldest daughter. Grandma GG confided in my mom about the struggles she was having parenting her daughter, Delilah, my aunt and my mom's baby sister. My aunt, who was 15 at the time, had run away from home. My grandparents had reported her missing but later found her living with an older guy who had his own apartment.

They had found them experimenting with recreational substances, so my grandparents admitted her to rehab. It was very expensive, and my grandma felt like she was running out of options. If my aunt returned home to grandma, she might run away again and do as she wished, getting involved again in inappropriate behaviors. So my grandma was desperate and fearful of what would become of her baby girl, as any mother would be.

My mom had spoken to my GG about how God could save her. She and my stepdad sold themselves as if my aunt living with us could fix the problem and wipe away all the hurts and poor decisions my aunt had made. For some reason, my grandma trusted this plan, and my aunt came to live with us. I was the lucky one who had to share a room with her. My aunt appeared to be a pillar of strength and sophistication, and one would never believe the hidden truth.

My aunt got the royal treatment from my mom and stepdad, and I, of course, was the placemat they stood on. It made me even sadder to see the attention they afforded her, as it drew a bigger gap and stabbed into the loneliness I bore. I think my parents tried to highlight being Christians more by leading family Bible study and enforcing the Bible as an even greater means of control over me and Bethany, and my aunt was the onlooker, watching the awkward Bible story makeshift show on display, with us girls as the main characters.

I resented my parents more and more, as if there was any room to harbor more bad feelings. I would go to bed each night crying at first, trying to hide my sobs and not be seen by my aunt. I didn't want her sympathy, and there was nothing she could do to fix the problem anyway. My stepdad built a little plywood board to separate our beds, affording my aunt privacy. Don't ask me why she couldn't stay in the empty room across from mine, but they chose to put her in my room. She would hear me cry myself to sleep many times at night. Finally, one night she came to my side of the room and opened up a conversation, extending her sympathies. I felt as if she was starting to see the real picture, the picture behind the scenes, so I started to pour out my hurt and despair and shared details she had not presently witnessed as I pulled back the curtain of my parents' deceit.

Little did I know she was having these same discussions with my grandma GG. As the school year came to an end, and my aunt prepared to return to Texas, my grandma arranged with my mom for me to stay the summer in Texas, staging this rescue to help me do chores and buy clothes for my first year in high school. Little did I know at that time what was building behind the scenes of my life. I was so elated to go stay with GG, grandpa, and my aunt. I had stayed with them many times during my childhood and felt relieved just to escape my parents' harem. I felt some survivor's guilt thinking about leaving behind my friend and her mom, but there was nothing I could do but take advantage of the opportunity to save myself.

WHO IS CLANCY?
WHO AM I?

*W*hile we were planning on packing and preparing for me to go to Texas, my mom, my friend Bethany, and I were in the kitchen baking a cake. My aunt had left to spend time with some friends from school. As I was gathering and mixing ingredients, my mom casually stated, "Clancy," your last name given to you at birth, "is not your dad." I stopped as if time had frozen. She had captured my attention. She said that was my birth name only, which means my mom had married him while she was pregnant with me.

Turning and looking at her, I said, "What?"

"You didn't think Clancy was your dad, did you?" she asked. "Your real last name, or real dad's name, would be "Ski.""

I was stunned and speechless. The name I carried my whole twelve years of life was suddenly a lie. I wondered why the person I longed for had left me. I never got to meet him and wondered if I looked like him and where he was now. But it was all an empty void of a lie. Now it made sense why my parents would make scoffing jokes about my nose, calling me Ski and making me self-conscious—relating my Polish, well-pointed ski nose to my, unbeknownst to me, genetically rooted DNA. I am not sure that either of my grandmas knew the truth about my biological dad. I later found out from my grandma Olive in Kansas that Clancy always kept in touch with her, writing letters, calling, and checking on me from afar. He always worried about me and how I was doing. In my later years, this helped me find comfort, knowing someone out there really loved and cared for me. Later in life, my grandma asked permission to share my information with Clancy. I was able to find him and answer some of my own mysteries and questions, finding solitude in knowing my life mattered to someone, even if he wasn't my dad.

CHORES FOR CLOTHES

 $\mathcal{S}$ ummer came, and my GG, my aunt Delilah, and I made the long trek to Texas so I could stay for the summer and do chores to earn money. As we drove down the driveway and headed across the hills and valley, I vowed not to look back as Lot's wife did. I didn't want to jinx my release and was only looking forward to what the summer would hold. When we arrived, my Grandpa Frank greeted us in love. We entered the house with what belongings I had in my mom's old red suitcase. I was escorted to my place for the summer, sleeping in the room I requested when I was eight, and my grandparents had bought this house while I was staying with them for the summer. Now I would return again to sleep in my aunt's waterbed. It wasn't always perfect, and in a funny kind of way, despite my parents wanting to save my aunt, it was, in fact, my aunt and GG who saved me.

My aunt continued to have friction with my GG, and I distinctly remember the screaming matches between them as I hid behind the rocking reclining chairs in the living room. My GG pounded on the bedroom door as my aunt would throw curse words and disrespectful slang at her very own mom. I never understood how she could treat her mom that way and get away with it. It was terrifying to be a part of as I tried to disappear and hide.

I spent the rest of the summer days doing chores, such as vacuuming, dusting, cleaning the bathrooms and kitchen, and mowing the lawn. My GG would try to be creative regarding any chore she thought I could do, keeping a checklist of how much money I earned before I returned home. I spent my free moments being a kid, swimming in the elevated pool outside and trying to learn tennis with my aunt at the park. We would ride our bikes across the railroad tracks and go to the local store to buy candy periodically or make a quick trip to the store to get something for GG.

My grandparents still owned the RV, and since it was summer and my grandpa had a vacation, we got to take some long weekend trips to Rockport, Texas, and to San Antonio to visit my other aunt and cousins.

I loved going to Rockport, Corpus Christi, and taking the ferry. We would go fishing for crabs, and my grandparents would cook a crab feast afterward. I couldn't bear to watch them place the live crabs, with their hissing noises, into the hot water. Maybe this moment was reminiscent of my parents' escapades with the chickens, and I would turn my back and focus on the allure of the beach, the sound of the waves, and the beauty around me instead.

We also took another trip to Arkansas that summer and got to mine for diamonds at Crater of Diamonds. No diamonds were found that day, but in 2021, a person found a notable diamond in size. The park's reputation was built on someone finding the largest diamond ever discovered in America on this 37-acre park. Well, we were hopeful anyway. Sadly, the summer came to an end, and back to Kansas I went.

CHILD LABOR AND A
TRUCK STOP CAFE

*O*got my first job at a truck stop waiting tables at the age of 13. I needed money for clothes, necessities, and extras before I started high school. Plus, I just wanted to escape the country. It was a tough first job. I manned the front of the cafe, taking orders, serving food and drinks, registering, cleaning up, delivering food, prepping all the condiments, and mopping before the owners came. The owners would come after the dinner rush and scrutinize the uncleared tables and half-filled condiments as I was scrambling in circles, frazzled. That was one of my first lessons in how to multitask and work efficiently for pennies on the dollar. I can understand how children in less fortunate countries have to drop out of school when they work because it was starting to take a toll on my productivity in school, my schoolwork, and my body. There was one other employee who cooked and did dishes in the back. We sometimes passed a word of encouragement to each other as the food plates slid across the slick silver platform, as if separating us by two worlds.

Many times, we would have some retired farmers sit for hours waiting for pots of hot coffee refills while they got caught up on the latest weather and crop production or the latest bid or battle at the barn auction. Occasionally some crude younger guys made mocking jokes, make a mess, and leave me a penny tip in a dirty coke glass. What an insult for a young girl already trying to find her place. Based on their crudeness and mannerisms, they probably didn't have much luck in the dating realm either.

SECRET EXPOSED

*O*started the ninth grade. After only a few weeks, I was pulled out of class for a personal call from my grandma. She inquired about my home life with my stepdad and asked if I had been mistreated and abused. Apparently, my aunt had been telling my GG about what she saw when she was staying with us. She asked why I didn't talk to her about these things during the summer months and asked if I wanted to live with them in Texas. I was shocked and elated at the same time. Now the school was involved. I'm not sure whether it was my GG's intent or if the school contacted her. She said she was coming to get me but was working on a plan.

The following Friday at school, we had a game, and the band was required to attend the event. My dad sent the lady that lived with us to pick me up. I stated I wanted to stay to be a part of the band. Grace had just driven from the country per my stepdad's instruction, so now she had to return without me, which she knew would anger him and place her in jeopardy.

After we argued and I refused to go home, she left angry. I started crying, realizing the trouble I had caused. One by one, my friends—the one who gave me the cassette tapes, the one whose brother was my friend, and my fellow friends in the band—circled around me as I started to weep uncontrollably, fearing the consequences waiting once I got home. My friends and classmates sought the teacher's help, the teachers sought the principal, and the principal called the police.

Once the police arrived, they called my stepdad. Little did he know the explosion that would take place on the other end of the phone. It was as if the years of my childhood in Kansas started to unfold before everyone's eyes in the band hall that night. The police told him they had his daughter and I was not coming home that night. I could hear him through the phone's mouthpiece as he yelled vulgar words to the authorities. My GG was called next, and I heard her reassuring words that she was coming to get me.

MOMENTARILY A
CHILD OF THE STATE

Once again, the townspeople's suspicions of oppression and abuse at the hands of this professed ordained minister were confirmed. How could a godly person behave in such a way? I was loaded into the police car and driven into the night for an unknown distance to a foster home. I was now in the custody of child protection services, CPS. I had no toothbrush, only the clothes on my back and my flute instrument in tow, clinging dearly as if the tunes of hymns were carried in my head. My parents had been able to run and thwart this action in previous years, but now it had all unfolded that dark night in a small town in a little unknown place in the middle of the great Midwest.

I don't know how many days it took. I don't think I ever got to go back to school again to say my goodbyes, for that was it, cut cleanly off like a knife, never having a chance for closure. My goodbyes stood in my head as a flurry of mixed emotions, feelings of guilt and separation, and lack of closure all cut clean away. Did my grandma Olive in Kansas even know where I was and what had happened? I cried myself to sleep that night, burying my head in a pillow of unknown origin in a room lined with single-bed cots for others like me. It was like I was living in a movie where the camera kept rolling, but everything else stood still in time as I waited what felt like weeks for my GG to find and rescue me.

Other children resided in that group foster home in a small town. I'm not sure where it was located, but it was within walking distance of many things. The children would come and go freely without much adult supervision or guidance. I was given a toothbrush, but I'm not sure about clothes, as everything was pretty much a blur from the shock. One of the fellow kids took me to town, walking as if it was a tour of survival. He started to school me on the next chapter of this hard luck life as we walked to what was like a bar and video arcade. He was teaching me the ropes of the streets and showing me the whereabouts. This taste of freedom opened a door of curiosity and intrigue and served as a deterrent to the guilt I was feeling.

A CURSED PRAYER

*D*espite police warnings and the restraining order against my family, grandma picked me up and took me back home to get my few items. I only had what seemed like a matter of minutes to gather what I could throw into black trash bags, piling them in grandma's car—all 12 years of pictures, memories, yearbooks, and souvenirs from my travels from the East Coast and my RV trips with grandma. I was still in a state of shock and just reaching for whatever was in sight. I often thought of my special memories left behind in those moments of feverishly packing years later. It's a constant reminder of the separation from my mom and the memories I harbored through my stuff, all left behind.

My grandma gave me one last chance to say my goodbyes to Grace and her daughter Bethany, my mom, and lastly, my stepdad. My stepdad, wanting to be king and have the last word to protect his honor, suggested a circle of prayer. I did everything I could to hold in my tears and remain strong. I don't remember much from that prayer, but his ending words still ring true in my ears: "I am giving you my permission to get involved in sex, drugs, and rock 'n roll." It was as if he set forth a verbal curse on my life moving forward.

As we traversed what seemed like the longest road trip of my life, even longer than the Oregon one, my grandma drove forward to Texas. My aunt Cindy, Olive's daughter in Kansas, was pregnant and had just delivered my new cousin. I hadn't yet had the chance to see her, so I begged my GG to make one last stop to see my cousins and say my good-byes to them and my Grandma Olive. They lived on a hill just outside of town. But no, my GG only held the path straight to Texas.

Later my grandma Olive told me my stepdad had followed my grandma GG all the way out of town just to make sure I couldn't see my grandma or cousins one last time. As we drove down the highways, rubbing sounds on the tires concerned my GG as we traveled on the journey that led to my new life. Upon arriving in Texas and being greeted by my Grandpa Frank, my GG realized the weight of all my stuff was bearing down on the car and tires and causing the friction. It was as if the weight of all of my childhood years of abuse and scorn was mirrored by the car that carried my burdens and delivered me to my freedom.[9]

Friends: Keep the faith, putting one foot in front of the other, leaving the pains of the past behind you, and courageously facing the fear of the unknown ahead of you. As you move step by step away from your past, remember not to let it define you. Use it as reminder to cultivate and grow you, like the bitter stench of ammonia in fertilizer transforms to the brilliant flowers it produces proudly poised in the garden.

9   If this chapter touched you and you would like more information to help on your own *Quest*, see page 312, **Bullying.**

Chapter 13
WHAT DID I DO?
LEAVING MOM

THE CORD IS BROKEN

*O*was living in Texas at age 13 with my grandparents and 16-year-old aunt Delilah. I was not permitted to go to school immediately because my grandma had to show the school she had legal custody. My GG contacted my mom to obtain a letter stating she had relinquished her parental rights, and off we went to the bank for my GG, me, and the notary to sign the document. I must have been out of school for what seemed like a week, waiting and trying to process what had just happened.

I found out later my parents had to pack what belongings they could and were chased out of town by the police. The town wanted revenge, and jail time was in the documents for them. They fled all the way south to Tennessee. I still wonder how they got there out of all the states possible. Left behind were Grace, our neighbor from North Carolina, and her daughter Bethany. They were abandoned in that old country house left behind on the hill.

I sat in my new cold, empty room that I cherished on so many prior engagements, looking around as if in a void. I couldn't contain it any longer and started to cry. I hunched over, holding my head in my hands and bellowing as if my stomach would turn inside out. What had I just done! What had just happened? Everything I hoped and prayed for had come to fruition, as I was free. But oh, how I didn't feel free.

That spirit connection formed from birth through the womb and umbilical cord was finally severed. My dreams of a mom's tender hugs, touch, comforting words, and gentle understanding were all gone. I always longed for those days of mommy and me, always hoping my mom would somehow revert back to the one time I remembered. I always blamed my stepdad for changing her and taking her from me. All those days gone, poof, as a glimmer of light goes up in a thin line of smoke when the candle is snuffed out. It was all gone. My mom was gone from me forever, and it was all my fault. No going back, no looking back— it was final and written. I's dotted, T's crossed.

What would become of Grace and her daughter Bethany, whom they abandoned too? Maybe it was a bit of survivors' guilt for them being dragged out to the Midwest and then left behind. I blamed myself not just in that moment, day, or week but in the months and years that followed. Many of my actions and choices in my adolescent years were made to silence the voice of blame, sadness, anger, and guilt in my head. I was walking around in a state of shock, which has made it harder to recall the events during this time.

A KID'S BEST FRIEND

My aunt had a cocker spaniel, much like the ones I had growing up. She would come into my room and snuggle beside me, comforting me as if she sensed my sadness, deep grief, and feelings of abandonment. She would follow me into my room and I would close the door behind her. Her stints of visitation grew longer and longer, eventually leading to overnight sleepovers. This prompted anger and resentment from my aunt, as she blamed me for taking her dog. I don't think she realized the comfort and compassion this innocent little creature brought me as she looked at me with her big brown eyes and soft, squeezable floppy ears and head, as if she saw right into my soul. Finally, my grandma would come retrieve the dog to appease my aunt. I knew it was only fair since it was her dog, but it prompted more feelings of abandonment and loneliness.

Not long after that, someone who lived in an apartment had just gotten a Shetland sheepdog and couldn't keep it. My grandma asked me if I wanted the puppy. I didn't know what breed it was, but I said, "of course!" I think my grandma understood the comfort a dog provided me and the yearning I had to fill that void with man's best friend. The little dog was six to nine months old, but I didn't feel an initial connection. This pup had small beady eyes, pointy ears, and long, skinny snout as we made our first soul-to-soul connection. Little did I know the sorrows, struggles, milestones, and adventures we would both share as we journeyed through life together.

FOLLOWING THE LEADER

*A*fter that long week, my grandma and grandpa went out of town that weekend. Maybe they thought they could trust my aunt with me and with the house. My GG had a hobby of making ceramics and selling them at festivals out of town. Little did I know my aunt had planned a party, a very awkward party with two boys who brought alcohol and marijuana. As the guys and my aunt smoked the not-too-familiar cigarettes, it took me back to a place, a memory of a far-off land of many years prior, so I drank. After a few drinks and trying to drown my thoughts, I somehow ended up in bed for an even more awkward moment with some boy I didn't know. I looked up at the ceiling and talked to him with a nervous energy, probably not making sense at all, passing the time. I didn't even know how the night had gotten to this point. I could hear my aunt outside smoking and laughing with the other boy. Fortunately, that night I had a pass that preserved my childhood innocence another day.

THE CURSE IN ACTION: SEX, DRUGS, AND ROCK 'N ROLL

*L*ater in the school band, I established relationships with three friends, Abbey, Brianna, and Cate, who lived nearby. They invited me to their house, and we nurtured the friendship around our commonality of playing an instrument.

Abbey's boyfriend was on the football team. I longed to have someone love me and be as sensitive with me as her boyfriend was with her. She was a bit older and had a car. I would go to her house or with her to the boyfriend's house after school. On one occasion, after they went upstairs and I was left alone, I took a bottle from the boyfriend's parents' liquor cabinet. It looked like water, and I drank it like I was drinking water, gulp, gulp, gulp, wow! That was a strong drink, and not long after that, I lost consciousness. It was as if I was drinking away my sorrows.

The next thing I remembered was walking and falling down the street with the boyfriend holding me up and my friend walking on the other side. They were hoping to have me sober up before I had to go home and his parents got home. My friend took me home that evening, and straight to my room I went. My retreat and escape.

Brianna had her driver's license and a scooter. She would pick me up and we would buzz through the community on her scooter up and down the streets, surveying the streets for kindred souls like us to hang out with. We found a couple of older guys outside talking, and since I was extraverted, I introduced myself and my friend Briana. We would come back each day and cultivate what I thought was a relationship. One weekend evening, he had asked me to come into the house. He took me to the bathroom and kissed me and laid me down. That night, I lost my innocence. I gave my innocence away to someone I thought would be my boyfriend. I thought giving myself away would make him love me and commit to me. I never had anyone teach me about dating or any role models for a healthy relationship. I only saw what my friend had and wanted that. I tried to call him several times afterward to no avail. He did not return my calls. I didn't understand. I was 14 years old and deeply yearned for someone to love and accept me.

I continued to seek the wrong kind of attention, mostly from older boys outside of school. Most boys in school were established in their own cliques, and we didn't have much in common. I was always looking for the next social gathering. One night, my friend Abbey and I were invited to a small party by two older guys. We were flipping quarters into a cup to determine who would be the next one to take a drink. One guy pulled out a pill and offered it to my friend. She said no way. I could see her shaking her head, looking down and flashing her eyes. I figured it was because she was driving. Even though I didn't know what it was, I stepped up and said, "Give it to me! I will take it." I wanted attention and wanted to wash away my sorrows.

Somehow, I ended up leaving the party with the two guys instead of my friend. My memories of that night are faint, like poor reception on an old TV fading in and out. I remember driving around a neighborhood seemingly in circles, parking where there was construction and an empty open house. We got out of the car and walked into the house. The guys were secretly talking among themselves. Miraculously, I made it home that night. Looking back, I don't even know why my friend let me go with these guys by myself, but the most important thing was I made it home. In today's world, I would have been a missing person, never to be found again, purposed for another underground intent. Despite the circumstances, I know God had his hand on me that night.

My other friend Cate would invite me to sleepovers. I often stayed the night on Fridays. My friend would always say how cool her mom was, as her mom and dad were usually unwinding from the long work week. I remember the liveliness of the house as her parents would play rock music and their laughter would carry through the house. At some point, her mom asked my friend if she wanted beer, and my friend said sure! She bought us a pack of beer. We sat in her room, centered around the beer in the middle of the room. My memories of those nights were me drowning my sorrows by throwing back each can of beer until I passed out or threw up, whichever happened first. I woke up the next morning and went back to the house as if nothing had happened. I always felt as if it was a hidden form of recovery and coping. It couldn't have lasted more than a semester, and the jobs I acquired at a young age quickly became my next distraction for those lonely nights. One golden egg that came from those days is that now I do not like beer, neither the smell nor the taste.

NEIGHBORS WHO
MADE A DIFFERENCE

The previous summer when I had stayed with my grandparents, I was asked to babysit the neighbors' two boys. The lovely couple perfecting their second marriage sang in a band on weekends at least monthly, and sometimes more often. They had shared custody, and the dad out of state also kept the boys most of the time. The boys were in town the latter part of the summer before school started and they needed a babysitter. Little did I know babysitting for this couple would lead to a lifetime of love, support, encouragement, and a new extension of my God-given family.

Two houses over was a foreclosed abandoned house. It was a decent house, nothing out of the ordinary. But I remember the day when I saw the truck and the new neighbors moving in. I'm not sure how long it was before we officially introduced ourselves, but I know it couldn't have been too long because of their outgoing and exuberant personality. They had two boys almost the same age as the first couple. Over the years, this brought all of us together.

It must have been early spring of my ninth-grade year. The weather was perfect, not too hot. Beautiful white cotton ball clouds floated against the blue canvas sky. I remember the day very well, filled with laughter, cheer, and hard work. That day, a connection was made that changed the trajectory of my life forever. The neighbors had a pool that was in dire need of some TLC, and I volunteered to help the lady of the housework on it. Her husband was working at his custom cabinet shop, and the small kids were inside playing while we uncovered this pool layer by layer. The pool had wooden boards followed by a metal grid and a heavy layer of plastic. It must have been abandoned for some time, as the layers of plastic were broken and cut. Being weathered from the wind, some pieces disintegrated in our hands as we picked them up. Some had fallen in the mucky water below us. It was like we were the archaeologists and this was our dig site to excavate in the next two days.

We pulled the top layers off down to boards we used as balance beams above the pool. As the water slowly drained, it would reveal the hidden treasure, such as the screens for the house windows, a bike, a giant-sized trashcan full of trash, bowling balls, and a jockstrap. We laughingly joked there would be some type of body to match the jock strap. Lucky for us, there never was. Little did I know at the time helping her unearth those layers in that pool that day would be symbolic of all future relationships and the impact this family would have on my life. They would help me unearth all my childhood layers of hurt that would be brought to the surface and healed. In fact, I may only be able to share this book with you today because I processed my feelings so many years ago sitting in their dining room as they wrapped me in their love.

I am so blessed and thankful for these two families because I know I would not be who I am today without their impact on my life. They became my confidants and mentored me. They role modeled what a true family unit in my eyes should look like. Their forgiving love and acceptance were mirrored by a sense of calmness no matter the magnitude or severity of the problem. The nights of drinking and passing out soon became a distant memory in ninth grade, as I was able to talk to someone whom I felt cared about me.

OFFICE WORK WITH A
MAN WHO MIRRORED
A PATRIARCH

That summer, they hired me to be an office secretary. I rode to work every morning in the work truck with Abraham, and he was like the dad I never had. As we talked about life and cracked jokes, he would advise me on dating and school projects. He would share the latest stories about his cabinetry projects. I got to see what his expertise and trade were as he created beautiful artwork with his brother. It gave me an even greater appreciation for my grandfather William in Kansas, who was also a carpenter and prided himself in the cabinets and homes he built. It was like having a piece of my grandfather in this individual as I sat in the front seat enamored and in awe, watching him talk each morning.

They took me under their wing and had the confidence in me I never had. They believed in me more than I believed in myself. In the office, I learned how to schedule their appointments and work projects, organize their paid and unpaid invoices, file their documents, and be the face and representative at the front desk. This afforded the brothers the focus they needed to make their creations.

Another job I had in ninth grade was delivering flyers or door hangers for a famed pizza place that is still my favorite to this day. It was a nice way to be outside, learn to read maps, and get familiar with the community and neighborhoods, plus it gave me an excuse to be out of the home. I never would have imagined all those days of reading maps and tracking streets and pathways would only foreshadow and condition me for my six-month trek through Europe in the years to come.

REGRETS AND
RESENTMENTS

*F*riction and conflict were building between my aunt and me, and I think she started to regret her part in bringing me to live at her house. My grandma began withdrawing from the relationship we were forming due to my aunt's resentment toward me. I started to feel more isolated, alone, and guilty for having to live with them. My aunt was the boss of the house, and she would project harsh words and actions toward me just as I had seen her do to grandma during my previous stays with them. At first she tried to hide her anger and corner me in my own room, grumbling threats under her breath. I always wondered if my grandparents could see how she treated me.

Grandma had my aunt take me to school and pick me up and had her take me with her to activities she desired to attend. We went to Motley Crue and Bon Jovi concerts, which rapidly changed to suddenly being banned from attending concerts and such things because my aunt complained she wasn't permitted to do such things when she was 13 or 14 years of age. It was a very confusing time not only for me but for my grandparents, since the games of the playing field were constantly changing. I think this gave grandma some confidence that Delilah would not do certain things while her niece was tagging along. But honestly, I don't think it mattered to my aunt much, as she continued to do as she wished just as she had that first weekend night.

BODY IMAGE DISTORTION

I was very insecure and easily intimidated by my aunt. My insecurities ran deeper than the surface on several accounts, including the morphed and distorted way I viewed my own body. My aunt was picture perfect to me, and I placed her beauty on a pedestal. She had straight, long blonde hair, was taller than me, and she was thin. She could fit any type of clothes and often wore her size skinny Jordache jeans.

Oh, how I wanted to be like her. I had idolized my aunt from childhood, a bond that formed over being pen pals. I was alone and had always wanted a sister. I would watch her eat and wonder how she kept her physique. I would skip meals and save my lunch money in an attempt to cut calories and be thin, as I often compared my body to hers. In my mind if I didn't eat, saved calories, and did lots of exercise, I could lose weight and be skinny.

I was always more shapely, with most of my weight in my hips and legs, even as a child. My GG would always reflect on how she remembered me as a kid trying to fit into my aunt's passed-down skinny jeans, wondering why they would be skintight on me. I would starve myself all day on many days, breaking my fast with nachos at school or a Reese's after skipping breakfast. I would go to work at Dominoes and eat pizza when allowed as a reimbursement for the miles we would walk dropping door flyers. Those days of watching my mom diet and binge eat soon became my pattern, as I tried to find the physique my body was not made for. This unrealistic pattern of eating, poor body image, and obsession with being active followed me years later.

ELUDE AND ESCAPE: INCLUSIVENESS IN BABYSITTING

*O*babysat for both families as often as I could. It was more than a job but the connection and escape I longed for. And if I wasn't babysitting, you could find me at their house in the evening, processing life past and present or just sitting back watching TV with them. It was a well-sought-out place of refuge for me to escape the turmoil at home and in my head. Eventually, those evenings of babysitting turned to sleepovers, in part to avoid disturbing my grandparents by coming home late, and also simply because I didn't want to go home. They eventually took me to parties after their nights of bowling. We would laugh and make jokes about the great escape. Looking back, this was really an important part of my development in my teen years. They gave me a sense of freedom and trust while allowing me to explore and make wise choices through the love they role modeled. Most healthy parents would walk their own teens through this part of their development. They made me feel included and accepted when they invited me to such gatherings.

HOMECOMING DECEIT

*O*n tenth grade, I attended homecoming with my friend Abbey and her boyfriend. I was asked to go with her boyfriend's friend, who was also a football player. We went separately in our own cars but sat together and hung out at the dance. I didn't really know this boy, but I longed to go to homecoming and be engaged in school activities. I wanted to go and be social, spending time with my friend and dressing up like the princess I wished I could pretend to be for an evening.

I think my date longed for something else. Upon completion of the night, he attempted to kiss me and prompt some action in his truck as he took me home. I didn't feel a connection, and we had little to talk about. I didn't do well in sports growing up and had little knowledge of football. I didn't feel he understood me or my background. I thanked him for the evening, and we parted ways. I felt guilty for not kissing him, as if I owed him something for taking me to homecoming. He didn't seem to be happy when he left.

Following homecoming, Abbey called me and had the discussion only a parent or doctor should have with a girl. She told me about planned parenthood and birth control. She explained what it was and said I should start using it. At that time in the 80s, underage girls could make an appointment to see a doctor. You would go in and answer a series of questions about STDs, how active you were, and your income status.

They would talk about the risks and consequences of having multiple relationships and discuss symptoms associated with the onset of these diseases. Most girls were almost always guaranteed a yearly prescription of birth control and a female exam for free or for a nominal price. After that discussion, it was as if a light came on and I had awoken from a daze. I made a pact that I would protect myself that day. I didn't have a boyfriend, and it was not necessary to take birth control at this time, so I waited, trying to slow the clock of time.

Unbeknownst to me, extensive lies and rumors started to spread through the football world about me, as this group started to cackle and laugh at me. Several boys from the team sat behind me in biology class making crude jokes and talking about me. I sat in the front and ignored them as they repeatedly threw their daggers of harsh words at me.

THE MOMENT I SCORED

During the semester, we had a project due, which Abraham helped me with, but of course, what else does a dad do? I researched trees. I wrote a paper about the different layers of growth and how each year weathers that tree when it builds its core layer by layer, adding strength as it gets taller and reaches the heavens. Each layer's thickness resulted from the amount of water and nourishment it received, producing bigger or smaller bands sealed by each season. Abraham, being a carpenter, helped me cut a slice of wood and laminated it, placing it up on legs so I could rotate and talk about each layer of growth.

When I presented it in front of the class, the teacher commended me on my project, and I got 100 on it. I think he knew the kids would have harsh words, as they brought me down each day. This teacher was my hero as he used this moment to elevate and praise me for my hard work on the project, highlighting the person I truly was. The kids continued to scoff and taunt me, saying, "your dad made that for you!" *Yes! That's right. My dad made that for me*, I thought as I walked back to my desk, beaming. I'd had a small victory; I was the one who scored that day.

A MOTHER'S DAY BLESSING: YOU DON'T EXIST

That following Mother's Day, my grandma was on the phone and asked me to speak to my mom. I dreaded the moment; I had nothing to say to her. I picked up the phone.

"Hello?" I said.

In her joyous voice, my mom said, "Hi." Then she said blatantly, "You don't exist. No one in Tennessee knows you were even born."

She said she was adopting foster kids. I wondered how she could even get kids. She didn't even take care of her own daughter? Would they even let her have those kids if they knew how she treated me? I was floored. I kept hearing the words *you don't exist* ring in my head. It was as if she was trying to break me down more and elevate herself.

THE LONGING FOR A MOTHERS LOVE

In the tenth grade, my other friends were Dina and Linda. Dina lived nearby and stood out with her provocative attire and loud personality. Her single mom always seemed to have a different boyfriend around. Dina loved to go to parties, and many of her friends were boys. She always knew where to go for excitement and to get the attention she desired.

She knew how to woo most people, including my GG. My GG loved her, and when I stopped hanging out with her as much, she would say how nice Dina was, as if to encourage the relationship. Linda, her friend, was a product of two parents who were divorced and didn't get along with either. She would ping-pong between both parents and use her leverage against both of them. I observed her calling her parents for money and threatening each of them with unkind words until she got what she wanted. I observed her meeting up with older guys at parties and clubs. She was the passive friend and would often be quiet and have a glossed-over look until the cycle repeated itself again. She would call her alternate parents again, threatening them with unkind words and stringing them along until she would get more money.

I watched the cycle and felt so bad about how she treated her parents. I could hear her mom's pleas on the other side of the phone as she would say she didn't have money to give. She seemed to be crying out in despair for the return of her daughter. I can honestly say I learned what not to do from both friends, and our friendship was short-lived. Once I started driving, I had more control and options for where I could go and what friends to hang out with.

PARTY AND POLICE

One night Dina and Linda asked me to go out with them. She told my GG I would stay the night and hang out with her. I had no idea what was to follow. Some guys picked us up at her house to go to a party. As we drove, playing music, singing, and laughing in the car, the moments stretched into an hour and things seemed very unfamiliar. I asked where we were going, feeling apprehensive. We were going to a party in Channel View, driving from Spring, Texas. We pulled up to a shanty of a hotel, and I was ushered in. It was quite lively, with loud music playing, and the room was lined with older guys holding their beers, and a big cooler was the centerpiece in the middle of the room.

My first observation was that we were the only three girls there in a room full of guys. It was a little awkward as I watched my jovial friend laugh and flirt with all the boys. I remember that night well since I didn't like beer and that was the beverage of choice. I don't even recall drinking. As the night progressed, a very loud knock on the door trumped the music. The guys peeked out and yelled, "It's the police!" My heart jumped as I panicked and ran to the bathroom. I slid behind the door penciled in a small space between the tub and the door. I could hear several policemen talking to them as I tried to hold my breath.

One policeman pushed on the door and didn't find me. When he left, I sighed a bit. What if they arrested us? My GG would disown me. Thoughts of being kicked out and homeless flashed through my mind. Where would I go? Where could I live? How did I get here? I didn't even know where I was! A second policeman came and slammed the door into me. I must have whimpered as the door kicked back. I was found. I thought I was going to pass out in fear as I held my breath. The last acquaintance I had with a policeman was sitting in the back of the cop car as I went to foster care.

My body was frozen in fear as I was advised to sit down. The policeman quizzed me and said there was a reported runaway and that I fit the description. I wondered if my GG had reported me missing even though she knew I was with Dina. Did she somehow know where I was? *Maybe that was a way to get rid of me*, I thought, as all these random thoughts flooded my mind. Eventually, the police left me and told the boys to drain all the beer and throw everything away as they waited and watched until every last beer can was drained. They marched to the dumpster, eliminating all evidence of a lively night.

The cops told them to keep it down and walked out, closing the door behind them. As the door closed, I felt a sense of relief. I could breathe again. My first get-out-of-jail card was spent that night. Oh, but the night was not over as I lay sandwiched between these guys I didn't know, wishing I was home in my own bed or at my friend's house where we were supposed to be. I could hear panting, groans, and wrestling just a few feet away from me as I pretended to be asleep and dared not look up. The night came to an end not soon enough as the sun rose, and we were released and taken back to my friend's house.

PEOPLE PLEASER

I was a people pleaser, scared and too weak to tell people no. I wanted people to accept and like me. I had no boundaries to protect myself physically and emotionally, as I was never taught what boundaries were. Every person in my life had crossed those boundaries and taken my innocence in some way or another, starting with my mom and the men in her life. This prompted a lifestyle that would often lead to me putting myself in unsafe circumstances and situations, never thinking of what could happen as a result. I was selling myself out to others who had no value in my life, but I was too broken, too young, and too naive to see it. I only longed for love, and in my mind, surrendering to others would provide what I so needed. I didn't know how to protect myself. Even though I had my own relationship with God and Jesus, I was very empty inside. I would talk to Him, but I searched externally to be filled with the love that was modeled through secular eyes.

DANCE "CLUBBING" SCENE

*D*ina and Linda also introduced me to the clubbing scene. A dance club called CARZ catered to underage kids, so it was the place to go. It was the first club in the industry, priming kids for bigger party scenes like club 6400 or after-hour clubs like Lizard Lounge, none of which exist today. One night we went out, and I met another girl named Valencia who went to my school. I saw her on the dance floor as her long hair and sleek body seemed to glide seamlessly across the floor. She appeared very confident in the way she moved and how she carried herself, very polished and distinguished. I was drawn to her and wanted to meet her. She was by herself and, although friendly, very guarded. We started talking and realized we had common interests and similarities. She was older than me, a junior in high school, and had her own car. We exchanged numbers, as if counting the endless days and years of friendship that would proceed us from that moment on.

MY FIRST CAR

Turning 16 and getting a job meant needing a car. My aunt had recently convinced her parents to buy her a second car. They couldn't sell her old Mercury Cougar for enough to get their investment back, so my grandparents set up a payment plan for me to purchase the car from them. I wasn't thrilled about buying her car, but they made it clear that was my only option. In junior high, I was able to drive myself to school and work. The car was a tank, a six-cylinder beast, and I could barely peer over the steering wheel even while sitting on two stacks of phone books and a pillow.

My friends and I would laugh, turning through winding streets in subdivisions as the headlight beams would project into the bedroom windows of the second floor. The headlights were like two eyebrows cocked in as much amazement as I had about driving it. At one point, the brakes went completely out as I plowed into the back of a car parked at a stoplight in front of me. Maybe that is why I still have dreams about pressing and pressing the brakes in desperation, but to no avail. Fortunately, upon inspection of his car, the man I charged into found the damage to be minor and sent me on my way.

I hid the truth from my grandpa once again, blaming myself for the car's malfunction. The passenger side leaked hot water from a slowly dripping hose, and crossing your legs in the wrong place would cause marked skin. The wipers and defogger didn't work, and in the cold of winter or rain, I would hand crank the windows to wipe the mirrors and windshield. It was a death trap waiting for an accident for sure.

A BIG SCHOLL

*O*loved being in school and was enamored by such a big school! As I walked down the hall, I observed so much diversity in all the extracurricular activities, posters of cheer lining the hallways, and the different faces of the students. Different groups co-existed: jocks, head-bangers, skaters, surfers, preps, cheerleaders, dance, and one group in particular, cosmetologists. That's it! I could see how my previous dream and vision could come to fruition if only I could be accepted into the program.

My aunt's friend was enrolled in cosmetology class, and she would always talk about it and show us her latest hair trends and appetite for alternating colors. She was in it for the long haul—two years and three class hours each day, to be exact. Her goal was a signed and sealed beauty license, which would thrust her out into the workforce armed and ready to face the world. I prayed I would get selected for one of the 12 allotted slots as the anxiety welled up inside. I visited my aunt's friend Deane when possible and made myself known not only to the teacher but to the art in its raw form, with no misunderstanding of expectations for the future class.

As I waited nervously, I continued to work my job at Captain D's, a fish fast-food restaurant, and continued to focus on my schoolwork and assignments. It was not acceptable for me to make any grade less than a B, as this standard was set in my younger years. I had decided to always complete my work, and it served as a place of meditation that filled my mind with positive thoughts. I also highly valued an education and knew that someday it would afford a better way of life. I wouldn't accept anything less for myself, as I was the only one who gauged my efforts in school. To this day, I even have a copy of my old report cards as personal monuments of the mountains I had slowly conquered each semester. I was my only competition.

Much to my delight, I had been accepted to the cosmetology program, just as I knew I would in the vision God had given me years before. I knew cosmetology would create an avenue to build a life for myself, and that would be my escape. Once accepted, I acquired a second job as a personal assistant to an independent hairdresser and her team. I worked on Saturdays, washing hair, rinsing perms and dyed hair, running the register, and booking appointments. I was watching and learning as much as I could, absorbing everything like a sponge.

My life started to turn for the better during my junior year of school. I met many girlfriends who harbored the same cosmetology goal as I did. I was finally in a niche of my own and starting to feel a sense of belonging, having an identity, and being someone in school. I met one of my lifelong friends, Dana, at that time. She came from a different school to attend classes during the second part of our day. We sat together as we wrapped our perms, practiced giving each other manicures, and painted our hair. She was my friend of reason as we would methodically talk about things and process life together. Our Sundays were spent driving to get our traditional chips and green and red salsa as we sat for hours sharing our innermost secrets about ourselves. She knew about my other friends and my early attachment to dancing.

STRANDED. CAR
BUT NO KEYS

One night I was asked to drive my two friends, Dina and Linda, to CARZ, a teenage dance club. We went dancing and met another group of people. One guy in particular befriended me and offered to hold my keys and license since I didn't have a purse. We all huddled, and a pill-like substance was passed out to everyone, known as the happy pill or XTC. And then we all went our ways to dance the night away. Since it was my first time, I remember the heavy beat of the music and dancing in my own rhythm while everything flowed so fluidly. It was one of the first times I really felt happy, as if the lights were smiling down at me. I felt a sense of superficial joy as if in a trance, dancing the night away.

As the night came to an end, I looked for the boy who had my keys and license, but he was nowhere to be found. I realized I didn't even have his number. I panicked about how I would get my car and drive home or to work. I had work scheduled for the next day and needed my car. I was supposed to stay the night with my friends. They had little investment in the situation and found others to ride home with, leaving me abandoned at the club. I started to panic and have an anxiety attack because I was one of the last ones standing in the club. The club staff took me to a back room and interrogated me as I explained that the boy had my keys and had left, and my friends had also left me.

They threatened to call the police and report me if I didn't have someone pick me up. They didn't care who came to get me as long as it was immediately. I cried in despair. I knew I could not call my GG or my aunt. Guilt and helplessness came over me, and I called my friend Dana. I had her house number memorized, and she was my last resort. I knew she would be home. Her parents provided her with a stable and secure childhood, and I knew they would understand. I didn't want to jeopardize our friendship or her relationship with her parents, but it was my last resort and I was betting on the odds to play out in my favor.

I called and her dad answered the phone.

"May I speak with Dana, please?" I asked.

"Do you know what time it is?" he asked in a monotone voice.

"Yes, but it's important."

"Ok," he said, "let me get her."

He woke her from her sleep. As I explained my predicament, she asked me all the details to aid in my rescue. She was my reason and my savior that night, as she brought me back to her house and I got the rest I needed to face the next day. She devised a plan to bring me back to my house that next morning. I knocked on the door and told my GG I needed clothes for work and I was with my friend having breakfast. I slipped the second set of car keys from the key holder behind my GG's back, grabbed my clothes, and ran out the door. My friend took me to get my lone car sitting in the parking lot waiting for me. I followed her back to her house and got ready for my nine o'clock opening of the restaurant, ready to work a ten-hour shift. Dina contacted the guy, and he dropped off my keys and license, sharing his remorse. I accepted his apology and we remained friends. That event secured my friendship with Dana. I realized what a true friend she was and parted ways in my mind with the other girls.

RESPONSIBLE FRIENDS

My relationship with Valencia started to grow as we found more to talk about and enjoyed the same passion for going out and dancing. In dancing, I found the freedom to express myself in each beat of the music. My heart and soul felt connected as I swayed, stomped, and moved to the rhythm. It felt as if all the bodies were rocking in unison and harmony, moving in a beat and rhythm of its own—an unspoken connection drawing us all together as the waves of music strung us together as puppets on a line. We had a superficial sense of family as we all danced, tied together in music. This invisible connection kept drawing me back as much as my weekends could afford between school and work, as those were my priorities.

Valencia and I made a pact, knowing the club scene had a very dark side. We made a pact to always stay together, much like the buddy system teaches in elementary school. We also promised to stay away from the hard stuff. My friend would always say it just takes once to try it and you could be hooked. It would call your name and suck you into the lies, ruining your life forever. We made a vow, a vow of friendship and a vow assuring me someone cared about me. They cared enough about me to entrust my protection over them as well. I had meaning and value.

Valencia's parents always knew where we were and when we would be home, another layer of protection and parental guidance I didn't have or know before. My grandma GG always knew when I was with Dana and Valencia. I could speak with confidence, knowing the plans of the night with no surprises. Having my own car and these newly acquired relationships gave me a sense of having more control over where I could go and not remain merciless at the hands of others. It was empowering, and I was starting to build a network that made me feel safe and predictable.

SUMMER
BABYSITTING JOB

The summer between my junior and senior years, I acquired a babysitting job for a single mom who had two kids. Her schedule was arranged so she could work long consecutive days and obtain her hours within a few days' time. I would stay at her house and sleep over, so I would be present in the late evenings and early mornings when she needed me. I continued to manage my job at the restaurant and was able to collaborate the schedule with my manager, which constituted a very booked and busy summer. This allowed me to escape my GG's house. With my aunt completing high school and continuing to reside at home, I felt that helped diffuse the tensions between us. Any additional time was spent going dancing with Valencia or having my weekly Sunday lunch with Dana.

My best friend Valencia went away to college my senior year of school, and I longed for the weekends she came back from Austin. I was mourning a loss again. I'd lost the connection we were building and no longer had that safe, secure net with whom to go out. My focus remained on my three jobs: the restaurant, hairdresser assistant during the day on Saturdays, and now-a popular hair product supply store, filling and bagging orders of hair supplies for local hairdressing salons.

I would come home late at night after work and often stayed up till midnight or later completing my homework. I continued to maintain my grades through it all and even graduated with honors once it was all over. I focused on studying and practicing cosmetology and prepared to go to Austin to take my exam, knowing it was important to pass the test. That was my lifeline after school ended and all I had, which heightened the amount of pressure I placed on myself. Dana and I started going to the park and walking and running to be more active. I would often go to her parents' house just to hang out and always went straight to the kitchen looking for the chocolate chip cookies her mom would bake. The cookies served as a conversation piece as I built a relationship with her mom. My friend hung out with me at Abraham and Lydia's house as if they were my parents. She built a relationship with the boys as I babysat them.

TRADED CARS

My parents came to visit during my senior year and brought a Fiat international car with them. It was a four-door modeled much like a Volkswagen. It had gray faded, peeling paint, much like an old nail polish job. I was advised that was my new car, and my grandparents took the keys to the 67 Mercury Cougar and gave them to my parents. I was mortified at the appearance of the car, thinking about how kids would make fun of me. Once again, I had no voice, no warning, and no choice in the matter.

Holding back my tears, I ran to Abraham and Lydia to process what had just happened. Abraham had changed jobs in recent years and was now working and teaching cabinetry in a trade school. As I discussed the events that took place, they shared my anger and wished the situation could have played out differently. Next, they embraced my sadness as we discussed my feelings and fear of facing rejection at school. Finally, as they always did, they saved me. They piped in with a moment of positivity to reach down into the abyss my parents had just thrown me into. Abraham had the answer: he could take the car to the trade school and have it painted! I knew if anyone could fix a problem and make something happen, Abraham sure could. We brainstormed and talked about what colors I wanted. I got a bright blue metallic car with hot pink stripes. My new treasure, thanks to Abraham and Lydia, and this time my stepdad couldn't destroy it like he'd destroyed my kite many years ago. I beamed with joy.

FIRST REAL BOYFRIEND,
I THOUGHT

$\mathcal{N}$ear the end of my senior year, I met a boy named Charles. I remembered him from school before he graduated. I always thought he was one of the popular guys. He would walk through the school with his arm around his girlfriend, both with bleach-blond hair and bronzed skin tone. He always caught my eye as we daily walked past each other in the halls during the previous school year. He gave me his attention, and I gave him my number. I went to his apartment during my free moments. He didn't have much to offer other than his time and trying to woo me with his kisses and affection. He didn't have a job but tried to play the card as a college student, stating he was taking classes at the local community college.

He told me his parents were divorced. His dad left his mom for a younger lady, trading his mom in for a new model. He despised his stepmom. I could relate to his pain. In his eyes, she had stolen his family, divided and conquered, leaving pieces behind—he and his older brother and his mom. His dad would pay for his schooling, as he was financially very successful, and his mom helped pay for his apartment while he went to school. His dad had the resources to help, but his mom, not so much, as she struggled to make ends meet for herself.

Charles had a very difficult time coping with this change in his younger years, as his family unit prior to the break was very stable and financially secure. We both bonded on this premise of loss and heartache and filled each other's gaps. I mourned his loss with him. We seemed perfect together. Little did I know he had a hidden secret, an addiction that ran very deep. What seemed like casual partying and a momentary release soon became evident as our relationship progressed. He was addicted to the same munched-up, grass-like substance my parents used to use.[10]

---

10 If this chapter touched you and you would like more information to help on your own *Quest*, see page 314, **Pregnancy Prevention.**

Friends: If you find yourself in a similar dysfunctional, life-threatening situation, don't feel guilty about leaving a loved one, no matter the level of abuse.

Chapter 14
REPEATED – A MIRRORED CYCLE OF CHAOS

HIGH SCHOOL
GRADUATION

*D*uring the weekend of my graduation from high school, my parents came into town. I thought they were there to celebrate my graduation and watch me walk across the stage. My mom was smiling and helping me position my cap and gown while I was lining up with my friends. I envisioned all of us going to lunch afterward to celebrate. Graduation lasted many hours, as our class size of almost 600 people marched across the stage. I was closer to the front of the line with my Cum Laude credentialing. I awaited my turn, excited and amazed at my own achievements. How did I manage to maintain several jobs, seven in total, with loyalty and a good work ethic? How did I train and study a trade in pursuit of getting my license?

The whole cosmetology class had gone to Austin for our licensing test, which I passed. I came back and interviewed with a Fortune 500 company and received my first apprentice job as a hairdresser at the mall. I overcame the emotional turmoil of separating from my parents and the personal attacks from my aunt while trying to dodge the friction in the home. All of this while not just completing high school but exceeding in grades and earning the cum laude distinction. I beamed with pride as I walked across the stage, accepted my trophy, and sealed it with a handshake.

KICKED OUT: NOT GOOD ENOUGH

Afterward, we went back to my grandparents' house. My parents and grandparents asked me to join them in the common area of the house. No lunch was served, just people all seated and waiting. I took a seat as my stepdad and mom started the well-planned-out meeting.

"You need to leave; you need to move out of your grandma's house," my stepdad said.

Then my mom piped in, "You never did anything."

All I could hear was, "You don't amount to anything. You need to leave. You are too independent," as the discussion seemed to last for hours. I tried to hold back the tears, recanting their statements as they ran through my head. All I could think about was where were my parents these last 3.5 years? How would they know anything about me? How was it their space to say such hurtful things to me? They didn't have to take care of me. I worked and paid for my own stuff, committed to school and being responsible where it mattered.

All I could think about was my aunt. It was all about her! She was pregnant, working at a local discount store, and they needed the space for her. I was the one being asked to leave when I was the responsible one all along. Oh, the irony! Yet I was the one who did nothing. After hours of the beratement, I fled to my room in tears. I couldn't escape them. Nowhere to hide, broken, humiliated, and powerlessly homeless. I was just a kid, 17 and homeless! At least I had my cosmetology license and a job, but still no money.

LAST RESORT – LIVING
WITH A BOYFRIEND

I left shortly thereafter. I had a few days to pack my things and grasp what happened on my graduation day as I tried to explore my little to no options. Charles said, "Come live with me." I hadn't known him for more than a few months and had apprehensions about it, but I felt there was no other option. He comforted me and provided reassurance as I shed tears and explained the situation. Once again, we found solace in our own rejections and insecurities.

MY FIRST PROFESSIONAL
JOB CUTTING HAIR

*M*y first real hairdressing job was at a hair salon in the mall, working as an apprentice. I was training to cut hair and had to complete the company training and take a test, which required a passing grade for me to work on the floor. I passed all but one of the required haircut styles. Call it lack of self-confidence, a transition in my personal life, and an avalanche fallout resulting in trauma, which almost cost me my career. I panicked and recanted my failure in my mind. I was advised to pull it together and return after practicing this required skill. This only delayed my opportunity to build a clientele and start making a salary that could harbor a minimal lifestyle. Although I wanted to crawl into a cave and sulk about my failure, I knew I couldn't give in. I was afraid of failing and failure, afraid of the fallout that would result if I couldn't get it together and pass my test. I had one more chance, and I knew my manager was cheering for me in my court. Miraculously I passed my test that day, that second chance. I overcame the fear as I hoisted my self-confidence and pushed forward. That day paved my future for the next 18 years of my life as I obtained the necessary skill to be deemed worthy of cutting hair in one of the most affluent and well-known companies.

NOT GOOD – APARTMENT LIFE

Things at the apartment were not so good. My boyfriend, Charles, was distracted and abusing marijuana. I went to work each day, but he was skipping classes and not doing the required coursework. He prevented me from seeing my friends, Dana and Valencia, when they came home from college to visit. As my career progressed, he even asked me to quit my job, which was not even close to an option. The more I progressed in my achievements, the more he regressed.

Finally, one day I was at work and got a call that Charles had gone to the hospital because of a drug deal gone bad. Some guys that he was buying and selling marijuana with pulled out a gun and tried to rob him at our apartment. In an instant, he jumped through a closed window as they shot at him. The glass had severely sliced his leg and ankle as he narrowly missed being struck by a bullet. He was getting the necessary treatment, including stitches and antibiotics, and would be home shortly. The police were contacted and filed their report as the apartment staff had to literally pick up the pieces by repairing the shattered glass windows.

I was overcome with fear. What if that had happened when I was there? What if it happened at night? Was my dog safe? Why was Charles not in school like he should have been? He was so fortunate to have an opportunity to just focus on school, but he let it slip through his fingers. In the following nights, I lay in bed restless and scared, feeling invaded and knowing the perpetrators were still out there. What if they came back?

"TRADED" A CLUNKER

My so-called trusty car from my parents was having mechanical problems and broke down, leaving me dependent on him for transportation. The only Fiat mechanic who could service the foreign car was downtown and many miles away. One day as Charles picked me up from work, we got into an argument about his lack of school attendance, job search, and addictions. When the car was stopped on the main road, either he kicked me out or I fled, jumping out of the car and running across two lanes of rush hour traffic. Tears streamed down my face as I panicked and tried to determine in which direction to walk—back to the mall, to work, or in the opposite direction to my friend's house.

As I walked those three miles along the busy road toward my friend's house, I ignored his cat calls as he drove beside me. Finally, he sped off in his anger. I tried to focus on my steps as something squiggled under my foot. It was a snake! It was one of my biggest fears, and I jumped and started running. A guy in a truck must have seen my reaction. He pulled up beside me and asked if I needed a ride and if I was ok. I dismissed his gesture and proceeded toward my destination.

When I reached Dana's garage, I found the phone and called her at work. I told her what had happened and that I was in her garage. She said she would be home from work shortly. I sat and waited patiently in the garage. When she got home, we went to her room. She told me I didn't need to go back and I could live with her. I was really torn and afraid. I was afraid for him and for her. I didn't want to jeopardize our relationship and wear out my welcome at her parents' house. It would be an indefinite time until I could establish my trade and be financially secure. I stayed the night, and she took me to work the next day.

Charles called me at work and promised to make changes, to go to school, get a job, resolve the addiction, and move away from the vicinity. That was my ultimatum, and he committed, much to my surprise. So back I went, and we moved to Conroe, just north of Houston. I had a 45-minute commute to work, but the peace of mind afforded me and a new start for him gave me some relief, though it was only short-lived. Going back to the relationship also threatened my friendship with Dana. I knew my days of crying wolf were numbered, and she would only step in to help a limited number of times. But I gave him another chance.

My car would get fixed and then break again, leaving me stranded on the highways as I tried to go to work. Several times I was picked up by strangers and either taken the rest of the way to work or home, while the car was towed downtown again for repairs. The repairs took longer and longer, and I became more dependent on my boyfriend. We would ride the long distance back and forth to my work on the highways and busy roads by motorcycle, whether it be rain, sun, or cold.

ALMOST TAKEN – DESPAIR

*D*epression set in, as I was totally vulnerable and dependent on him. He hadn't changed his behavior despite the move, my only source of transportation kept breaking, causing every dime I made to go to costly repairs, and I felt trapped and isolated from my friends. I hated the munched-up grass addiction he was feuding with, as it reminded me more and more of my parents and the resentment toward them and him I buried deep inside.

At one point, all I could think about was dying. I wanted to end my life to escape the torment. What reason was there for me to go on at this point? There was no light and no escape. Why didn't my mom just abort me when she had the chance? I would always question why I was even born if this was all life had to offer me. I had tried but failed. I didn't have the courage to push hard enough on my skin and catch my main artery in hopes of bleeding out. I sunk to the floor and cried, envisioning no future. I wasn't able to escape the chatter of worthlessness ringing in my head from my family and now my boyfriend.

We got some food the next day on the way to work, and he spied my wrist and grabbed my hand. "What is this!" he exclaimed, as I sobbed out the truth—my cry for help. He passionately stated that he loved me and to let him know if I ever felt that way again. For a moment, I thought he really cared and my pain subsided, but only temporarily.

Finally, it was decided my car was irreparable due to a bent frame and should become scrap metal, leaving a less-than-desirable profit toward a new car. I had to have a safe and functioning car to get to work each day, so I went to the Honda Dealership and asked them for the cheapest, brand-new reliable car I could afford. They showed me a blue Honda Civic with bare bones and an AC. It didn't even have a right mirror or a radio, but I didn't care. I had confidence in a vehicle I knew would take me where I needed to go.

I had no credit and needed a co-signer to purchase a new car, a Honda, which was rated a highly dependable car. I took a chance and called my grandma, who convinced my grandpa to co-sign. I had promised to pay the car off. By paying the car off in a timely fashion, I could repay them by improving their credit score in return for previously living with them. On one hand, I felt I was repaying the debt, and on the other hand, I was the one more indebted.

I grew tired and depleted. Work weeks were long, and the weekends seemed to run together, with twelve-hour days leading into the next too quickly. It was dark going to work and dark leaving; having no glimpse of the sun made the days run together. Once again, work was my escape from the perils at home, but the commute was getting more difficult. Another lease had passed, and we decided to get an apartment closer to my job. We moved for a third time together. My confidence and career were starting to flourish, and Charles's confidence was waning. This was apparent in how he treated me and his fat slurs.

A WORD OF WARNING

One night I went out after work instead of going home. In the bathroom, I ran into his ex-girlfriend. I couldn't believe it. I said hi as she opened up and started warning me about his character, behavior, and the violence he would bestow upon her. I admitted he had not used physical violence against me, but I had seen him hit other things, including the walls, breaking some of my own items or turning on his dog and mine. We would get into arguments, and I would escape to work. While at work, I got calls several times that someone had my dog. Apparently, Charles would take his anger out on my dog and chase her away. Several kind souls found her and called the number on her tags. This happened on several occasions, as my dog would run as if looking for me to escape to. I am so thankful she was never hit by a car or endured an accident. His ex's words of warning cycled through my head. I stayed guarded, telling myself I would never allow anyone to hit me again.

ONLY JESUS SAVES

However, I felt it was my purpose to help save him. I knew he needed church and God. I asked my clients about the churches they attended and planned for us to go. Church was extremely hard for me to attend. It took me back to the days of the religious abuse I endured in the name of God and the Bible. I was instantly guarded as I walked in and sat in the pews. I started breathing deeply and shaking as anxiety welled up inside me during the song service. I did all that I could to finish out the service, but I couldn't go back because of the deep internal struggle and pins and needles I felt.

I had my own internal relationship with God. Why would I need to go to church if it was supposed to bring peace and this is what I got? I tried to share the message of God and salvation with him, but I couldn't do it at my expense. We never returned to church again together. All I could hope was that the seeds of freedom were planted, waiting for nourishment and his own growth, in the right season. Only Jesus could save and help him overcome his addictions and hurts, giving him the power to change his mindset and life.

My grandmother must have sensed the tension and known something wasn't right, as she had walked this path before. She invited me over for dinner and cards. She would make my favorite Czech dish of homemade noodles and chicken soup over mashed potatoes. After dinner, we would play cards. We would often connect and play cards as I was growing up before I lived with them. During one hand, grandma looked up and asked if everything was ok. She said if he ever hurt me, I should let her know. I had been living away from home for about 1.5 years, and quite frankly, I was stunned when she mentioned it. It had been a rocky road that was getting rockier by the minute. I filed her response and look of concern away in my brain for a rainy day. Then I changed subjects and talked about my job and my achievements there.

My best friend, Dana, was now attending classes at A&M and invited me to attend the bonfire. I knew there was no way Charles would let me go, and at this point, I didn't care. I missed my friend and wanted to see her. I went after work, arriving just in time to see the blazing spectacle that stretched many stories high. I am glad I went because shortly afterward, a tragedy occurred, and the famous bonfire became a historic memory for most. We had a great time connecting and laughing, and the crazy part was that one of my clients was her suite mate!

A TUMULTUOUS NIGHT

The sad part was I had to go home. I already knew there would be turmoil, and I braced for the predictable. As I walked in that early evening, Charles jumped off the couch, his eyes lit with fire. He was extremely angry. I tried to bring my bag and items and greeted my dog while avoiding the daggers of hostile words. He followed me, bumping his body aggressively into mine as I turned to avoid him. I ran up the stairs to the duplex to escape and just go to bed. But his anger was only elevated as he increasingly pushed himself into my circle, my personal space. Next thing I knew, he was trying to throw punches, wailing his arms uncontrollably. I ran into the closet and tried to hold the door closed as he pushed his way in. I was cornered and afraid as I felt his fury. I bent down on the floor, curled up, and covered my head as I had learned in the annual tornado drills in North Carolina. He aimed for my head and back as my arms covered what part of my head they could. He hit me several times; I'm not sure if it was his hand, fist, or foot—maybe all of them. I didn't fight back; I only lay defensively, trying to protect myself and pray.

This was it. If I could only escape the night and his outrage, I would leave. I wasn't sure where I would go, but I would find a way. I was done trying to help him, and I wasn't going back to being physically abused again. The verbal abuse, paired with the physical abuse, was the final straw, and I decided that night to draw one of my first boundaries and not accept that for myself. On the outside, I was a fat, cheating hoe who played mercilessly on the ground at his feet. On the inside, God was giving me the mindset to say no and not look back. I didn't know how, but only God knew how to make that miracle happen. I just had to walk in faith.

Charles left me locked in the closet all night. I just lay in a ball on the floor and cried, briefly fading in and out of rest, but on high alert in case he came back. I didn't know if it was night or morning as I slowly cracked the door. It was daylight, and everything was quiet as I pondered my escape. Where were my keys and purse? I would grab them and my dog and run, run, never return. He must have been sleeping as I slowly opened the door and went to grab my things, but before I could leave, he awoke. Frozen with fear, I paused and continued to play out my scrimmage of escape in my mind. Miraculously I was able to get past him with my dog and keys as, in his wrath, he chased me out the door and to my car.

POLICE, FAMILY, FRIENDS:
AN ETERNAL ESCAPE

I was in my car. I had escaped! Now where should I go? My grandma's words rang in my head: "Tell me if he ever does something to hurt you," as I drove to her house. I knocked on the door, and it didn't take long for her to realize something was wrong. I broke into tears and said, "He hit me. I was locked in the closet all night. He hit me." My grandma called the police immediately as I sat in the kitchen. I cried and recalled the moments of wrath he lavished on my body and mind. My grandma looked at my back and took pictures of the marks to ensure there was physical evidence to back my claims.

The police came, made the report, and asked, "Do you want to leave?" I said, "Yes!"

"Is there anyone who can help you get your items?"

I looked around. My aunt from San Antonio and aunt were all in the kitchen, circling around me.

They piped in, "We can help."

One of them quickly ran to the two neighbors, explained the events, and asked if they could help. Why yes! Elizabeth and Noah, my first set of neighbors, could bring their truck. But where would I go and where would I put my items, clothes, and furniture? I was speechless, exhausted. Mentally and physically, I couldn't plan. All I knew was I wanted out. I was lucky this time because I had a choice in how and when to leave. Next time, I might not have been so lucky.

So off we went without a plan in my head, four cars in total. We followed the police back to the apartment after the report was filed. The policeman knocked on the door. This time I was on the right side of the door as Charles answered, looking dismayed; he knew the outcome. The policeman told him we were there to get my items. Maybe he was relieved at first, as he wasn't being arrested. Once the initial shock wore off, he tried to catcall me and hover while I scurried to pack my things. The policeman redirected him to another part of the house with his first warning to leave me alone or else. I will never forget the kindness of the policeman and my neighbors and aunts who stepped in to help me.

The policeman watched and waited as we carried each load of clothes or furniture pieces to the truck. He waited as we drained the waterbed my GG had given me. At the end of his shift, he said he had to go and would send another policeman to ensure our safety as we packed and loaded the remaining items in the truck. He left in victory that day, knowing he helped a young 20-year-old girl like me live to see another day due to making the right decision. He was vested in my recovery, which began with my step forward of independence and leaving the abuse behind. I had broken the cycle, another chain of dysfunction from my past, leaving it all behind, forgiving but not forgetting.

We drove back to my neighbors' house with items in tow. Now what? Where would I put everything, and where would I go? My neighbors said they had room for me to stay with them to help me get back on my feet. They had room in their garage for my items, and, most importantly, they had room in their hearts to help me, to see me through to the light at the end of this dark tunnel. I was speechless and in awe. For one of the first times, I really felt loved and cared for as they all huddled around me in support and genuine concern, elevating me out of the pit. It was as if God had sent them and lifted me on the wings of his eagles, drawing me up when I couldn't reason to a higher place. I cried in shock about what had happened, I cried in guilt for leaving Charles behind, and I cried with a sense of relief. That part of bondage in my life was over, and I will forever be grateful for my neighbors, my aunts, and that one policeman who rescued me that day.[11]

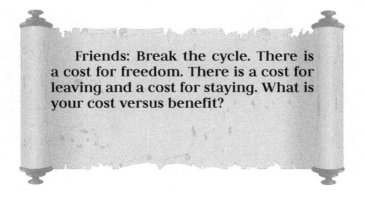

Friends: Break the cycle. There is a cost for freedom. There is a cost for leaving and a cost for staying. What is your cost versus benefit?

11   If this chapter touched you and you would like more information to help on your own *Quest,* see page 314, **Pregnancy Prevention** and page 315, **Suicide Hotline.**

Part Two:
SELF-ACTUALIZATION, PERSONAL GROWTH, AND SPIRITUAL HEALING

Chapter 15
ON MY OWN

INDEPENDENCE DAY

*O*was free at last. I could truly put my head down and rest that night. All of the burdens, bondage, and darkness surrounding me were lifted. I could come up for air and breathe a sigh of relief and rejoice in my new freedoms and liberty. Each day I would go to the salon, striving to succeed. I wanted to build my clientele in order to build financial security. It was more than just cutting people's hair; I longed for relationships. I longed to help others feel beautiful, handsome, and confident. I longed to help kids overcome bullying and not endure being laughed at. I longed to create coiffures as my clients joined in matrimony. I was excited and looking forward to focusing on my career and the growth it would afford me during this journey.

I saw Charles in the same week I left. I was cutting hair in the front chair on the elevated platform of the salon, with the glass windows dividing me from the main forum of the mall. I could feel eyes as I was cutting hair, just like the feeling I had when my stepdad would loom over me in my sleep. I looked up in the mirror and there he was—standing there staring at me. I was in disbelief, and my heart dropped as I tried to hold my composure and focus on perfecting my client's creation. Once I walked my client down and said my goodbyes, I had to find my manager. She knew the situation and was my strength and rock at work. We were both in disbelief that he was there.

He had gotten a job outside of Macy's department store convincing people to sign up for a credit card. I don't know how he was hired, but he was using this moment to stalk me! My coworkers were already screening the calls and deferring any requests from him, leaving a void of information, as this was how he got back at me. My thoughts went back to what the ex-girlfriend said. She said he had slashed her tires when she tried to leave him. I knew his potential and knew I should expect the unexpected. Seeing him in the mirror brought flashbacks of our last night, playing through my mind like a movie—the harsh words he would spew out and his attack on me as I escaped with the cops. He brought it all back. He brought it all to my work as I tried to push through and pretend everything was alright.

I asked my manager to move my assigned chair to the back of the salon. She agreed that was a good idea; however, my day was booked with appointments, and I had to wait until the end of the day to move. I had to push through and be strong and resilient, resisting his stares and projected thoughts of anger, sadness, and his hopes to bring me back. Even my own workplace wasn't safe. Oh, but this was my playing ground, and I knew I could outlast him. I had the support I needed to overcome.

We had a talk with mall security and explained the situation, including the police report. They were my mediator as they approached him and told him not to come close to me and to leave me alone. They also relayed the message that the police would be called again if needed. I'm not sure how long his employment lasted, but I know his days were numbered—maybe because he couldn't see me any longer. I also parked in a different location and entered through another store, making it harder for him to find my car during the Christmas madness. He eventually disappeared and left empty-handed from his pursuit, and I had a victory. Truly that chapter of my life finally closed, never to look back, never to date someone again with a drug addiction or violent background. I was getting stronger each day, and God was helping me as I realized I couldn't save him or others like him; only God could.

A COMPANY THAT CARED

My company was different, which is why I chose to work there rather than in a small family shop or starting out on my own. This company prided itself on education and training, and I knew I had a lot to learn to be the very best I could be. I was a blank slate and they poured into me. Not only was the hair-cutting technique important but who we were as individuals. The owners really cared about us and treated us like family. The company had 16 salons across the Houston area at the time, and the owners would meet with each one of us individually once a year plus have meetings in our salons and hold quarterly classes. They poured into our lives and treated us like family—teaching us, guiding us, and helping us grow as if we were their own kids. I soaked up every moment of every word like a sponge. I had truly found my place. My connection and my life started to make sense as I started to feel I mattered to someone. My life finally had meaning. I had waited and endured 20 years, and my life finally mattered. I was somebody. I was somebody others would request to cut their hair.

The Christmas holidays came and went, bringing good cheer, lots of work, and enough money to get my first apartment. I couldn't think of a better way to start the new year. I was so grateful to Elizabeth and Noah for their love and support in giving me a place of rest for my thoughts and a place to lay my head. I was grateful for the transition of staying with others in the event Charles tried to follow me home. As I recovered and started healing, I knew someone advocated for me, which gave me the strength to keep moving forward.

I was also grateful to Abraham and Lydia, who helped me transition into my first apartment. Abraham took me to buy my first furniture and put the security locks on my door to make sure I was safe. Both families helped me move everything back; only this time, it marked a new normal I never had. It marked a start to the control I had moving forward. No one could come through my door without my consent, and as I left that door, only my intentions would pave my future. It was my time and my choice. I had the choice to decide where I went and how people treated me as I started to create new lines and new boundaries I never had. It was exhilarating and frightening all at the same time. Would I pass or would I fail?

PHYSICAL TRAINING: STRENGTH AND DIET

One of the first things I did was get a gym membership. I never wanted to be the underdog again, powerless and weak. I decided I wanted to learn how to lift weights. I had tried cardio workouts doing exercise tapes, dancing, and walking, but now I wanted to be strong. So off to the gym I went, feeling fat and too embarrassed to even go in, with the old lineage ringing in my head and pushing me forward. I did what was familiar. I tried the elliptical machine and a few machines without any reason, and I then went to the weight area.

I must have looked lost and in need of help as a nice guy, Jerry, piped in and set another machine for me. We started with small talk, and he asked me to spot him while showing me his next move. He started sharing the first chapter of what I learned about bodybuilding. He took me under his wing almost immediately and asked if I wanted to join him the next day at the same time. I was in awe and shocked that he would take the time to help me. I agreed, and that set my new schedule at the gym. I had time to work out in the mornings since the mall didn't open until 10.

Jerry was very strong, his muscles defined and popping out without even trying. His nicely bronzed skin shined through his hard work. His smile and soft eyes told me I could trust him and I could do this. I loved working out. It gave me a new high I had never felt before, and I couldn't wait to get back to the gym. I could feel my body changing and getting stronger physically and mentally each day.

I became entrenched in working out and doing at least an hour of cardio each day. Trying to be lean, I turned to dieting next to enhance my body image. I would count calories and race to the gym to burn off the same number of calories on the machines. At the same time, I was always thinking about food and planning my next meal. I read everything related to nutrition. I didn't know the difference between scientific, sound nutrition counsel versus nutrition information from weight loss gurus, so I tried to practice it all. I used herbs and drops, diet pills, and protein powder shakes—all trying to sculpt the desired body shape I had in mind. I turned to a fat-free diet for many years and sent back food at restaurants if it came out glistening in what I thought was oil or butter. My work friends referred to me as when Harry met Sally and laughed at me in love whenever we went out.

I realized my passion during this time. I wanted to study nutrition to help others. I was drawn to it, infatuated, and couldn't get enough information to pacify my yearning. I thought of my mom's body image issues and inconsistent way of eating. I strived to do the opposite of everything she did since it didn't work for her, so it was up to me to find another way by trial and error. I decided to study nutrition when I was stable enough and could afford school.

As time passed, I was committed to my work, and the gym took up a lot of my time. In my free time, my friends and I would go out dancing for exercise and for the thrill of the beat. I would also host cooking parties, making fat-free meatloaf, lasagna, and muffins from my cookbook. I hid behind the idea of eating healthy or lean to justify my physique and hide my poor body image. It was as if I needed an excuse to justify eating real food.

TRAINING: SKILLS, RENEWAL OF MINDSET, TIME MANAGEMENT

*M*eanwhile at work, I was growing in my career, my skills, my clientele, and in self-realization as my mind stretched. At the quarterly and annual meetings, we had guest speakers such as motivational speaker Tony Robbins; John Paul Deloria, the owner of Paul Mitchell products; internationally acclaimed hairdresser Yosh; and the Fortune 500 owners of our salon, of course, just to name a few. Each had their own story of hard work and how they overcame obstacles that led to success.

We were shown that we could be someone, no matter our family of origin or amount of negative conditioning. We renewed our minds about who we truly were and how we had the potential to be successful with hard work or be anything we set our minds to. We learned not to listen to the chatter in our minds following the lies that were deeply rooted from childhood, which led to failure. We had the strength to turn our thoughts around and look toward a future of overcoming. They also shared their Christian faith and principles and their passion for helping us and our clients. I was striving to renew my mind daily. The old things would pass away or be buried, and the new thoughts would take precedence, pushing me forward toward a bigger goal.

We learned about books like *20 Things I Want My Kids to Know*, which highlighted dreaming big and writing your goals down while believing in yourself, striving each day, and taking steps to achieve small goals that led to big goals. It's funny looking back at the goals I had written, such as grow my clientele, finish two years of college, get accepted to U of H, graduate from college, get a convertible, and make a salary of $25,000, most of which I have accomplished to date except for the sports car.

Our company paid for our salons to do team-building activities and a ropes course to build trust and companionship. One workshop was 7 Habits of Highly Effective People. We also did a blindfolded test. We were paired up, and one of us was blindfolded while the other person, by way of their sight, sound, and touch, would lead us safely through an obstacle course. We had to surrender and depend on our senses to complete the test, making us literally lean on our teammates. We all had a good laugh weaving between barbed wire, over fallen trees, and around patches of brush, smelling the snapped twigs of cedar, and hearing the crunching leaves with each step. Once completed, we learned we could trust others, especially our teammates, and learned to lean not just on what I could do but what we could accomplish together. I believe that the workshop helped heal a part of me and allowed me to open up and trust others. I desired to be part of a bigger picture, a team, no longer just surviving and doing things alone.

The workbook taught time management and how to handle a schedule full of events, projects, and spontaneous crises. We learned how to prioritize while striving for long-term goals and how to manage our time, thoughts, and to-do list ranging from immediate and urgent, important and not urgent, and finally, not important and not urgent. Ironically, it helped us realize how much time we can spend thinking about the non-urgent and non-important, which steals our time from the important and keeps us from achieving our own goals.

Everything may be important, but not everything is urgent, and this helped pacify the anxiety and pressure I carried daily about overcoming and achieving. It taught me to take a breath, manage my time wisely, and not feel overwhelmed and give up due to the mounting pressure. Time is a commodity that we cannot buy more of, so we need to learn to manage it effectively. If we don't manage time, it will manage us. I practiced these time management techniques later when I was juggling work, school assignments, and having fun. My job taught me to take a life of chaos and disorder to a place of order, structure, and balance. This allowed me to achieve my goals and some peace of mind.

GOAL SETTING, TEAMWORK, AND DIVIDENDS

*T*he resources and love poured into us must have worked. Out of the approximately 16 salons at that time, our salon was number one for the most sales during the first five years I worked there. Each person had an annual goal of total percent of clientele, a percent of product sales, and a system to track lifetime earnings. At the end of each year, those totals reflected the salon sales, which were ranked overall. Each year, we won an allowance to take a trip. We got to go to New Orleans and Vegas several times. In addition, the top-producing hairdressers won a company trip with the owners. Everyone sought the goal of a company trip to play hard and seek more wisdom while being under the owners' wing. I had earned company trips twice, going skiing in Park City, Utah and being offered Wyoming during my first six years of employment in addition to the annual salon trips.

I was developing meaningful relationships with my coworkers and clients. As my feelings of connection and love grew for others, I felt others' love for me. I first met Sheila when she came to my high school to introduce the opportunity of working at the salon. I asked her many questions, intrigued by the potential opportunity this company could offer me. Little did I know when she saw me at the salon, she thought to herself, *Oh no. Not that girl, the girl who asked so many questions!* She confessed years later that she didn't expect us to become such great friends. She became one of my workout buddies as I shared what I had learned from my bodybuilder friends. We confided in each other our secrets from childhood and our passion and desires in love. Through exercising, we cultivated endurance in the gym, at work, and when we started studying our classes in college.

Sheila was very straightforward; if she didn't like something, she would tell you. I liked watching her verbally lay out her boundaries to protect herself and the livelihood she created. We had another friend,

Tabitha. We were all single and were like three women straight out of the movie *Steel Magnolias* in girl power. Tabitha was very skilled in artistry crafts and sewing, so she helped me ponder my decorations for my apartment. Tabitha had straight hair and practiced her creativity on my locked curls while offering a place of mental and physical rest between my busy lifestyle.

The three of us would go on breakfast outings on Saturdays as we braved what the day would bring, laughing and sharing moments from the week. We recapped each season, be it prom, homecoming, weddings, back to school, Christmas, or Easter. This was therapeutic and prepared us for the 12-hour shift that lay before us.

BUILDING RELATIONSHIPS.
PEOPLE WHO CARED

The clients became my family, and I'm still connected as kindred hearts to some from many decades ago. I am so thankful for the opportunity to meet and serve so many wonderful people. I was invited into their families as I watched them date, get married, start careers, have babies, and grow their families. I attended weddings and would visit some of them for holidays and birthday parties. They were an extension of the family I never had. They brought me lots of joy as God modeled what family should look like and slowly started to peel off some of my layers of the past and replace them anew.

Many of my clients knew of my background and were my sounding board of reason, providing words of wisdom when I faced difficult decisions. We would laugh, cry, smile, and hug as I perfected my arts and sent them out to face the world again, feeling beautiful and handsome. I was able to pour into their lives as someone was pouring into mine. I finally felt I was living my purpose. As I got established in my lifestyle and emotionally, I felt my desire of going to college was becoming more attainable.

I met another girlfriend, Sharon, at the gym. She was peddling with machines and lifting weights on her own. We started talking and started spotting each other's machines and weights. We bonded not only over the gym but also over dark secrets from our past relationships, as we had some commonalities. She was Cambodian, and I loved learning about her culture.

One Sunday after working out, she invited me to have dinner with her family. They were so kind and accepting of me and had prepared such a feast. I didn't know the names of the food, but I do remember some sweet sauces like fish sauce in Vietnamese food. The food was eye candy, with brilliant shades of red, orange, green, and shades of brown, along with different textures, inviting you in. It was oh so satisfying, sweet yet smooth and spicy, as I crunched the vegetables with minced meat and chewed what I called fish jerky.

Her family would share stories about how beautiful their country was as I envisioned myself going there. Visiting her family was like taking an escape to a mystical, faraway place. Once coming back to the reality of my routine, I started to long for our friendly tradition and my weekly escapes.

The following summer, Sharon invited me to stay at her sister's house in Orange County, California and go to Disney. I loved to travel and thought why not take advantage of a good opportunity? Plus, she was my workout partner, so we could work out together while away. Staying with her family in California was like stepping into a village far away. We shared a bed and room with her cousin. At night, the house was big and seemingly empty as her family retreated to their rooms to sleep. During the day, the house became alive as the men grouped in a large open space with beams of sunlight shining down on them from above. The ladies gathered in the kitchen and dining space with their pestle and mortar, grinding spices and fish making paste and sauces, and preparing their meats for the meal.

There was little furniture in the home other than beds, leaving an open feeling to the space. We would all sit together on the floor with the bowls of food lined up in the middle, all reaching, sharing, and eating as one communal village. I told my friend I didn't know there were so many people there. It was like they disappeared at night and magically appeared during the day. I didn't know the house had so many rooms to accommodate the three families that lived there. She explained that the only way the families could survive there with the cost of living was to coexist together, which made sense. Oh, the interest spiked by learning about other people and their cultures! I added Cambodia to my bucket list. What a beautiful world this would be if we could only embrace each other's differences!

A LONELY VOID: EXERCISE
AND BINGING

*O*ince I lived alone, the feelings of loneliness started to set in. I strived to stay busy between work, school, and going out just to avoid being by myself. Sometimes when I was alone, those binge-eating sessions would draw me to the pantry. I only kept what I considered healthy foods, such as fruit, fat-free items, whole grain cereals, peanut butter and graham crackers, or healthy snacks. During those moments, the healthy snacks became unhealthy, as I would hide my sorrows, loneliness, and lies of being fat in an indescribable number of calories. As if awakening from a food coma, I would relive the session in regret and set my timer to wake up earlier and go to the gym to burn off the calories.

Sometimes I would take my bike out at night, even at midnight, and ride beneath the stars. One night I saw a man hiding in the shadows near the apartments. As I kept riding around the block, I found him later walking and made sure to say hi and let him know I knew he was there. His presence made me feel that I needed to be alert, taking me back to a memory of walking in on a man stealing my lingerie from the washing machine. The news had mentioned a stalker in the area. Could that be him? I had to stay on high alert and decided it was time to go home.

My eating and exercise became a vicious cycle, so much so that my periods stopped cycling during my early twenties. I thought it was great not to have a cycle; now the medical world has a term for it—athletic amenorrhea. This can be caused by high levels of emotional stress, disordered eating, and excessive exercise. This continued for several years.

My friend Valencia was back from college, and we would go out dancing more often. We exchanged numbers with people in hopes of finding romance. I would invite some people I met to get a haircut. It was a safe place to meet strangers rather than bringing them back to the apartment. I would also ask the guys if they were in college to screen how close I would allow myself to get to them. Plus, in my mind, someone working hard and commuting to school should be a safe person. My goal was to complete college, and I would not stay on track if I dated someone who was not in college or didn't have the same goal.

I had worked at the salon for almost four years and had started taking preliminary classes at school, such as English and Math. I felt they were a waste of time but figured they were screening classes to see how serious people really were about attending a local college. It took that long to be financially stable with an established clientele. Once I had worked at the salon for five years, I could cut back on my schedule and take Saturdays or Sundays off.

TO HAVE OR HAVE NOT

*M*y friend's parents had a beach house, and we would often go on the weekends, leaving on Saturdays after work. We would arrive and find a dance club and dance away the evening. That night, I met Dan, who later became my boyfriend. He approached my friend and me and started talking. He was not shy, and as the lights shone on his face, I could see the sweetness in his eyes and his smile. I could sense he was genuine, and he appeared trustworthy enough to dance with. As we were mingling, I asked if he was in college. Of course he was, and he had a plan. He was studying chemical plant safety since his dad worked in the plants himself. His mom was a massage therapist too, which was closer to my personal goals.

We dated for a few years after that, which seemed pretty convenient.

He loved soccer, an offshoot of his parents' lifelong hobby of playing in the leagues. We had exercise and school in common. He would play on weekends while I worked. How perfect could that be? I didn't like organized group sports and was never sports-worthy growing up. I was always the last one picked for teams in PE. I would drive to visit him after work on Saturdays and stay at his parents' house and bond with his mom. I am not sure if I loved him or his mom more as I shadowed a normal family unit and would play out the lifelong effects of this plausible relationship in my mind.

When we had a serious talk about how I could move in with him and his family to go to community college in Texas City, I was caught off guard. He had already done the research and said I could study physical therapy or something close to nutrition. I couldn't believe my ears. Was he trying to change the degree plan I felt deeply rooted and connected to? Or was he trying to get me to move in to have control over me like in my first relationship? This raised a red flag, causing me to be more guarded in the relationship. His intention may have been purely out of his love for me and wanting me closer so we could progress in our relationship. But it could also have been out of selfish gain.

Either way, I felt threatened and guarded but could not communicate this appropriately at the time. I was not willing to give up my apartment, change salons and start over with my clientele and pay scale, change my career path, and leave behind those I had established relationships with, including Dana and Valencia. This was too much for me to stomach—too much change and too many triggers from the past. It wasn't long before I realized he loved soccer, probably more than I did. That was his passion. I had many passions, and I knew committing to him would mean losing a part of myself. Not only would it change everything I worked for but also my personal goals and dreams of traveling, riding bikes, going to the park, and engaging in activities that didn't just entail going to the soccer fields each weekend. Why was I the one giving up so many things to deepen this relationship without a lifelong commitment?

When it was convenient, he would stay with me on those few days between soccer matches at Meyer Park on the weekend so he wouldn't have to drive that 1.5-hour trip home. My relationship with Dan both pacified and intensified my loneliness. When I spent time with him, I was happy and full, but each time he would leave to go home or we would go back to our own lives, my feelings of abandonment would arise, causing me to intensify my cycle of eating, exercising, and experience more loneliness and guilt. What if he found out my secret? Would he still love me? Or maybe I was using that as a wall to divide our differences.

COMPROMISED

One night as I was sleeping, I had the windows open, and my porch door cracked to let in the nice, cool, dewy air and white noise of the other neighbors running their AC units. When I was a child, my parents would open my windows at night in the trailer to circulate air and turn on the fan, which created that same white noise that always helped me sleep better. Suddenly, I heard the loud parade of feet running from behind my second-floor apartment up the sidewalk separating our two buildings and then across the front building, separated by the pool and going to the office. It was a woman and a man who sounded like Madame Medusa and Mr. Snoops from *The Rescuers*, and the image of them running frantically past my apartment door flashed through my mind. As the woman was barraging the man to follow her lead, the voices became muffled as in a tin can, and a loud clanging noise was emitted into the air. They were in the mail room, and I could envision them prying each mailbox open and recovering the goods inside, wiping each cubicle clean, and adding it to their stash. Suddenly they ran back and paused at my porch, talking and looking up at my windows and door as if feeling threatened that they were found. The crackly, raspy voice of the woman commanded the man to keep watch to determine if their cover had been exposed and to do as he wished with the person on the other side in order to keep the secret.

She ran off with a vengeance, and I heard soft footsteps walking outside my window. I watched his shadow above my bed for more than an hour as thoughts raced across my mind. I lay still on my waterbed, barely breathing and praying my dog wouldn't start barking or get up to go outside. What now? I seldom checked my mail daily, probably weekly at best, unless I knew something timeless and pending was waiting. They knew I most likely lived alone and had my name, phone number, utility bills, and college and credit card information. Everything was in paper form. My life was in jeopardy at the hands of these perpetrators as the guy marched outside my window. I lay frozen and held my breath until his shadow finally disappeared with the rising sun. Terrified and shaking, I got up. Was the coast clear, or had he stepped away only to return and catch me? I closed all my windows immediately and found my living room door wide open, even more than I realized I had left it. Oh, how he could have climbed the banister and entered in a timeless fashion. How lucky I was!

I called my boyfriend in Galveston immediately to tell him what happened, and he scolded me for my carelessness. That next day, I went to the office and explained what I heard, but they dismissed my report. Later, the postman justified the details of my story, stating there had been a rash of apartment mailboxes being pried open and mail stolen. Not too long after that, a wrought-iron door was put over the entrance, and all residents were given a key to enter, confirming the landlord knew what I had said was true.

SAFETY & COLLEGE COST CUTTING

With this recent event being very fresh, living alone started to feel threatening. My boyfriend also got me thinking about his proposition and how I could cut costs and take more college classes. I knew I was on a very long journey toward college and wasn't in a hurry to complete it. I was realistic about the amount of time it would take to finish. I really enjoyed where my life had finally gotten to and cherished working with each of my clients.

One of my established male clients, Brad, was close to my age. He didn't have a place to live or any funds. We both shared the goal of wanting to take classes and save money, so I thought it might be a good idea to share a duplex. Since the mailbox event, my boyfriend agreed it was best if I wasn't alone. Living with someone could help save money, allow more time to focus on school, provide an added sense of safety while relocating, and squelch some of my lonely feelings.

BROKEN AGREEMENTS
PROMPT CHANGE

*O*t wasn't long before the roommate idea appeared to be a bad idea. Brad got a dog and didn't tell me. The dog must have had abandonment issues, as he started to run around frantically and damage things. While left alone, he did things such as knocking the TV off its pedestal, tearing up the bed, scratching holes in my brand-new comforter, and shredding trash across the floor. After three months, I was notified that the rent wasn't paid. I thought, *How could that be?* I was always very prompt in paying my bills, including rent.

I went to the office to investigate the situation and found out he had not paid his share of the rent. They had already given him a warning. I welled up with fear and anxiety, and all of my past fears of not having a secure and stable home came to a head again. I asked what I could do to preserve my credit, and they offered a one-bedroom apartment in the back. They could transfer my account and preserve my future residency. I had to act immediately and move right away.

As I was loading my personal items into my car, I went to Brad's room. I was aghast. How did I not notice his floor covered in newspapers that left a black smudge on the carpet and smashed beer cans? Some remaining beer left a wretched stale smell, taking me back to my beer-drinking days. This only prompted me to move faster in hopes of being gone before he got home. Seeing his room confirmed I was making the right decision.

I blamed myself again, feeling terrible about leaving him behind with an even bigger rent payment and bigger property as I transferred my electricity and phone service. I knew I was adding to his history of trauma and abandonment. Instead of helping make a bad situation better, I was making a bad situation worse. But I couldn't allow my credit and livelihood to go down under his irresponsible choices.

A friend helped me move the bigger items with his truck. My new apartment was in the back of the complex and surrounded by other units. I was able to park my car closer to the unit, which made moving easier than in my previous two apartments, and I felt more secluded and safer.

My porch faced the porch of another neighbor, whose name was Ramona. She was an older lady who was single and never had kids. She had her own cleaning business and was on her porch one day watering her plants while I was outside with my dog. We introduced ourselves and had a small chat that led to our friendship. She began to help me with my dog, letting her out and walking her when my days were long with school and work. We had dinner together after work and on weekends as we talked about our lives and relationships.

At this time, my relationship with Dan was fading. We broke up when one of my clients saw another girl watching his soccer games on the weekends, and it was obvious they were intimate. I was shocked he couldn't be honest and break up with me. I felt rejected and cheated on. Deep inside, I had already felt it wouldn't work long term, but I had the security of knowing someone out there loved me, and it was hard to let go as feelings of guilt and unworthiness crept in.

WORKING DISTRACTIONS

*O*continued to focus on school and work as a distraction. As each semester progressed, I would stand up in class at the beginning of the first session and ask, "Who wants to study? We can meet at my apartment." Not many students had their own place, and the dedicated ones found it useful to come over, so forming a study group was a successful venture. The classes were getting harder, and the only way I could survive them was to get help learning. I didn't realize until I was in a study group that I had never taken such classes as biology, chemistry, anatomy, or geometry before. All those classes are introduced in high school, but mine were replaced with learning about perm rods, solution, curls, and color.

The odds were against me, as I had to study even harder to grasp unrecognizable concepts. I pushed forward and prayed with each new perplexing concept, overcoming each test and moving on to the next semester.

BLINDED BY FORGIVENESS

My mom and I had started talking again. She and my stepdad bought me a plane ticket to stay with them at their place in Tennessee. We were reconnecting in a superficial way, and I was very guarded. There was no mention of the daggers thrown on graduation day. I chose to overlook the offense because of my yearning desire to have my mom's love and form a connection out of adulthood and maturity.

They had become foster parents and had two kids, which took me back to that Mother's Day phone call: "you don't exist." She had moved on and cheated the world into giving her these babies. I tried to push aside my feelings and accept this new world and the lie others saw in my parents as we made our first stop at a resale shop to buy toys. She was buying them toys as if to throw them in my face. She never cared to do that for me. I pushed down the thoughts with my swallows, trying to hold back tears as I saw her be the mom I never had.

Instead of running with these thoughts, my mind turned to lyrics: El Shaddai, El Shaddai, age to age, you're still the same. I had just gone to my first Amy Grant Heart in Motion concert in Houston. God is always the same; He never changes. I found comfort in these thoughts while wearing my concert shirt, feeling wrapped in God's love. At that moment, I chose to love, pushing forward and trying to forget the past.

AN UNLIKELY MEETING

One day I called my grandma Olive in Kansas, as I tried to follow up weekly with her. She was my rock, and we had many meaningful, soul-searching conversations. If I needed help with a recipe (before the internet), cooking meat, sharing my travel plans, what I was learning at school and work, or just catching up on her weather (because it always came our way next), we would just chat. I wanted her to be proud of what I was achieving, and she would always encourage me and motivate me to keep pushing in the right direction.

During one of these calls, she said, "Your dad, Clancy, has always called and kept in touch with me. He wants to know if I can give him your number. I stood frozen in shock. He was the only dad I had envisioned in my mind all these years. She said he always loved me and thought about me and wanted to make sure I was safe. Of course, my mother kept him away and never allowed the relationship all those years. Why couldn't she allow him to remain in my life? My life could have been so different to truly have someone who loved me and took me as his own, symbolized by the name I was given at birth. I was curious to meet someone who continued to think about me 20-something years later.

Clancy called me, and we arranged to meet for dinner one Saturday after work. He brought his lovely wife as we shared a meal at my favorite Vietnamese restaurant and shared our stories. He divulged how when he met my mom and she was pregnant, he instantly took me as his own child—loving me before I ever laid eyes on him. He talked about how he still loved my mom even though she cheated on him. Even after my mom left and we were separated by distance, he still loved and cared for me all these years. He also said I had a brother who was very protective of me. When my mom took me away, they were both heartbroken and helpless. Tears streamed down my face thinking about all those lonely childhood days and nights when someone out in the distance was reaching out in their own thoughts of love for me. A part of me resented my mom more for keeping him from me, a secret I never shared.[12]

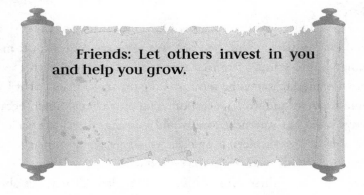

Friends: Let others invest in you and help you grow.

Chapter 16
FINDING AND LOSING
MYSELF IN EUROPE, 17
COUNTRIES LATER

I WILL NEVER BE THE
SAME PERSON

1995 was a very successful year at the salon as I grew my clientele and income. My annual achievements were honored that year at our conference, which resulted in a nice bonus accruing interest in the bank. I had paid my dues by working most Saturdays, Sundays, and long work weeks for the previous five years and was close to completing two years of community college. I was tired and broken from my failed relationship and needed a break.

My friend went to a local college and had plans to backpack through Europe when she graduated in 1996. She had been researching this idea for a while, and when she asked me to go, I didn't quite know how that would happen. I didn't even believe she would undertake such an adventure. Dana was a homebody who didn't usually take the initiative to explore unknown territory. As any good friend would do, I followed her lead as she processed, prepped, and planned for the trip.

I had been working since my first job in Kansas at the age of 13. I worked many jobs in high school and then invested in building a clientele for six years, working long days at the mall. Two years of community college were behind me as I pondered and contemplated the likelihood of going to a bigger college and continuing to succeed. But my best friend was planning to go to Europe and then move up north to teach and live near her sister. How could she leave me? How could she go on this grand adventure and then move away, never for me to see her again? I had to find a way to go. I knew I had to pay my own way and make it happen somehow.

PREPARATION FOR A
BACKPACK ADVENTURE

*O*set out to prepare for a six-month trip to Europe. First, I asked my manager to plead on my behalf to see if the owners of the company would allow me to take a leave of absence. I then applied to British University North America Club (BUNAC), which grants college students under the age of 25 a work visa. Everything took longer since I had to send in a handwritten application by snail mail.

As I waited to see if I was accepted, I checked the flight information. It was just under $600 to fly to London from Houston with an open-ended return ticket, which meant our flight was scheduled to return six months later. During that time in 1996, the euro pass was approximately $750 to travel unlimited for three months to about 21 European countries. A Eurail pass covered 33 countries in total- including Great Britain.

Next, I had decided to sublet my apartment. I wanted to help a young hairdresser like myself who might need their own place starting out. Someone within our company from another salon. The renter agreed to keep my dog with the apartment. My neighbor Ramona agreed to oversee the rent and my dog Nicole since I continued to pay part of the rent. The salon owners not only agreed to let me go but also had connections that would let me work at Vidal Sassoon in London. I thought about the offer in depth and what my future lifelong goals were—either hair or college. As much as I loved hair, I knew working at the salon would entail working long weekends and nights, which would make it hard to travel. I already felt burned out from committing so many long work weeks for the last almost six years and really wanted a job that would allow me to travel, so I declined the once-in-a-lifetime offer.

HOSTELING NEAR AND FAR

*O*had a few months to notify my clients, and a couple of them offered to let us stay with them or their families while abroad. One in Chelmsford, England and one in Greece. While we continued planning, we visited the youth hostel in Houston to get our annual membership, which allows you to stay at any location but had some age requirements similar to the Eurail pass. In the Houston hostel, we met some people from Japan and Austria. We took them out to some common places in town while learning about traveling and their hometown countries. We asked questions about using the train, finding and staying in other hostels, and the different cultures of traveling. Each hostel had its own set of rules. We took them to an all-you-can-eat buffet and watched them make several trips back with heaping high plates saying in astonishment in their accents how cheap and abundant the food was. Apparently, all-you-can-eat buffets didn't exist in their countries based on the cost of food and living, which I later experienced firsthand. America wonders why we have an obesity epidemic. We took them back to the hostel and said our goodbyes, planning to meet again.

When I spoke with my mom in preparation for such a faraway trip, she reminded me not to fall in love with a foreigner and fail to return to the US. She said they would only hurt me, reflecting on her own life. She made me promise to call her collect as I entered each country so she could hear my voice and hear about my travels. I vowed to call no matter what.

REALITY SETS IN –
CURRENCY FOR A LOO

*D*ana's parents dropped us off at the airport—two young, careless girls going into who knows what for the next six months. No hotel or car reservations booked, only a community hall to show up and look for jobs held up by pushpins to a cork board and an endless amount of train seats going nowhere for the next three months. We were so naive and had no map or itinerary, other than a few friends who volunteered their homes in sporadic countries.

We arrived in London after an overnight flight, feeling exhausted and exhilarated, and then reality set in. I had to use the bathroom, commonly known as a loo, which required English pounds. Having only American dollars and coins was a rude awakening. We needed to exchange money into the local currency. Next, we needed to take the train from the airport to get to downtown London, all the while dragging our next six months of belongings up and down the stairs, escalators, and bathrooms

We also had to search for food. During our visit to a local cafe for our first real meal, they brought out a small teacup saucer plate with a minimal amount of iceberg lettuce and a slice of tomato and cucumber. We both looked up at each other at the same time—that was the salad? As if it was a garnish for the meal. The main course, spaghetti, arrived next in a kid's portion, but we were famished from traveling and transporting our belongings.

Once we paid the bill, we counted all the unexpected expenditures from the day. The train ride from the airport to downtown, the three-day tube tickets, the bathroom, lunch, water, and snacks all cost ¾ of $100 in only a few hours' time. I panicked. How could I survive spending that amount of money in the next six months? We called my client's mom,

Wanda, from the iconic red telephone booth. She invited us to her home, so we got another train ticket to travel outside the city to the suburbs. We arrived at her house late, and she prepared some warm, homemade English bread pudding. I have never liked soggy stuffing or mushy bread-type recipes, but this was the best bread pudding I had ever had. It was like I was breaking the fast of my fear of eating and my mindset of getting fat with each delicious bite.

We shared the stories of our 24-hour adventure over the breakfast table. Ms. Wanda stated we could keep our suitcases at her place until we began our travels abroad with our Eurail pass and needed our wardrobe to work. We took our showers and settled in for a quick night's rest before heading back to the London airport and flying out to Greece for our first 16-day destination with my clients and friends, Greg and Andy. Dana questioned my judgment, saying, "Who are these people? How do you know they will be there? What if they aren't there? Where are we staying?"

I didn't quite have the answers to some of her questions, but I reassured her. I had known my client for the last four years, and every summer, he went back to Greece, his country of origin. During the flight, we sat next to a couple of older ladies with thick English accents. We asked them about their culture. The stewardess had just passed out some free wine and drinks, which we all partook of. We were enthralled just watching them talk and listening to their lively travels. We must have been lost in time, startled when the stewardess wanted to take our cups and drinks for landing. Suddenly the ladies said, "Throw it back," and their drinks were gone just like that as we all giggled.

SMITTEN BY THE
STRIPES OF BLUE SKIES
AND WHITE PURITY

On the landing, armed military paraded the tarmac, all containing FN Minimi weaponry, which was quite intimidating as we walked down the stairs of the plane onto the tarmac. We were then ushered into a bus that drove us to the building. I felt like a prisoner of war for a brief moment as we all followed suit. Our party awaited us in the building, and I sighed in relief.

Andy was from Athens, and he invited us to stay in his flat with his dad—a gourmet chef in Greece who fed us like royalty. He would bake lamb while roasting potatoes, basting them with olive oil and squeezing fresh lemons every so often. Each time he opened the oven door, the smell of herbs and citrus wafted through the air as if I had never smelled it before. He made Greek salad and fresh feta cheese with homemade crispy, but soft, bread served with homemade meatballs. Everything was so delicious, and we did not want for food. We got to eat the raw Mediterranean diet before it was the acclaimed diet of choice for heart-healthy weight loss management in America years later.

They took us to the Acropolis and the city, and I learned how little I knew about pertinent history. I realized how much I had missed in high school by taking cosmetology and trying to survive. I didn't comprehend the magnitude of this great monument and the stories it shared. My friends were great and well-versed in their country's culture, and we quickly learned to love Greece as much as they did. We would visit street cafes for an afternoon frappe or shaken coffee with sweet milk. I hadn't drunk coffee much before, but this soon became one of my favorites.

My friend's dad packed us a very healthy lunch and snacks as we set out to the port and loaded a ferry in search of the Greek islands. Our island of choice was Santorini. It was an overnight ferry, and we watched them board all sorts of cargo and supplies to take to the islands. We sat on the deck with other backpackers as the stars magically appeared and the Greeks sang traditional songs and shared some of our delicacies. It was a very magical place as the sun rose over the bodies of land that appeared on the horizon. Santorini was known for its three beaches—one with black sand, one pink, and one warm beige in color. The island itself is built on top of the volcanic remains from many thousands of years ago and has the most amazing sunrises and sunsets, as if God is smiling directly at you.

Soon we loaded a bus and headed to Thessaloniki with Greg to stay with his family in the city. They were very welcoming as his mom greeted us with hugs and kisses as if all her kids had come home. We stayed in the flat and ate our meals on the veranda. Lines of string stretched from flat to apartment flat, as we sat eating and looking out across the ravine of the hanging clothes. It was as if mesmerized and, in a trance, watching the clothes blow in the wind like flags flapping and waving back to us making music in the wind. We would go get Greek pastries and coffee for breakfast. As we walked down the sidewalk, my attention was caught by a van driving behind us on the sidewalk honking its horn. The Greeks drove without rhyme or reason, crossing each other's path, honking, yelling, and hanging out windows as if to direct the traffic around them. Nowhere was safe, not even the sidewalks.

We learned about Alexander the Great and the battles fought and won. This city has a rich history dating back to BC and sports several monuments linked to Greek mythology. We visited the amphitheater where Paul preached and walked on the very grounds of famous Biblical people. I could relate to Paul and his life's journey in many ways. Once we left Thessaloniki, we went to Chalkidiki, or the three fingers, where the beaches were. The crystal-clear blue beaches were the most amazing I had ever seen.

Sadly our 16 days of Romance ended in Greece. As we said our goodbyes, Greg's mom gave me a laminated card of Jesus and gave my friend a cross, telling us to carry them with us everywhere we went. She must have prayed our way through Europe because, looking back, I know some things may not have ended so well. I will forever be grateful for my friends who poured out their love in sharing their families, country, and rich history with us. I was very sad to leave, but 21 other countries were waiting to be explored as we boarded our planes back to London.

A TATTERED BUCKET LIST

A nice gentleman was on the plane who was well-traveled in Europe. Once he knew we were backpacking, he mapped out a three-month voyage with highlights of each country and city to see on a napkin served by the stewardess. This outline became my travel bucket list, and I was able to fulfill most of the places on the list. We flew back to London. My friend really wanted to teach a semester and was investigating her potential opportunities. Once she realized it was off-season, we set out for the mainland of Europe through the cliffs of Dover to Bruges and Brussels, Belgium. It was quite the contrast from the Mediterranean's warm sunrays, inviting beaches, and a plethora of fresh breads, veggies, cheeses, olive oil, and meats. It had its own old-world charm, with medieval-era buildings and cobblestone streets leading to the windmill-laden canals. As we walked the path through the city, I envisioned the history of horses and carriages that would parade those streets. My favorite was the purest chocolate that melted in one's mouth, silky and smooth.

There was something very humbling about putting a few meager belongings in a bag and wearing them on your back like a turtle, drawing attention to oneself unknowingly while marching through prominent streets that came alive. Surrounded by the voices of the city streets, I walked down each cobblestone step as voices of my past collided with voices of the city's past. Layer by layer, I realized I don't have to care what people think anymore. Am I smart or pretty enough? Did I say the right words? I visualized someone watching me eat only to label my physique as "well-nourished."

I Indulged in the purest chocolate slowly melting in my mouth as each layer of "I cannot care anymore what each person thinks of me" invaded my thoughts and helped me find a newfound confidence. I found value in the smallest morsel of chocolate, quenching my thirst for sweetness just like life, seeking to be satisfied in the mindset of how we all got here, and a much bigger canvas on display in front of me took me away from the self-centeredness of my limited self-conscience and timid reflection.

I was still running the race set in motion as a child while watching my mom run. This time, this nervous energy and inner drive to overcome followed suit as each map and train ride continued to lead me on this path of self-discovery and conquering each country etched on my bucket list written on that airplane napkin by a stranger and tucked into my knapsack.

As we ventured across Europe, our list took us from Danish windmills and Belgian mouth-watering chocolate morsels to miniature mermaids in Sweden, over to the battle of the north and south while trespassing between the once-divided walls of Berlin, Germany. It became clear our interpretation of the Europe tour was different for both of us, as evidenced by her decision to part ways at the Berlin Wall. *Why wouldn't my friend want to share the same journey?* I wondered. Just as the wall came down in Germany and the people flooded unknown territory and ventured to the other side, so did all my childhood feelings of abandonment come flooding in as I watched her turn away to a different path. The very irony of unity for the Germans during this new era captured our separation at the very same place, triggering my isolation, loneliness, and threat of safety.

As I stood there alone in a foreign country, my fortitude crumbled, not knowing in which of the other three directions to go. This journey was about one's own self-actualization, as we had walked different paths in our own lives and each had our own milestones to conquer at our own pace. It took all of my strength as I dug deep to face my childhood hurts. I picked up my bag, stood tall, and moved forward. With thoughts of being alone, vulnerable, and without reason, I turned back to my bucket list and headed to the train. There was no time to pity myself, and my timed train ticket was ticking on my budget.

It's funny how we are taught to find value based on how much something costs, using a monetary means to elevate things and people. Sometimes we have to realize that we can't elevate based on money or misrepresent the reputations of others. How often we do not appreciate or find value in things that come easy or cost us little either monetarily or in energy, leaving us to fail to take advantage of those opportunities or people around us.

EASTERN EUROPEAN
ROOTS

*O*n the 1990s, Czech Republic was in a sense being reborn post communism and before the eastward expansion of business and modern influence, finding a new realm of freedom and exploration. It was a hidden treasure where a meal with an after-dinner warmed cognac and a night in a hostel was less than an Andrew, or five dollars. I sat on the mountain slope with the castle fortress as if protecting my back, watching the stars twinkle over the river below and the city skyline, a beauty untouched by any war. I pondered on my newfound discovery, having the eyes to see my own value—undiscovered, unappreciated beauty—and all I had to offer. I felt a soul connection to this place, maybe because my family lineage was part Bohemian Czech. This was the closest I could possibly be to a family I had never known. I felt a longing, placing value on the priceless meaning of beauty, tradition, heritage, and family.

Before moving on to my next destination, I took one last stand on Charles Bridge, asking an elderly lady to take a picture of me with the statue of the crucifixion behind me. The statue was engraved with Czech words speaking of our redemption. The elderly lady, not speaking English, kindly obliged to my beckoning request, smiling and nodding her head in sheer joy while not looking through the camera hole. She was too excited to say she didn't understand, to think a young American like myself believed in her ability to take a picture, accepted her, and gave her a chance to overcome a small task to one but mighty to others.

This lady had seen the days of communism and likely was never able to learn to read or write. Books were banned and not allowed to be owned or in one's possession. For you see, that is how communism works, to keep power over you. How can one have control of their own lives or advance in wisdom and knowledge while reliving the past in stories with a promise to never repeat the bad cycles but only to move forward. She was living that breakthrough moment in time now, as she could embody these physical symbols of freedom with the potential to enjoy the fruit of learning how to read and write. But at this moment, someone believed in her.

FAMILY AND A FOREIGNER
BREAKING BREAD

*O*walked through the small alleyways with the smell of leather, fresh baked bread, and window shop views of colorful gelato.

"Americano, Come join us; come eat. There's always plenty," I heard in a thick Italian accent as I looked over my shoulder as if I thought I was invisible.

I motioned to myself with my hand to my heart and said, "Are you speaking to me?"

"Why yes, of course. You aren't from America?"

I guess the blonde-haired, blue-eyed Texas girl traveling alone shone like a penny reflecting in the bright, heated summer sun. I gingerly walked toward them, in awe of their foreign greeting. They each stood one by one to introduce themselves and politely placed a kiss on each cheek, with my permission, motioning to an empty seat as if they had prepared for my entrance. I was filled with curiosity, as I asked questions about our own connections, traditions, and, of course, each course of food being served. Pasta with scallops, pasta with clams, pasta with fish was served with a carafe of homegrown wine to chase it all down. We studied each other as each course was presented and consumed while watching the evening night casting its shadow as if each course had its own shade. I found joy in catching glimpses of a warm family dinner and for one moment, which I wanted to last a lifetime, feeling the unconditional loving embrace of family and learning to trust again.

A SHARED COST-
EFFECTIVE FLAT

*O*had an appointment to meet my Austrian friend Alex in his homeland. Our first introduction to hostels and the Austrian culture was in Houston. Now I had a chance to experience it firsthand as a rapidly approaching car pulled up to the disembarkment platform at the train station. My friend jumped out and greeted me ever so kindly. That same car shuttled us back to his apartment.

As we approached the wide concrete steps, I asked, "Where's the elevator?"

He said, "Silly girl, there is no elevator."

His loft was simple but necessary, and I understood his awe of American living and standards. The concrete stairs led to each open breezeway with doors for each Ikea-sized loft—none of which had a shower or toilet. Each level had a shared bathroom at each end of the hall, while each loft had an assigned basin, holding each person accountable for their own cleanliness. His room was small and quaint, affording a small fridge, cooktop area, and living space that converted to a sleeping area. My thoughts raced about American standards and how so many have higher expectations than what they can afford. Why couldn't these simple infrastructures be built to support our lower income status, providing clean, simple living for those like me with little or nothing, struggling to earn credit and rights to improve their livelihood? How much would it improve our American culture and economy to meet our people where they are with what they could afford as they proudly worked those entry level jobs? Maybe creating this type of infrastructure in America would help target some of the depression and hopelessness and give this population a foundation to build on. Maybe this could even help solve some of the problems that lead to unnecessary gun use and violence in America. And just maybe every weary, wondering heart could be blessed and sing their own song of music, finding peace and rest.

REUNITED FRIENDSHIP

As I said my goodbyes and boarded the train, I saw Dana curled up sleeping. I hardly recognized her or believed my eyes! We sat together and shared our stories and adventures, renewing our relationship in an unspoken forgiveness. We vowed to meet again in London once our train passes expired and our work visa began. What odds, as we parted ways when the train whistle blew, leaving a future calendar date to meet again etched in our minds.

THE GYPSIES' THWARTED PLAN

Oftentimes when backpacking, the days are full of adventure, leading to less time for intercountry travel. It's common to travel at night and sleep on the train for no added expense. One night in particular after meeting some fellow backpackers, we boarded to travel the French Riviera only to arrive in Spain the next day. We shared our European adventure travels. We laughed, in awe of the beauty around us, until night set in. Two girls were by the window, and two guys were in the aisle seats. We intentionally pinned bags between us and the window and on the overhead racks.

As we slumbered and the darkness lay around us, we were awakened by the sudden screeching of train brakes. Everything was still and quiet when suddenly two disheveled guys, otherwise known as gypsies, suddenly appeared—cornering us in and eyeing our bags. The girls, of course, were barely moving yet very watchful. Suddenly, both guys stood their ground. They were taller and hovered over the two men with a mission, and like scolded dogs, they ran.

I couldn't help but think of some of the stories. Did they have a knife like most did or, in today's terms, would it be a gun? I was forever thankful to meet these independent foreign travelers who all stood together for one test in time to conquer evil. Victory one and all was saved as our individual missions were completed.

THE ROMANTIC DANCE OF
A BLOODY TRADITION

Madrid is a city of two sides, a commercial city full of modern-day hustle and bustle museums and cafes paved the sidewalks. In contrast, another side reflects a living relic of romance past—bullfighting, flamenco, paella, sangria, and the afternoon lull of Spanish siesta, leaving a boarded-up vacant city by day and a vivacious music-filled atmosphere drawing into the late hours of the night. Close to the hostel was a small paella cafe with bullfighting posters pasted like art on display lining the walls.

Many of us agreed to go fetch a hot pan of paella, and since no one could eat that alone, we rallied up a group to go eat. Upon our arrival and sheer delight, this cafe was indeed that of the locals, as a well-known bullfighter decided to join our lively group. He shared his stories of savage encounters with the bulls and invited us to see his performance. We were intrigued, entrenched by this Spanish charm, and all set out to the coliseum to partake of this romantic offering the next day.

Soon our excitement turned to fear as we watched the torment of this poor animal. We tried to remind ourselves of this cultural entity passed down from many generations as the man woos his woman. To this day, there has been a constant tug of war as other countries have tried to silence this practice on behalf of animal cruelty and an ongoing clash of cultures. As we parted ways, the bullfighter vowed to keep in touch and remain pen pals as the journey led me back to London to start my work.

GIVING LIFE: A CORKBOARDS' ROSTER FOR HOUSING AND EMPLOYMENT

he first task at hand was finding a permanent place to live for the remaining months of work. Dana and I met on orientation day as we scanned the corkboard for our preferred job requisitions. I was living in a shared hostel, which had multiple beds in one room. My space was my bed and under my bed, with a weekly or monthly fee, I could hardly afford post travels. I couldn't wait for my first check, as funds were low. Much to my despair, the British income is paid only after a month's work, and if you are starting a new job, it is further delayed. How would I survive? How would I eat?

With no one to call to rescue me, a sense of homelessness started to sink in as images of the past of homeless young American backpackers on European streets flooded my mind. I had a job working on Oxford Street in a high-end mall; however, I couldn't remain homeless in order to maintain my employment. Childhood fears of homelessness arose within, causing great anxiety and propelling me to work harder and overcome as I discussed other potential living situations.

During my stay at the hostel, many people came and went, and one led me to a pub on Baker's Street. Someone there was resigning their position to continue their travels. There were rooms located above the pub where foreign travelers seeking a bed could reside and work. I was offered the job and could learn to pour a Guinness Four Leaf Clover beer in the wee hours of night and keep my day job. My dollars were dwindling and being so close to Oxford Street saved the cost of taking the tube each day as well. My main staple of porridge each day filled my belly and the cost of a two- to three-pound lunch at work helped stretch my scarce pennies. It was a simple way of life to afford the British culture and way of life.

Our mail was sent to BUNAC, and we were able to send and receive letters from family and friends near and abroad while having a permanent address to receive important documents. One day I received a postcard in London from the Spanish bullfighter. The front of the postcard had an image of a man modeling tequila, and next to the image was a scratchy, barely legible English statement reading, "A lot of little Pedritoes" along with the bullfighter's name, Pedro. I realized this insinuated a marriage proposition and a plethora of children. Although his adoration for me scratched onto this liquor advertisement was quite flattering, it brought about a sense of entrapment, being barefoot, pregnant, and having no way to escape and return to my country of origin. Although the invite was flattering, it reminded me of my mom's second marriage with an abusive German man and the reason she wanted me to call from each country just to ensure my safety. I couldn't imagine the thought of giving up my American heritage to live in Southern Spain, surrendering all aspects of vulnerability, which could have been an optimal life experience or a situation I may not be able to escape. I couldn't live my life erroring on the unknown.

THE CONCLUSION TO A
BRITISH WAY OF LIFE

As the days and seasons passed, it was time to return back to the states and say goodbye to my temporary British way of life. A sense of emptiness and lack of belonging started to replace the once-filled sense of self-awareness. I was a nobody caught between two worlds. I wasn't British, and I wasn't the college hairdresser I left behind. There was no purpose, no fulfillment, and no opportunities to help others. My life was meaningless. My identity was left to the observation of others. The fragrant experiences beheld by my senses, viewed by my eyes, processed by my brain, and tasted by my mouth had all come to a head, leaving what was now a void. I was ready to go home and recreate a new me, a world I left behind, never to be the same person. But who was I now? I was feeling sad as I said goodbye to friends, leaving the superficial life of being someone to go home and be someone newly defined.[13]

> Friends: Challenge yourself to learn about people from a different culture. We can all learn acceptance by seeking to understand others. It might be fun!

---

13 If this chapter touched you and you would like more information to help on your own *Quest*, see page 312, **Bunac.**

Chapter 17
ACCEPTED!

A STEP CLOSER

*W*hen I returned from Europe, I was so excited to see my friends and clients. I was a hairdresser and student, the identity I had worked to create for myself over the last six years. This was how I defined my importance and how I felt needed during this time of my life. Helping others feel good about themselves gave my life meaning. It wasn't long before post-travel depression set in. My eyes and brain had gotten used to being visually stimulated by so many beautiful things and constantly learning. I was used to changing my diet, eating so many culturally diverse foods, and meeting so many new people. Now the monotony set in as I worked at the mall and returned to school.

My boss noticed and pulled me to the break room and shook me with her words. "What is wrong with you?" It took me a second to reason. What is wrong? I longed to be back in Europe. The adventure had ended and coming back was a hard adjustment, but I had to get a grip on my life and refocus on my long-term goals of finishing college. My boss woke me up that day as I transitioned between two worlds.

LETTER OF ACCEPTANCE

*O*had completed my community classes and couldn't take any other classes until I went to university. I had applied to the University of Houston since I knew I could commute to school and still work. I will never forget the day I checked the mail and got the letter. I was accepted! I almost couldn't even comprehend the words as my vision of completing college, starting a career, and having a family raced in mind. It was finally happening. I was the only person in my mom's family to get a college degree.

A VISIT BACK TO THE
PAST IN OHIO

*O*stayed in frequent contact with my mom and stepdad. I longed to build the mother/daughter relationship I never had. Later that year, my parents asked me to fly to Ohio and spend Thanksgiving with them and his parents, whom we visited annually for the holiday. I was obliged despite not being sure what to expect and a very heavy college workload. There was a final test in all four of my classes after the break.

Once there, I had a burning desire to ask my stepdad's mom about my childhood and the abuse I endured from her son. I was trying to understand his past. His dad was the mayor of the town; his family was stable, with brothers and family intact. She acknowledged the abuse and remembered finding me hiding and crying once in the washroom. I asked her what she did. She did nothing because she didn't want to get involved and chose to close her eyes. It was her son after all. She gave me what I needed that day—confirmation of the past and a closer step to healing and moving forward in my life. It gave me the motivation to finish school and break the chains of the past.

LONGING FOR A NEW RELATIONSHIP

I was searching for more. I was told on many occasions to go back to church— from the high school student who invited me to his AWANA youth group meetings, to my clients' invitations to visit their churches and divorced friends who sought refuge in the church. I knew I needed church and needed to forgive my mom and pray for her. I just didn't know how to do it. God was building an awareness in my heart, as He was calling me. As I pondered on the community of church and God's people and wanting to find someone special, I knew I needed to put myself in a different social clan. How could I expect good things in life if I didn't forgive my mother and myself and put myself around good people?

I often reminded God of the hurt I had endured in the name of church. I knew from my own relationship with God in the Pentecostal church that it is all about our personal relationship with Him and our Savior, Jesus Christ. It's not about the people and the buildings. We speak to God in our own heart and mind. God is always there waiting for us to speak, listening to our thoughts and hearts motives. But I also knew how powerful the blanket of prayer, community, and the love of God could be. At this time, I realized my identity wasn't my career, what I did, or my achievements but about being a child of Jesus' family and finding meaning in a much bigger realm.

FAMILY LINEAGE

I reflected on family. I knew my Grandma Olive in Kansas with a bad hip wouldn't always be around, and my time with her and Grandpa William would be limited. I needed to make time each year to see my grandparents and treasure these last years and bar any regrets. I had several broken relationships, none of which led to a lifelong commitment or marriage. I pondered on the opportunity I had to meet Clancy, my dad at birth. I had lost the opportunity to having a loving father and role model during my childhood years as I sought for the father I never had.

SURRENDERING THE PAIN

*O*often cried out to God. I always felt He was with me and felt closest to Him in nature and his Garden of Eden. I always felt close to God in helping others. I cried out to Him, saying, "You know I can't go to church, as it is too painful. If you want me in church, you need to make it happen." I cried myself to sleep many nights, overwhelmed with loneliness and bewilderment, and often had thoughts of finding a lost dad, pursuing a dream of getting married and having a family. Would these dreams ever really come true?

I often downplayed the dad portion with little thought that I would ever really know where I came from and where I belonged. I was on speaking terms with Clancy and his family. I had just seen my third stepdad for the holidays as I tried to build the relationship we never had. I couldn't even imagine finding my biological dad. From my mom's declaration many years ago, I checked the computers at school but gave up easily. Either I had the wrong spelling or an endless list of people had the same name, which thwarted and delayed my search for years to come.

> Friends: Despite the acceptance we find in our education, jobs, and imperfect families, they do not define us. We are part of a bigger picture, a bigger community, as individuals of a much higher power who beckons for our attention and accepts us just as we are.

Chapter 18
CROATIA: A MISSION TRIP

UNDERSTANDING THE
REAL REASON FOR HOPE

My dear friend Denise had gone through a bad divorce. During a haircut session, she confided in me and invited me again to a singles Bible study group and a special meeting. Reflecting on my need for God and the community, I asked God if this was His beckoning, so I accepted. We met on a Sunday evening in a small, warm, personable setting at a church in Houston. It was very cozy and did not have the structure of a traditional sanctuary. I could feel a blanket of peace as I entered the room. Everyone was very friendly, social, welcoming, and seeking a relationship with God our Savior. I was able to find fellowship with people close in age, those going through the same struggles and loneliness of singlehood and finding comfort in all my life's madness.

The singles leaders presented a Croatian mission trip opportunity to the group and, for those who qualified, grants to assist with the cost. Fortunately, I was able to go with my dear friend Denise and best friend Valencia from high school. We were assigned prayer partners and began our trip with orientation, a prayer, and our daily Bible study while jour-naling. Our plan was to help rebuild houses destroyed by an unnecessary war of touting independence in the early 1990s. As we toured the towns, we learned about the unnecessary violence of innocent lives lost, brave men, untrained soldiers, women, children, young teens, and how fami-lies barricaded themselves trying to avoid the bombing.

Pictures of debris and devastation served as a reminder of the coun-try's fight for freedom, lining the streets like a walking memorial in hopes of history not repeating itself. When we helped clean up the streets in the communities, families would greet us and offer the finest espresso and cookies as a thank you. Many people fled their homes to seek refuge. The Serbians took over, staying in these homes and retreating once war was completed, leaving the broken remains of what was once a beauty symbolized in the sparse flowering roses on a spindly bush. The roses reflected the family that once lived there before having their world turned upside down as the home remained empty and broken. Did they lay victim to the war or retreat and move to sheltering countries, leaving behind everything they once worked for only to start over? Others fled and took refuge in these abandoned homes, commonly known as squat-ters, hoping the original owners would not return.

Our group would meet each evening at a cafe on the Danube River to recap the day's work and worship our Savior. One evening before dinner, my friend and I ventured for a short walk. Two boys, approximately 9-12 years old, were playing soccer. One had blond hair and blue eyes, and the other had brown hair and brown eyes. Both had light skin. My friend, who had warm brown hair, eyes, and skin, jumped into the game, kicking the ball to speak an international language of sports. Suddenly both kids started to aggressively kick the ball at her and chase her. She retreated quickly with fear in her eyes, feeling threatened. Were the kids taught segregation as a remnant from the war? Were they taught to recognize those different from themselves and react out of trauma faced years prior from the war? Clearly there were differences, which raised its ugly head in that moment of innocence.

HUMILITY IN SERVICE

These survivors took refuge in a large building housing several floors and several small one-room apartments. On our final night with them, they volunteered to serve us in the main kitchen and community living space. Oh, how humbling this was, as these ladies and children took their only scant offerings and refined them into homemade bread, soup, and a lavish meal. They expressed joy in bringing us their finest in gratitude for our service, and we shared hope with them. Who were we to receive so much from those who had so little to give but gave above their extent of wealth in pure joy and sacrifice? How many times have I withheld sharing, giving, and helping others when I had the power to do so much more? Our Savior always has a way of revealing Himself to us in the least expected way, growing us and shaping us to do his work.

Some may ask what we accomplished when we couldn't build. We planted seeds of hope, sharing God's love. We shared the love of a Savior, one who rescues you in a storm as He comes in and sends others to help pick up the pieces and let you know there is love and one is not alone. Embracing one another's hurts through empathy, providing comfort and fellowship listening to others' hardships without fault or prejudice. Looking for opportunities to heal the brokenhearted and rebuild trust in humanity by just being present. My relationship with God, my Saviour, was restored at this time. Never had I felt as close to God as when He helped me shed the trauma and layers of religious abuse and trust Him again just as these survivors did.

Slowly, God started to peel off the onion layers of religious abuse and took away the unease of attending church. As life progressed and time passed, I graduated U of H and started to attend the sought-out computer-matched nutrition internship at Sam Houston in Huntsville. I started looking for a closer Bible study group, which led me to The Fellowship of the Woodlands. Little did I know how much I would need God and Jesus as my protector during my next stage of life, all of which brought me closer to Him again as I hid in His shadows.

Friends: Sometimes just being present and helping others process their own traumas is all we need.

Chapter 19
GRADUATE SCHOOL

TRYING TO DISPEL
THE DARK CLOUD

*I*t was extremely hard to successfully complete the curriculum due to many years of taking classes in college that I had no exposure to, such as chemistry, calculus, advanced English/math, due to being in cosmetology. My Savior knew my needs and weaknesses, providing people I could study with who helped me overcome this learning deficit. This enabled me to move closer to my goal and never give up on the journey. Through constant prayer, meditation, collaboration, and hard work, I gradually got one step closer to completing a Bachelor's Degree in Nutrition and then a Master of Arts degree.

As time passed and several haircuts later, I began dating Walker. I'd been cutting his, his brothers, and his dad's hair since the age of 17. We had always been friends, but he was attracted to me on a different level and admitted he didn't know why. Maybe he was enamored by my recent travels abroad, as I shared many stories during the haircuts. Maybe he saw the light of my renewed relationship with my Savior. We dated on several occasions, which led to a committed relationship and cycles of breakups and getting back together.

It seemed Walker's mom didn't want me to succeed in my nutrition internship application, as she deterred my efforts and told me I needed business, not nutrition, classes. After one break up, I almost resigned my efforts, distraught to find I would have to apply for a 6- to 18-month program while attending school and working for free in the internship program. Voluntary hours would be clocked and recorded in nursing homes, hospitals, outpatient doctor offices, children's daycare programs, rehab units, etc in order to gain experience while studying for the nutrition certification exam. I was afraid and questioned how I would survive during this time without working. I had no parents or family to fall back on. I almost passed the deadline to submit the handwritten application pleading for acceptance into a program, any program, questioning my career path decision, which was clouded by doubt and confusion.

Walker even bought a house in Houston so we could be together and reassured me I could go to college, which would help complete my nutrition internship. I had given up my lease, donated all my belongings except my clothes, and transferred my mailing address. We were not married or engaged, but he reassured me that he wanted the relationship. I was committed, although I knew inside it was bold to commit without a formal, nonverbal commitment from him. I knew better. I wanted more in my life than what my childhood offered and what was mirrored to me. So it should have been no surprise when he changed his mind and didn't call me, didn't return my call, and left me hanging, homeless, and distraught.

Fortunately, I was able to move in with my best friend, who was house-sitting indefinitely, and continue to go to school. She was my rock and provided support when I needed it, unlike the previous track in my life. My heart was filled with gratitude as she helped me pick up the pieces. I was devastated and felt all my dreams were crashing down back to square one, confused and questioning my purpose and God's plan for my life. I was in the process of determining which nutrition internship program to apply to after completing the bachelor's program while continuing to work in the salon. After almost giving up, recognizing there was no financial way I could work for free and complete a program, let alone get accepted without any working hospital experience, I prayed for a sign.

ALMOST A MISSED OPPORTUNITY AND FUTURE

The internship was a difficult process of applying to several colleges with a complete handwritten notarized application pleading my case for acceptance in dietetics. The deadline was approaching when my classmate Betty gave me a pep talk and woke me to my senses, reminding me of all the work I had invested in nutrition. With an impending deadline and her step-by-step instructions, I completed my application and college plan with only minutes to spare.

I had another moment of triumph when I got a letter of acceptance and the call. I was accepted to a college that was new to pioneer the nutrition program with a master's degree and a business minor. I wanted to personally thank my friend Betty for her encouragement. I don't know where life may have taken me if I hadn't finished my nutrition plan. My Saviour sent my sign, the messenger, and created a path where there was none. The clouds of confusion lifted as my vision was clear and my feet were on the right pathway for my life's purpose.

Once again, like clockwork, Walker would come back to the salon and book a haircut with me only to initiate the relationship again. He would often say that his mom didn't want him to date me as the reason for ending the relationship before. His family was financially inept, and she wanted him to marry someone whose family had monetary gain or influence. His mom would show me pictures of a lady who always made kind gestures toward her, whom Walker said his mom wanted him to marry. One time I saw this lady outside the salon window as if watching me. I mentioned it to Walker as an affirmation of his mother's wishes for her son.

While dating, it seemed there was a dark cloud. I had thoughts of his mom following me as I would pass her on a lonely, wooded street while going to school. Why was she following me and tracing my steps? Why did I keep going back to this unhealthy relationship? What was drawing him back to me? Why couldn't I just say no? Oh, how I longed for a relationship and to be loved. Doesn't love overcome all obstacles? Aren't all things possible with God?

LEARNING/A LATIN ADVENTURE

I continued to focus on my new goal, my master's nutrition program, focusing on excelling in my grades. One of the teachers brought to my attention a study abroad program in Mexico with potential reimbursable grants. The teacher provided the grant information, and I got approved for financial assistance. Walker encouraged me to go and learn about the culture while studying business. He purchased a plane ticket and planned to visit.

Everything seemed to be on track until the day before leaving—the grant money had not transferred to my account. How could I leave for a month without money to go? The college had computers set up in the gymnasium to help students complete their summer class registration. They pulled up my account and found the grant money went to another student with my same exact name. At the moment of discovery, all of the computers blinked and turned off at once, and the attendee looked up in disbelief. After what seemed like hours, the computers eventually regained consciousness and my account was retrieved. The attendee reassured me the funds would return to my account and encouraged me to complete my college plan in Mexico.

ROBBED AND FOLLOWED

W hile studying in Mexico, Walker came to visit. When he left the following day, I was robbed. I was standing on a bus surrounded by a group of guys rubbing and pressing on me. Suddenly the bus cleared, and an old man motioned that my backpack was open. Once I got to class, I bent over to retrieve my paper from my backpack and realized I had been robbed. They got my purse, which had keys and a map to where I was staying, along with my driver's license.

The following day, I came home from school and a man was standing on the empty street in front of the house. He was looking down and kept looking at me as if trying to identify me by my stolen license. As I went into the house, he crossed behind me and walked up the hill. I stood in the window watching him, sensing his intentions, standing still in time, frozen in motion, fearing the notion of going to the outside world.

I still had some classes to complete before going home. Walker and I would talk long distance on the phone. I called him from a corner phone booth to discuss the event and the impending danger around me. He stressed, with fear in his voice, don't go out alone; don't call me. Just come home, baby. Just come home alive. Don't get kidnapped." I felt like he knew something I didn't. He also had Latin roots and knew the dark ways of the impoverished countries—how many times Americans would get kidnapped and held ransom for money. Without a ransom in return, they would disappear, never to be seen again. He knew the potential harm for a young blonde-haired, blue-eyed girl in Mexico. I could hear it through the telephone wire. It was pretty evident I was being followed. By the grace of God, I made it home safely, and Walker greeted me at the airport.[14]

> **Friends: In this world, we must all watch our kids and our own backs—Diligently, Prayerfully, Faithfully, and not fearfully—protecting who we love and protecting ourselves by putting on our armor each day.**

14   If this chapter touched you and you would like more information to help on your own *Quest*, see page 314, **Safe Horizon.org-Stalking** and page 315, **Suicide Hotline.**

Chapter 20
BATTLE OF GHOSTS

A HOLY GHOST VERSUS
GHOSTS OF DARK NIGHTS

At the dusk of night, I entered the church, praying the darkness stayed outside. After anointing my forehead with holy water, I prepared my own vile to wage the battle at home. Among the quiet glowing embers of lit prayer candles, my prayers rose to heaven in the smoke, breaking beyond the constraints of this physical world.

I was actively seeking God during this time and back in church by His grace. I knew I needed God as I sought His guidance and His plan in my life. I introduced Walker to church as well. I knew he needed God and Jesus in his life. He needed salvation and a chance to lead his own life and make his own decisions. An underlying cord or sense of bondage seemed to tie him back to his family, keeping him from moving forward. He would always say the church felt so peaceful.

One day we went to a record store. He loved records, especially jazz and anything vintage. He knew my favorite singer was Amy Grant, as we had been to one of her concerts in Houston and he had bought the recent Hymns and Faith tour CD for my birthday. He looked through some stacks and, out of nowhere, pulled out an Amy Grant record. I was delighted. We went back to his place and played the new find on his record player. One of my favorite songs I replayed was "My Father's Eyes." Even as a child, I loved that song. To mirror my Father's Eyes could mold me into his child and what I had become.

At one point Walker told me, "I know God is your Father. You never had a father." That random statement caught me by surprise for someone who hadn't been introduced to church and God before. I stopped for a moment and thought, *Why yes, God is the Father I never had. He takes care of me, providing what I need when I need it.* I always thought of God as a supreme being, but in this tender moment, I realized I always had my Father with me. Walker could see the light in me, and maybe that is why he kept coming back, not for me but for the light.

A PRAYED FOR
CONFESSION

My coworker and friend Rona invited us to a revival of praise and worship at her church. By this time, my relationship with Walker was struggling and I couldn't quite put my hands on it, which drove me closer to God and church. During the sermon, the pastor would speak in prophetic examples, directing the message to individuals in the sanctuary. The pastor said someone's mom was a witch and wished someone harm. I knew that was directed at me. I held my breath and prayed for the truth to come from him. We left that night, and as soon as we were in the car, Walker confessed his mom was the one. He repeatedly said she didn't want us to be in a relationship but that he didn't agree and he loved me.

I already felt that his mom wished me harm since she would try to eliminate me from his life. It wasn't my fault he kept returning to the relationship. It was my fault for allowing it to continue, but at this point, I felt God was using me to show him His light and praying that he could be set free from a life of bondage. In return, I was being haunted at night. I would awaken to my dog jumping over me back and forth, as if chasing something in mid-air. One night as I was sleeping, I saw an overwhelmingly big creature lifting my shoulders up and trying to bring my body to himself as if he was trying to enter my body. I started to pray and plead the blood of Jesus over my body and mind, stating in my spirit repeatedly, "I rebuke you in the name of Jesus." I began to sing the old hymnal, "What can wash away my sins? Nothing but the blood of Jesus" repeatedly in my sleep. Finally, I awoke as if it was a bad dream. The air was thick, as if I was gasping for breath. Sitting up in bed, I looked around the room, and suddenly the bedroom door caught my eye as it slowly opened as if the spirit was leaving. Seeking refuge and comfort, I called the local radio station for prayer and to hear the voice of reality while trying to retain my own mental sanity. Following the prayer, I turned, shaking in fear, and played my Amy Grant Legacy Hymns of Faith CD. The lyrics repeatedly filled the atmosphere as if a choir of angels sang, "I Need thee Every Hour/ Nothing but the Blood of Jesus." I was exhausted, my body was aching and hurting, my spirit was tired, and I knew I had fought an unexplainable battle that was won by pleading the blood of Jesus.

WAS IT A CURSE OR A STRING OF BAD, UNEXPLAINABLE EVENTS?

Following that night's event, I pondered back to mysteries past, wondering if it was possible all of the recent bad events could have been all of Walker's mom's bad wishes toward me. As I drove home from college, a gust of wind flipped my car 180 degrees, facing oncoming traffic on the highway in the dark of night. Was my car wreck a means to get rid of me? What about Mexico and my grants? Were the robbery and potential kidnapping all a prayer of deeds gone wrong? Pictures taken that night were developed and showed a shadowy presence over my bed, confirming another presence in the room that night.

All of the stress was causing havoc on my body mentally and physically, causing my female cycles to cease and become irregular. After a visit to the doctor, I was diagnosed with perimenopause at a young age. My thoughts started racing. *Will I ever get married or be able to have kids?* When I expressed some of my battles with my mom and talked about school, an ugly truth was revealed. A statement I will never forget resurfaced all of my childhood hurts and distrust for her. If I kept her in my life, I'd constantly be subject to her manipulation and ways. It was a turning point. I knew if I ever had children or a family, I could never trust her, as I knew she would try to sabotage it, as I had seen her do so many times as a child. My focus was to finish my nutrition internship. I had worked so hard to get accepted into the program and complete my degree. My internship was everything, and church and school were my distraction from the swirling chaos around me. If I did not complete the program, my degree would be worthless in the workforce.

The graduate program was coming to a close as I worked my final clinical rotation in a hospital. I would go in early in the mornings and read, research nutrients, and get ready for each day's assignments. During that rotation, a doctor allowed my assigned dietitian mentor and me to witness heart surgery. The doctor and team made mention of "napkins" to capture any blood loss, which was very interesting and lightened the seriousness of the surgery.

MORE HOURS NEEDED

*U*pon completion of the required hours to fulfill my rotation, the intern director alerted me that the voluntary hours completed were not approved by my preceptor at the hospital. During that last hospital rotation, there was no initial discussion of expectation of goals, no weekly check-in to determine progress or completed tasks, and no checklist to complete, so it came as quite a shock. The college director also advised that in order to graduate and complete my program certification, it was necessary to find another preceptor and complete the necessary hours. I wept once again, running through my mind all the what-ifs of failing and not completing this program. I reached out to one of my previous RD mentors who worked in a local rehab hospital and pleaded my case. Fortunately, she agreed to accept me and document my work hours.

All information was submitted, processed, and approved, including a complete vaccination record. Since I had no vaccine record from childhood, I had to receive the vaccines again as an adult. It was actually a fortunate opportunity to acquire more experience and better equip me for my future role as a dietitian. Little did I know it would also lead to an 11-year part-time job later. My classmates graduated that fall; however, my graduation would be complete once my final hours were submitted. I did not attend my graduation and walk with the other classmates since there was no one to help celebrate the achievement. This only put more salt in a sore wound, reminding me of my high school graduation, feeling alone and isolated. I focused on working in the salon again and completing the necessary hours, and my program verification was awarded that spring. It was ten long years before my Master's Degree in Nutrition was finally completed.

BREAK AWAY

After this series of events, I decided to no longer pursue the relationship with Walker. I felt it was best to concentrate on school, my job in the salon, and studying for my certification exam. This time I did not return his call. In the dark of night, I heard someone scurrying outside as the leaves and brush shuffled about. I slowly got up to look out the window and saw Walker running away from my window down the street with a small dog driven by a leash in hand. It was clear he was continuing to stalk me, years later loitering outside my window, shuffling the leaves beneath him. I reasoned in that moment it was over, and my boundaries were being constructed. We never had a clear agreement to part ways, but that last view of him made my decision even more poignant and permanent. I placed my trust and rest in the hands of the God of all gods. I was no longer going to be a part of this crazy cycle. Walker knew the right path, and now there was only one person who could save him. That wasn't my burden any longer. I had to save myself.[15]

> **Friends: We try many ways to escape the darkness of night and of our minds, but the only escape is through a ghost who is the holiest of all.**

---

15   If this chapter touched you and you would like more information to help on your own *Quest,* see page 313, **KSBJ Contemporary Christian Music, Streaming, Prayer,** page 314, **Music for the Soul Lessons,** page 314, **Safe Horizon.org-Stalking** and page 315, **Suicide Hotline.**

Chapter 21
MET MY SUNSHINE

LOVE FINDS ITS WAY

*I*t was a very dark time. My spirit was tired of running and fighting an invisible battle. I questioned my own existence, as there were many times I thought about how I could escape everything so easily and be in Heaven at peace. I questioned why my mom had to carry my birth to fruition. Why did I have to be born when everything seemed so hard? No matter how hard I worked to understand and change, it seemed an uphill battle. My life seemed to mirror Job's in the Bible. I had lost everything and struggled to move forward, seemingly slipping farther and farther backward each time. What difference did my life really make? No one would miss me. There was no puzzle piece my existence fit into.

I would meditate on the words to the song "I Can Only Imagine." I'd imagine how the gates of heaven could welcome me with loving hands that did not exist on earth. Oh, what an escape and reprieve I sought, only to keep waking up each day and continue the battle. No reason seemed adequate enough to purge my existence, so I existed each day. Each day was a prayer to God to turn my life around for the better, a prayer to make something from my ashes, to live and come out better than the beginning, only to help others who have been in such a dark place like myself. I meditated daily on the verse "For I know the plans I have for you" as I pondered God's promises and tried to justify the meaning of my existence.

I continued living with my girlfriend Valencia, who was absent on most occasions since her job was in south Houston and the house was north of Houston. She had bought her own house closer to work and was in the process of moving out. Another gentleman took residence in the home, and I continued to rent a room. I began attending the singles Bible study at a nearby church, where I met Adam, my future husband. At first, we didn't talk to each other much. We talked at each other as we each shared our interpretation of the Bible study passage.

CONFIRMATION IN COMPANIONSHIP

*W*e both came from dark places and sought Jesus as our refuge. We soon found we were both seeking God during the lowest part of our lives. One night Adam followed me home after work to study together. As we approached the house, I saw the gentleman who had recently moved in, filling the role of managing the home's financial matters. He was walking through my room, all shades pulled up and lights on in the house. As we entered the house, the new renter was extremely distraught as he exclaimed repeatedly, "There was a man in the house!" He stated he had come home early from work and saw a man in the house. The new renter, who was wielding a gun, projected his voice, stating, "I have a gun," as if to warn the stalker of his demise for entering the home, walking through the home room by room in search of the trespasser. He appeared very shaken. I watched him as he anxiously continued to investigate each room in the house. Once again, all the thoughts of being followed and tracked by my ex were confirmed. I thought he had moved on since I had seen him that night; however, that thought was disproved.

My new friend Adam and this innocent bystander stood there as my witness to the torment I had faced for so many years as I tried to move forward. My ex must have found the spare key my friend had always left outside, and who knows, maybe he even made his own spare key. The next day the gentleman replaced all the locks and keys to all the doors. I felt relieved that I wasn't losing my mind to the reality of being tracked for so long. The new locks locked out the ghosts of the past.

Not long after that, I moved in with my friend Denise, who invited me back to church. She had been inviting me over to her house for about a year now, providing a healthy meal, a place of refuge, quiet, and rest, as each Sunday, I would take a nap on her couch. It was a much-desired rest, replenishing sleep and peace in a safe place that prepared me for the week to come and helped me face the never ceasing spiritual war at night. The nightly mental and spiritual battles led to stolen sleep and peace of mind. When I told her about how my ex continued to follow me, she offered her apartment room for rent. I quickly obliged and sought escape in the clutches of her sanctified home. Adam had met Denise and was invited to visit often, as we continued to renew our own minds and seek healing. Denise's home was a secluded, quiet, safe place in the wooded area outside of Houston.

STUDIES BOTH SPIRITUAL
AND SPECIALIZED

*O*had completed my college curriculum and nutrition rotation hours and acquired my Master's Degree in Nutrition, with a minor in business. My next goal was to pass the nutrition exam and acquire my license. I had been studying for my nutrition certification exam but continued to fail it and submit another payment for the retest. In Denise's home, I could strictly focus on my studies, clear my mind, and find peace in God's nature, feeling free from the oppression and dark cloud that previously surrounded me.

The Women's Singles group at the church close to Denise's house introduced me to the Beth Moore Bible studies. Her studies spoke to my heart as I drew close to God and was reminded that I was a special creature and truly had value in my Father's Eyes. This same church brought Adam and me together, as he attended Beth Moore's Bible studies with me. We started studying books about God and forgiveness. Studies like Daniel helped me process and understand God's hand in difficult times of life. One big takeaway was how God delivers us, as in the story of Shadrach, Meshach, and Abednego. God may deliver us by walking alongside us through our fires, He may remove the fire, or He may take us out of the fire completely by taking us home to be with Him.

We never know God's final plan for our lives, when our purpose has come to completion. Our trials aren't for us but for others around us. It's like a domino effect, each one setting a chain reaction or impact in others' lives for an ultimate purpose. Just as Abraham was willing to sacrifice his only son, our lives and suffering may be a sacrifice to help save others in God's kingdom. Unfortunately, we are so wrapped up in our own suffering to look up and see God's purpose in our own stories and the impact we have on others' lives. Sometimes as we overcome the fires of life, God gives us back an opportunity to help pull others out of the same pit we were once in. Beth Moore's studies primarily focus on women and healing. Adam joined her live studies, and she would address her audience as her "Beloved Ladies and children of God." We would have a nice chuckle as he was one of the few men present, as we embraced God's message pertinent to our own situations.

I reflected on the examples, words, and promises in the Bible many times. These studies healed each of our own hurts and hearts, renewing our spirits and minds with a new outlook on our lives. Adam came side by side and walked me out of that darkness in God's fellowship as we helped bear one another's burdens.

Adam had a completely opposite background from me. It's still a mystery how we came together in a relationship. We often say that only God could have brought us together. He had the family I always hoped and prayed for. Adams' parents were still married and lived in the same house he was conceived in. He had a typical family of four, with his parents and two siblings, himself, and a brother. His parents both came from a long line of Catholic and Baptist believers, each holding their own beliefs and convictions. His family of origin came from a long line of stability, and neither grandparents divorced.

As the Bible says, those who are God-fearing can feel God's blessings for generations to come, whereas my broken family, living outside of God's guidelines, passes down curses for generations to come. Were my trials a result of the sins of my forefathers? Whatever the case, I was going to do my best to overcome and break the strongholds passed down by generations. Adams' parents financially supported him as any good parents would do, providing a stable home, parental guidance, clothes, and basic necessities, including college, and most importantly, role modeling a personal relationship with Jesus. He had all the things in a family I longed for and hoped for.

KINDRED HEARTS, DISTINCTIVE DIFFERENCES

Adam had no fear and had not experienced the level of trauma I had experienced. His vision of the world was a colorful canvas with equal opportunity, painted with no shadows or darkness to match his outlook. He was much younger than me and had fewer life experiences. He had a good heart and was willing to help others, even if that meant putting himself at risk. We often talked about our backgrounds and differences as we studied books on healing, and our kindred hearts grew closer together.

Adam was on the verge of reinventing his career and going back to college to get his teacher's certification, and I was pursuing changing my career from working in the mall to working in a hospital or clinical setting. I was able to emotionally and financially support him on his journey and help him achieve his goals. Adam was there to support me as I developed a better understanding of my life and belongingness. We dated through the seasons. Each season offered one of growth as we both dug into the layers of our own hurts and offenses, learning more about ourselves, each other, and God.

Adam met my grandparents in Texas, GG and Frank. As he got acquainted with them while eating and playing a game of chicken leg dominoes and a card game of nuts, we would hear about all their camping adventures. He met my grandparents in Kansas, William and Olive, as I had started an annual holiday road trip to visit them each year. We would sit in the basement laughing and joking, watching movies, and eating grandpa's fresh popped popcorn. Both sets of my grandparents fell in love with his personality and were both happy I had met a special person I could move forward with.

During one of our road trips to meet family, we heard the song "You are my Sunshine." We would sing this song to each other, reflecting on how we had found happiness even when skies were gray. These words and phrases reminded us of our dark moments before Jesus brought us together at church. God used each of us to bring light and healing to the other.

We would reflect on how each of us individually was the light to the other during our darkest moments of despair and low points in life. We reflected on the lyrics: no matter how grey or dark life was, "You are my Sunshine." We voiced our first promise of commitment as we sang, "Please don't take my sunshine away." As Jesus was fusing our souls together through love, acceptance, and closing our open wounds, our nickname for each other became "Sunshine."[16]

---

16 If this chapter touched you and you would like more information to help on your own *Quest*, see page 314, **Living Proof Ministries.**

Friends: While some people may let us down and hurt us, God can use others to heal us. He can work through others to be his hands and feet and provide their love and support to walk us out of darkness into our own sunshine. One may ask, *How can I find my own sunshine and have a good life?* Surround yourself with good people, which may include getting plugged in to a local church, Bible study, or community group.

Chapter 22
THE MOMENT WE
FOUND FORGIVENESS

FREEDOM, AT LAST!

I was reconnecting with my grandma GG on a personal level. She came to visit me, and I would give her haircuts. We had our most private and heartfelt conversations during that time. My Grandma apologized for my childhood and the time I was asked to leave the house. I knew she was genuine in her sorrow. I told her I knew she did what she could for me at the time. I also thanked her for being bold and standing up to my mom in bringing me to Texas. I told her that Texas forever changed my life. If I had remained in Kansas in the Midwest, there was little opportunity for me there. I would never have had the opportunity to get my cosmetology license and cut hair, which provided the resources for me to go to community college and then a nationally recognized college, University of Houston. I would have never had the opportunity to work abroad in London and travel to Europe for six months, learning about myself and so many other people, cultures, and food. I would have never been able to study in Mexico, learning about business and living with a local family whom I called Mom for a short time.

I was very grateful for Grandma affording me the opportunity that life brought me. I thanked her and said that enduring many hard things made me who I am today. I would never change the person God created and molded me into through all of these life experiences. I worked too hard to get to where I was in my life to look back and have to start over. I told Grandma I was sorry for anything I did that made her worry or upset as a teenager. I then asked if she ever knew my biological dad or his name. I didn't really expect an answer but figured it was worth asking. She paused and stated she remembered meeting my dad, whom my mom had a two-night fling with. She said she believed his name was Warwick "Ski."

Well, I knew the last name since my mom had told me when I turned 13 that Clancy was not my biological dad. My mom had previously made jokes about my "ski" nose, which didn't make sense and was humiliating. Their occasional jokes made me self-conscious about the physical differences that alienated me from my mom and stepdad. Since my mom had already told me his last name, I knew my grandma must have held the mysterious key to my existence this whole time.

The following evening after work, I couldn't get myself fast enough to my grandparents' neighbors' house, Lydia and Abraham. They were like parents to me, and anytime I felt sad, or had an obstacle I needed to work out, their couch was like my therapist chair. They kissed me as I entered and sat on the couch.

They were watching their TV shows, and I just blurted out, "My grandma remembered my dad's name."

"Really?" Lydia said, as she looked at me in disbelief, as if all this time the secret was hidden and buried beneath lock and key.

I knew what she meant. I could have known my dad and potential other family members. All this time I lost, we lost. At the age of 34, I was dismayed at the memories that could have been. After sitting there in shock as if to say *did this really happen*, Lydia jumped up, went over to the computer, and started googling his name. I watched her search and sift through the multiple names. In less than 30 minutes, we had the information I needed to contact my biological dad. She narrowed it down to the one person who would carry the DNA to my belongingness and my ski nose. I hugged her and smiled, leaving with a full heart. I left that night with a written address and hope for a new future and a new chapter in my life.

> Friends: Look for opportunities to forgive and be forgiven. It will be life-changing, and remember, it all points to a greater purpose. Your blessings may be foiled by your unforgiveness.

Chapter 23
THE ORIGINAL LETTER

ONE CHANCE TO
WRITE A LETTER

*N*ow that I had my supposed dad's name and information, I pondered how I should introduce myself. Should I call him? No, that was like the movies, and he would just deny me and hang up. Or if his kids or wife answered, maybe the message wouldn't be relayed back to him. How does that work? "Hi, I am your long-lost daughter you never dreamed about having," smh. Those were only my dreams; my world was the one turned upside down, not his. As far as I knew, he never even knew I was conceived. I pondered and thought about all the ways I could be rejected. So many times before, I had talked out every opportunity and its outcome in my head, making myself mad. I just knew I couldn't handle another rejection and being shunned by some man and his potential family I had never met.

I knew I had but one opportunity to introduce myself, and only one, so I needed to make the best of it. So why not write a letter? Yes, that's it. I could introduce myself, and if he chose to answer, then the mystery would be solved. If my letter stirred up dissension in his life, he could throw it away, never to have to revisit the thought again. I could protect myself from one more rejection. I wrote a letter, one last heartfelt plea, releasing all my years of not knowing whom I belonged to and where I came from. Laying out on paper the history that led to my existence was like healing a broken heart, whether or not He answered.

SNAIL MAIL, THE LETTER

The letter, dated 12/15/2004, is as follows:

Dear "Ski,"

I pray that you would read this with an open heart and mind. I think I may know you and you may know me. And if you are not the person I am looking (thinking) of, then I am still probably related to you in some way.

Let me explain: My mother is "Jo," and this is the story, to my knowledge. I know every story has two sides, and I don't for one minute discount your side if you are the person I think you are. My mother was approximately 22 years old, and the year was late November/December 1971. My mother crashed (without invitation) a Polish wedding and met a man with the last name "Ski." Later my mother found out she had conceived me. She told me that she knew when she had sexual relations with you, she knew she would get pregnant. But she also knew she wanted me (or shall I say, a child). She told me that you gave her money to have an abortion, but she wanted to have me. She opted not for the abortion as I am here writing you. She also said that your family didn't want to have any contact or relations with her or me. I could understand to some degree—my mom probably was a little crazy then and may have put pressure on you and your family. I am not writing you this letter in hopes of having you be an instant father I never had or to have you fix the past. I am writing you this letter out of curiosity and medical concerns. I would like to know if I look and act like you. My spirit and disposition are nothing like my mother's. Thank God, as He has spared me.

I have taken an active interest in studying nature versus nurture, or shall I say genetics versus environment. I really believe that sometimes genes play a greater part in the people we turn out to be. I say this because my environment and influence were not always the best growing up, but I know that I have turned out far beyond what one's expectations may be. I don't say this to make you feel bad for not being there but rather to commend your side of the genes. For this may have been my saving grace for who I am today, and of course by God's power and all the people He has put into my path along the way.

I would really like to know what you look like. People say I look a lot like my mother or even my grandfather and her dad in Kansas. But there are definite traits that I know do not resemble my mother's side of the family.

I am also very concerned about any medical history, background, or problems that are prevalent in our genes. I take active concern by trying to take care of myself. I have a Master's Degree in Nutrition and am quite aware of diseases and preventative measures.

A little about myself:

I was born on 9/11. That's been an eventful birthday! I have no brothers or sisters, as my mother could not have any other children. I think it was a blessing from God to protect other innocent children, although I didn't think that growing up, as I was always alone. I left my mother and stepdad when I was 13 to live here in Houston, Texas with my grandfather and grandmother, GG. I don't really feel I need to get into all the details of how my mother opted to raise or treat me, but I know I am a better person now because of what I have learned.

I lived with my grandparents until I was 17 years old, at which point I moved out. I started working as a hairdresser at 17 in a salon in a nearby mall. I have now been there 14.5 years and am the top hairdresser. I used my haircutting skills to work my way through college, which took me about 9.5–10 years. Like I said earlier, I now have a Master of Arts degree in nutrition with a minor in business.

I have been very blessed to have been able to do a Work Abroad program in England for six months in 1996. I also studied abroad in Mexico for one month in 2002. All of these things I have accomplished on my own with no help from anyone. I am very self-sufficient, independent, and have never been married or had any kids. I am still working as a hairdresser and am taking a break before I change careers. It's nice to just work and not be running all over the place.

I have always thought about you, wondered about you. I often look at myself in the mirror and try to envision what you would look like. I have polish customers, as I even look at them to see common traits. I even have a polish customer who could pass for a direct relation to me, such as mom, sister, aunt. I find it very intriguing to understand her culture, as she is a direct descendant from Poland. It makes me feel as if I belong somewhere.

I hope you can find it in your heart to contact me, even if you are not my father, just to let me know. If you are, please respond the best way you can—any response would be good.

Sincerely,

Jessica Clancy

May God Bless you

MY "SKI" NOSE

*M*y father returned the call after several weeks and admitted a lady had called him saying she was pregnant after their encounter, only to get into an argument and never talk again. We arranged to meet in person. He came to a local Chili's restaurant at the mall near my job. My friend from work went with me; after all, he was a stranger. As we approached his vehicle and he stepped out, I gasped in delight. "I have your nose," I exclaimed! He chuckled and smiled. I had found a puzzle piece to my existence. I knew in my heart and soul connection he was the one. He had the same wife since the phone call 34 years earlier. They had two boys, which meant I had two younger brothers. The three of us went inside to catch up on the years missed and put the two sides of the story together.

One of the first things he reassured me of was he did not give my mom money to have an abortion as my mom had told me previously. They had only talked by phone afterward. He had mentioned his wife and he had always wanted a daughter. It was as if God placed that desire in their heart, preparing the way of acceptance for me as my life unfolded.

My dad's sons, my half-brothers, thought it would be best to take a DNA test, so my father met me at work a week later as we sat in the parking lot and pressed our individual DNA on a tiny strip of paper pressed into a test tube. The boys never desired a sibling, so it was quite a shock to the rest of the family. They were happy and content, never longing for other siblings. The DNA test came back 99.99987% positive! I was filled with excitement just to see someone who looked like me, who I knew was my flesh and blood.

As a dietitian, I really desired to know of any genetic disease and history I needed to be prepared for. My dad told me his father died at a young age, in his 50s, from heart disease, and high blood pressure was prevalent in the family. The family, although shocked at the new discovery, welcomed me into the harem. My dad came from a very large family. His parents, my grandparents, had ten children, two of whom were deceased. The other family members were aunts and uncles, and most of them were married with kids. One deceased aunt who passed away young in a car accident looked very much like me, which partly caused the family to accept me. It was like God was giving them back a piece of their loved one through our reunion. My family had just multiplied ten-fold, just like the story in Job. God allowed him to lose everything and then blessed him with ten additional siblings. My story was the living Job, and this was only the beginning of God's restoration of my life.

Friends: If you want to find a missing parent, write a letter to introduce yourself. Write the letter in a way that doesn't put pressure or obligation on them to meet your needs. Highlight your achievements and who you are as a person—an individual with a purpose, someone of importance. Even if he/she doesn't find value in who you are, let that person know you are valuable.

Part Three:

BUILDING THE FAMILY
I NEVER HAD

Chapter 14
THE COURTSHIP BEGINS

A VISION FINALLY
COMING TO PASS

*A*dam and I just celebrated our 15th wedding anniversary on an Alaskan cruise. We cruised over the still waters looking at snowy-tipped mountains, creating an adventure to remember with two kids, Grandma, and mother-in-law in tow. I pondered when it all started. Our first date was either when I agreed to go to church with Adam instead of meeting him there or when we bought Phantom of the Opera tickets individually and agreed to go to the show together. Either way, our official date began our history in the making.

I wasn't even sure he liked me or I liked him until a discussion over morning coffee with my friend Denise.

She said sheepishly, "He really likes you."

"What? No, that's not possible," I said. "We are much too different, and what about the age?"

"Really, Jessica! He likes you," she said as she grinned, recognizing the benefit of finding someone who really found interest in me for who I was and not because of what I could do for him or what he needed from me.

Her words ran through my mind as I started to watch his intentions and mannerisms instead of staying in my own bubble.

To test the relationship, we planned a road trip to visit one of my clients who had moved to a suburb just north of Atlanta, Georgia. After many hours driving and watching the sunset, we finally arrived at the first destination Gulf Shores, Alabama. We arrived just before the stroke of midnight, setting the tent up in a minefield of dark trenches barricaded by red tape post-hurricane flood waters a month earlier. Waking in sweltering temps after a sleepless late night, I thought if he could still like me after this arduous adventure, he may be the one. I meandered to the bathroom, carefully trodding through a minefield of red-lined sinkholes. I started to visualize what life could be like if my heart knew he was the one. If one can endure the difficulties of traveling, which is a small glimpse of how one handles adversity and still get along, this might just work.

I also loved to travel, and traveling wasn't always easy! It was in my blood to travel, but as an adult, I was learning to travel to satiate the itch of moving while finding stability and longevity in my career. The most important thing that minimized the anxiety I generated from my childhood was stability and long-term job security with a home base, so traveling became a way to express the steps my forefathers taught me.

From the moment we met, it was like the heaven gates opened and blessings started to pour into my life. I was learning about my dad and his family and discovering my genetic predisposed mannerisms while healing a deep inner wound of alienation. Adam was there as I met my dad, stepmom, brothers, seven other aunts and uncles, and many cousins. My instant family accepted me with love and mercy.

TWO WORLDS COLLIDE

Adam and I decided to introduce our families at a local Texan steakhouse. As we approached the restaurant doors, fresh barbeque-grilled scents of meat and excitement filled the air as the unknown was about to be revealed. Adam's parents were entrepreneurs and had a cafe in a small local historic shopping center established in 1838 near Houston. Many festivals, events, and celebrations would generate a frequent following of liveliness and support family bonding. Early spring in the south, mudbugs or crawfish would emerge from the hidden troughs and make their debut, prompting the crawfish festival, where people boast about sucking their spicy heads. Adams' parents would make the Texas traditional crawfish boil and etouffee as families would come from miles around to be a part of it. Not only did his parents participate in one of the most traditional festivals in the south, but they also bought lit-up mugs, cups, and toys for both kids and parents, and sold anything that glowed to weekend festivals across Texas and Louisiana.

My dad, an entrepreneur himself, designed t-shirts and hats, purchased novelty purses, and Mardi Gras beads, preparing for each weekend festival and selling the flavor of each season. One of the most famous quotes on his t-shirts was, "If I would have known I was going to live this long, I would have taken better care of myself." He and his wife still say this a lot and both laugh at themselves. Festivals included the Rattlesnake festival, Mardi Gras, Crawfish festival, and even the Strawberry festival. One thing about Texan families, they always find a reason to celebrate!

As I listened to them sharing stories of events they worked on, they started to finish each other's sentences. Wait! There was a common denominator. These two families had been crossing paths and eating etouffee and crawfish while sporting the famous crawfish boil shirts and paraphernalia. A memory appeared in my mind as I listened to their jovial laughs and common workspaces. I recalled walking the streets and attending the crawfish festival once in high school. A man was yelling out, "Step up, get your T-shirts here," as they hung from the table and waved like a ripple. I saw a man of his stature standing at a table where the road ended and curved to the left as the finale of the festival's pathway disappeared into the distance. I myself had crossed paths into these two colliding worlds. They knew each other, sharing the same stories, streets, and festivities. Little did they know that our two families would soon become one!

FORGIVENESS LEADS TO
SHOWERING BLESSINGS

As Adam and I studied forgiveness, healing poured into my soul. It was possible to start letting go of my independence and heart to trust someone with my feelings again. The biggest impact of forgiveness starts with letting go of anger and hurt toward people as a result of injury and trauma. Finding relief in forgiveness set my spirit free. It does not mean saying the wounds didn't happen or don't exist, and it can be granted to an offender in several ways. Forgiveness isn't for the offender but for the victim. It doesn't mean forgetting the hurts and letting the relationship continue as if there were no boundaries crossed.

It's releasing that person, setting them free, releasing the past hurts, and redefining new boundaries to protect oneself and one's family. Those boundaries may include dealing with that person in a limited capacity, not letting them into your personal circle. Forgiveness may be given in person or over the phone. If the person is unapproachable, as in my case, or has died, it may be written or released in prayers to Heaven, releasing the person and the hurt to God. Only then can we begin healing and absorb our blessings. If our cups are full of anger, sadness, resentment, revenge, etc., we are blinded from seeing any silver lining or blessings as a result. They roll off our hard shells, unable to be absorbed like a hard, dry, drought-ridden ground. One by one, each person's offense was forgiven, released, and recorded in the Heavens, setting my conscience free and releasing me from the lies of the devil. As I recalled all my offenders, releasing them in forgiveness, God reminded me to not only forgive others but also to forgive myself. As God reminded me of this simple truth, one must remember to forgive others and themselves. Have you received your blessings from releasing your forgiveness lately?

Adam and I knew we wanted to be committed to each other, but I had reservations due to his age and his inopportunity to do the things I thought he wanted to do before getting married. I didn't want to get married to someone who might one day feel they had been cheated in life, to resent the commitment, hard work, and responsibilities of being selfless. I was very guarded and had previously avoided getting married to someone out of fear that I would end up like my mom. Adam assured me he wanted to get married. We had a mutual agreement about God, church, family, our careers, helping others, and even eating vegetables.

A MOMENT OF FAME:
THE LUBY'S TOUR

*A*dam insisted I pack a weekend bag when he picked me up for Sunday church service. After church, we ate at Luby's Cafeteria. As we entered, we saw cameras and a line of people laughing and cracking jokes. We were asked if we would like our picture taken, which could potentially appear in the Luby's cookbook. He looked at my 5'2" self against Adam's tall, thin 6'2" physique and said, "Sure, why not. Feeling exhilaration for a potential two seconds of fame, we agreed and waited our turn.

They asked us to look at each other while they asked us about our own Luby's experiences. I often ate at Luby's for lunch between my client appointments. It was one of the only healthy places to get vegetables in the mall, and besides, they had my favorite dessert, carrot cake. Well, Adam had a noteworthy relationship with his grandma. Between college at A and M and Houston and the surrounding vicinities, he and his grandma would visit all Luby's and eat a cherished meal of either chicken and dumplings or chicken fried steak smothered with southern gravy. Those interviewing us found out Adam was on his own Luby's tour as we laughed and shared a look into each other's souls. Later, we received a picture and a congratulations on our claim to fame on page 50, right across from the sauce recipes. The irony of it all, I don't even know how to make gravy or sauce!

Following the Luby's lunch, Adam drove to Galveston for a surprise getaway. It was a well-thought-out surprise, planned meticulously with all the brilliantly glowing colors of red and green at Moody Gardens. As we walked along the Christmas-themed display of Jesus' birth and the cold brisk winter wind blew off from the ocean waves, Adam got on his knees and presented a ring of commitment under the Festival of Lights as the Angels sang "Oh Holy Night!" At that moment, I knew my life mattered and had meaning as serendipitous tears streamed down my cheeks. He had planned this whole surprise for me, and this very day and moment was even captured by Luby's as an eternal reminder.

A PRINCE ON A QUEST
FOR HIS PRINCESS

The dream of being married was forever on the forefront of my mind; however, the image was different from most young women. The one thing missing was the princess. There was never a costume to try on and pretend to be, never an image to play the most valuable character of the forever fairytale dressed in a sweetheart ball gown lined with layers of tulle, gliding across the floor as if floating. The image was void, as if I was not worthy of this moment in time. As I fought back the childhood feelings of insignificance, I responded, "Yes, Yes, I will!"

Later that evening, Adam shared the story of how his plan of seeking my hand in marriage came to light. He found himself, a city boy, driving down dusty, tree-framed and knobby oak wood-carved picket fences. Stretched barbed wire lined endless country roads as he searched for my newly discovered dad and family. My dad never expected a young man like Adam to appear from over the sloping hill and shady overbrush covering both sides of the street, appearing as a mirage, only to ask for his newfound daughter's hand in marriage.

They both sat in awkward silence, pondering the meaning of such an acquaintance, which neither was expecting. They sat side by side while Adam waited for the right moment to discuss his plan. Awkward for my dad, as he never envisioned walking someone down the aisle and giving her up in marriage. Awkward for Adam, a city boy who had journeyed to an unknown territory in the countryside to meet with a man who was a stranger.

After Adam finished the story, I said, "Oh, but did you ask Abraham?" gingerly reminding him about my neighbors, Lydia and Abraham, who had played a patriarchal role in my life.

Caught off guard, Adam said, "But I asked your dad."

"Yes, but I have known Abraham for 20 years and he mentored me. Let's call them and ask."

So we called to share the good news with Lydia and Abraham.

As Adam shared with them the story and requested my hand in marriage, Lydia squealed in delight and Abraham offered their house and resources for a wedding ceremony. After that call, Adam apologized for his confusion regarding the obligation to call them, but realized that nothing in my life mirrored normalcy. It was ok. Everything was ok as I voiced an answer to the request for commitment in an astounding repetitious "Yes" as the night's moon reflected over the waters. I knew I wanted to be married and have a family but never envisioned what that would look like.

One of Adam's first obstacles pertaining to our relationship and planning the wedding was his family. His family wanted a traditional wedding, even if that meant paying for it. After some wedding planning, we decided to return to the place of engagement. A deluxe but limited guest ceremony package and honeymoon were planned for a carnival cruise adventure leaving out of Galveston. Adam stood up to his parents for the cost-effective decision of paying for the wedding ourselves

Adam and I agreed to plan and pay for the wedding ourselves. I always dreamed of being married and having a family but never had the confidence of what that ceremony would look like. I never had that mirrored in my own life or was taught what the expectations should be. I always knew that it would look like what my fiancé and I could afford, nothing grandiose with artificial expectations. We agreed not to have a big wedding with a lot of debt. In fact, our wedding and the blessings bestowed upon us far exceeded my life's expectations.

His parents agreed to support us with a rehearsal luncheon the day before, with a welcome of our names and best wishes flashing boldly on the city street sign. Our entire wedding party of all 50 guests were included in the adventure of a destination wedding. Never for a moment would I have changed that day's events. Each cruise thereafter is as if living our wedding day and commitment all over again as we share that with our kids and hopefully generations to come.

EMBRACED BY FAMILY
AND THE COMMUNITY
WITH LOVE

We had not one but three marriage ceremony celebrations. My clients wanted to celebrate with us and show their support. As offered, Lydia and Abraham helped plan a blessing ceremony in which I wore the dress again. My friend/coworker Yuan and husband Peter, who was a minister, presented us and blessed our union. They were dear to my heart, as they had been praying for me and helping me walk through the dark shadows before I met Adam. The other celebration was at my dad's. It felt like the entire Polish community was there to support our union. Wait, that community was my genetic bloodline! They all formally welcomed us with open arms and showered us with loving words and acceptance.

> Friends: What traditions, routines, recipes, or habits do you practice that have been passed down from your family? Or are you creating your own new traditions, creating your own legacy as I have done for my family?

Chapter 25
STRUGGLES: FAMILY PLANNING AND INFERTILITY

LEARNING TO TRUST
GOD FOR MIRACLES

*D*uring our first year of marriage, we were able to buy and build our first home. Shortly afterward, we traveled with the church on a mission trip to Honduras. Having experienced the joy of having our first home, we wanted to share that opportunity with others during this mission trip, helping purchase items and build a home for a family. Working with the families and seeing the children reminded me of my yearning for my own children and family. Building relationships with these children as we taught Bible school and the story of Jesus calming the storm and walking on water while gluing blue-dyed macaroni on precut boats kindled my motherly instincts. Coming back from the trip, Adam and I discussed my desire to grow our family with urgency since I had female complications and a previous diagnosis of perimenopause with prescribed progesterone use.

PREGNANCY, LOSS, AND INFERTILITY

Following the trip, we tried to have kids, knowing I was getting older. Shortly afterward, a positive home pregnancy test and an initial doctor appointment confirmed our first child and pregnancy, and we left elated. I started shopping, nesting, and envisioning all the preparations to welcome our first child, who would make us a family instead of a couple. The next follow-up appointment presented us with an ultrasound at six weeks. The sonographer took pictures and started to introduce us to our baby when, suddenly, she got up and left the room. We sat in silence.

The doctor came in to review the baby's positioning and suddenly stated, "There is no heartbeat."

What? We looked at him in disbelief.

"You can either go home and wait to pass the baby, or you can have a medical procedure to remove the dead child," he said.

Images of giving birth to my six-week baby passed through my mind. I couldn't bear to see the baby being expelled into the toilet. That image would certainly haunt my mind forever. We agreed to come back and have the procedure done. My baby boy had an extra set of chromosomes, which made his life not viable. I wept, as part of my inner being was lost with my baby. My husband comforted me as best he could. I longed to have the family I never had, so we tried again and successfully conceived. During our second follow-up and ultrasound, we received the same bad news—no heartbeat. I wept while Adam comforted me. We went through the same process, leaving behind my 13-week baby girl with an extra set of 23 chromosomes, or 69 instead of 46.

Despite the mourning process and the cycle of failed pregnancies, I finally passed my nutrition certification exam after five attempts and obtained my registered dietitian license. Work was always my escape during hard times. This led to transitioning from working at the mall to working at a hospital, with a completely flipped work schedule. It was a very intimidating time, and I was very fearful of failing. Once again,

I ran the hamster race, throwing myself into work to thwart failure and hide how little I really knew about working with computer programs, food production, and memorizing the guidelines for a renal and carbohydrate-counting diet. On top of this, I managed a small sect of employees and found myself in a grand hospital greeting patients each morning with their daily meal requests.

So along with the loss of the babies, moving, a job change, and learning a completely new field, the next few years brought mixed emotions, full of joy and sorrow. But we didn't give up.

CAMPING WAS OUR ESCAPE

My love of nature and seeing God's creation rubbed off on Adam. We started camping and eventually bought a travel trailer and joined a Christian camping club that met monthly. They were older than us and served as mentors. It was like camping with my grandparents again. Camping was a distraction when the relationship became difficult. It was an escape and a way to cope. It was also a time to strengthen our relationship by relieving stress and being close to God in nature while trying to recover from the loss.

THE WRONG DIAGNOSIS

A year passed, along with my next job position. I was working in a Houston county clinic teaching patients about healthy eating and how to manage any nutrition-related disease. Soon afterward, I started having lower abdomen pain and spotting. I mentioned this to my good friend from work, Nurse Tessy. She suggested I see a doctor who specialized in colon problems. When I went for the checkup I was

admitted immediately for observation and was told I possibly had a ruptured cyst. Then I was sent home.

The following week, a colonoscopy found I had a spastic colon. As
the pain continued in intensity, I tried to resume my daily routine. That
morning on the hour-long commute, I barely had the strength. At the
clinic, I lay on the floor in my office, thinking about how things felt as if
they were spinning. Slowly pulling myself up, I staggered into the clinic
manager's office, unable to form any words. My manager got a wheel-
chair and whisked me to triage, stating I had a greenish-gray appearance.
I was advised to go to the nearest ER room, while my in-laws made the
rush-hour trek to rescue me.

We met with the gynecologist who had diagnosed me with a ruptured cyst, and she laid me back on the examination table. The pain was
so tremendous as she offered a hand to help me up and off the table.

"Dear, you are fine," she said. "Just another ruptured cyst."

I asked, "Did you check my urine?" I remembered all the other times
my doctor had checked my urine.

"No, but you can leave your specimen for review," she replied.

As I got redressed and left the office, my specimen remained in the
sink, untouched. I returned home with extreme spastic pains that lasted
into the evening. I would continue to reposition myself as if the pain was
creeping upward, pressing on nerves and sending shooting jolts of pain
down my legs and the entire length of my body. At one point, I got up
and started walking, only to collapse and hit my head on the table. Adam
rushed me to the hospital, grabbing a bucket with a blanket and my few
belongings. I held on to him as he led me to the car.

The ER admitted me right away around midnight. For the first test,
I urinated in a cup and we sat in a cold exam room, awaiting the results.
The doctor entered and said, "You are pregnant!" I wept! I knew immediately what that meant as he walked out, returning a few minutes later. I
had just experienced a ruptured tubal pregnancy. I knew the severity but
was so weak, tired, and distraught from the ordeal, I was almost relieved
just to have a diagnosis.

The operation occurred later that day around 3p.m. After a procedure that should have been only a couple hours, I came to around 11 p.m. I could hear voices murmuring, "Is she alive? Will she make it?" I slowly opened my eyes and saw enumerable people standing over me. The staff thought I would die, as my heart rate dropped to extremely low levels, the blood pressure was hypotensive, and hemoglobin was 4.6 (normal is 10–12) and hematocrit 13.7 (normal 34.9 to 45.5), all of which were life-threatening ranges. They watched, suspecting my vital organs would stop and shut down, but I came to.

They drained almost three liters (coke bottle size) of clotted blood from my abdomen and small-framed body. The pictures taken and later shown to me by the doctor revealed how my entire abdomen cavity filled with blood and the several blood clots formed to create a life-saving cauterization, which helped stop the bleeding. Who really knows how long my internal bleeding prevailed, but I was still alive to share the story

My gynecologist knew of my dark medical past. At the next follow-up appointment, she said, "You should not and cannot have children." Were my three babies now waiting in heaven? What now? How will family planning look? Adoption? What were our options at this point? We didn't have money for in vitro or other fertility treatments. I could hear my mom's words that severed our relationship, "I never thought you would have kids," since she could have no more of her own running through my head like a verbal curse placed over my life.

This was another very traumatic experience, and my vision of not having a family flashed before me. It was devastating as I pondered my life's events that got me to this moment in time. If only I hadn't waited so long to try to have kids. I was mourning the loss of my three babies and wanting nothing more than to have the family I never had and the babies who left me. I felt depressed and withdrawn, adding another layer of trauma and feelings of a broken promise to my dreams.

I went to my doctor upon release from the hospital and asked for antibiotics because I had a cut on my nose from the fall. The doctor took one look at me, tested me for autoimmune diseases, and provided the requested antibiotics. She found I had a slightly normal but low thyroid level, which was treated with meds and a diagnosis of hypothyroidism.

FOURTH TIME WAS
OUR CHARM

One year later, I was pregnant at 37. Although it was a high-risk pregnancy, it was a miracle. I was in my third job, climbing my career ladder and commuting to a South Houston outpatient clinic and the world's renowned trauma hospital, Ben Taub, in Houston's medical center. I had many doctor appointments and was working a second job on weekends to save money, preparing for a three-month maternity leave. I was tired and not sleeping well, and scared every time I went to a doctor's appointment, afraid there would be no heartbeat. As the doctor pressed the ultrasound machine on my belly, my son would look up as if he was saying hello each time and reassuring me everything was as it should be. The doctor tested me again and found I had an autoimmune disease called scleroderma. Because of my high-risk history and age, they had to monitor the pregnancy closely. This lack of sleep, lengthy commute, additional workload, and responsibilities of nesting started to add pressure and strain on our marriage. We continued to go to church and believe in God's plan. Our family and friends supported me on this journey, which did help ease the burden since I was coming from a place of not having family and support during difficult times. However, it still couldn't remove the previous layers of trauma and how I was coping.

We had at least four baby showers with our family, jobs, and camping club grandmas, who even knitted and made homemade quilts and prayer blankets for our son. Others stated they didn't want to plan the shower until we were closer to his due date to ensure everything was ok

The doctor was hoping I could carry him until 38 weeks. My fluid dropped to dangerous levels at about seven months, and there was a mention of inducing earlier than expected. However, by God's grace, my fluid improved. I was able to carry to 39 weeks, and they did a C-section.

Our baby, Beau, was born at six pounds, grunting when he was delivered. As the doctor whisked him away, Adam followed to ensure all was good. When we left the hospital, he was all of five pounds, small enough for Adam to hold in one arm like a football. He was perfect in every way. We must have had 31 guests come to visit and meet him at the hospital, including my dad and newly found family. We were so happy to share him with all of those who had helped pray for his existence.

SEEMINGLY ENDLESS
SLEEPLESS NIGHTS

He was very small and would only eat small amounts. The doctor's prescription: wake and feed the baby every two hours for the first month. This added more stress and lack of sleep to the mix. At one point, the night was broken by Beau's cries of distress. Adam arose in his slumber, still groggy and loosely coherent, got up, and walked past him slightly, leaning his body parallel toward the bassinet, and then continued on his mission to the water closet. Even as the cries lingered through the air, I arose to find the multicolored, thin hospital baby hat had slipped down over his eyes, nose, and mouth as he wrestled to break free. The lackadaisical attempt to provide safety to the newborn instilled a sense of distrust in Adam, as Beau was vulnerable, innocent, and left to fend for himself.

During the following months, Beau had several ear infections and would cry in the middle of the night, preventing us from getting much-needed sleep. The doctors attributed the infections to the daycare he attended. We sought out an in-home licensed daycare provider to minimize the spread of germs and illness. She became a lifesaver for our son and family, building a lasting relationship to this day as she took our son as her own. Beau's nightly whistling and clicking sounds were later diagnosed as Laryngomalacia. This meant the upper flap at the top of his esophagus had not formed all the way and was not properly closing. This complicated things, as it competed for my sleep. These clicking noises were a constant reminder for a dietitian who "knew too much." I would envision the milk draining into his lungs instead of his stomach, leading to a sort of pneumonia or aspiration and a lack of oxygen.

After several rounds of antibiotic treatment for ear infections, Beau was finally approved to have surgery and correct the problem. He had two separate rounds of surgery to place tubes in his ears. The initial surgery helped remedy his issues for the first year until they grew out; the second surgery led to a tonsil and adenoid removal, which seemingly helped correct the problem. The doctors reassured me the multiple rounds of antibiotics over the years did no harm. Today, 11 years later, my son is diagnosed with type 1 diabetes, and I wonder if there is a correlation? Some research indicates truth in the aftermath.[17]

> **Friends: Females, don't wait too long for a family plan if possible. It just makes things more difficult and dangerous.**

---

17   If this chapter touched you and you would like more information to help on your own *Quest*, see page 312, **Food Assistance,** page 312, **Family Support,** and page 315, **WoodsEdge-stream church, prayer.**

Chapter 26
KID AND CONFLICT

LEARNING TO PARENT
WITH SELFLESS LOVE
AND PATIENCE

There was conflict between Adam and me, and I didn't understand why the relationship changed once we had a child. Emotionally, it was very difficult for me to cope; it was probably due in part to post-pregnancy depression, lack of sleep, and living out the memories of lost babies, realizing I had almost died. I always envisioned my husband embracing our new baby with joy and acceptance, helping as needed while supporting my emotional needs. Emotionally, he was withdrawn, and I felt like I was weathering this emotional storm alone.

Later during our marriage workshops, Adam admitted to his disparagement, stating, "After two years of dating and four years of being without children, I was not ready to share Jessica with kids. When we had our son, it was a strain on our relationship. Beau was very sick his first year of life, and I grew weary of doctor visits. After the losses Jessica endured, she was fearful of losing our son and was overprotective of him. This caused division in our relationship. We didn't want to bring a newborn to church and then couldn't bring Beau when he was sick, so we started to get into the habit of not going. This only exacerbated our relationship problems. I wasn't ready for the sacrifice of time, sleep, and energy necessary to raise our son. My wife used to ask me why I loved her. During the hard times, I had difficulty coming up with reasons, so I would think about my commitment to her and say, 'because I choose to.' Once my son grew out of his health problems, we began regularly going back to church and got plugged into a Married with Kids class."

The marriage Bible study classes were like attending a support group, which helped leverage the conflict between us. It helped us understand some of our problems were very common among other married couples with kids. We also recognized some of the conflict was due to our differences in gender, upbringing, outlook on life, and how to handle stress. All of these impacted how we viewed parenting. We were slowly starting to communicate better and recognize those differences. Without our marriage Bible classes, I am not certain we would still be married now. Adams' statement was profound and gave me relief, knowing that we both shared a part in the conflict that arose after our child was born. I was also very encouraged that he recognized his difficulty during this transition. I found comfort in his confession and knew that he loved me and was willing to continue to work on our relationship and family.

INFERTILITY AND
CLOMID SHOTS

Once Beau started school and overcame his illnesses, we decided to try to have our second child, although I didn't enjoy the first pregnancy and pondered on how the next would be. After a year of trying, my doctor suggested a relatively affordable treatment called Clomid, which tells your body to release eggs, increasing fertility and the chance to conceive. It required weekly shots and frequent doctor visits for up to six months. Adam did not like anything medically involved, including needles. Despite my fear of needles going back to getting stitches as a child, I chose to blank out the memory to replace it with the desired outcome of holding another baby. My RN friends at work would administer the weekly Clomid shots.

Adam later expressed he wasn't even certain he wanted another child, and we had more sleepless nights, as before. I felt little empathy from Adam during this time and felt I was enduring this fertility ride all alone. I didn't want to stop at having only one child. I didn't want my only child to grow up alone. When we would cease to exist, there was hope for a sibling to share his life with. Maybe as an adult, they could carry part of the family traditions and legacy together. Finally, we decided another biological pregnancy was a thing of the past and sadly ended the treatments.[18]

> **Friends: Expect changes in your relationship when you have kids. Each person changes the dynamics of the family mold, and each person needs their own time or way to adjust.**

---

18   If this chapter touched you and you would like more information to help on your own *Quest*, see page 312, **Family Support** and page 315, **WoodsEdge-stream church, prayer.**

Chapter 27
BECOMING A FOSTER PARENT

OVERCOMING HURDLES
FROM THE PAST

*G*od was healing our broken relationship, growing our faith as we moved closer to Him and preparing us for our next challenge—adoption. I always had a passion for helping others and giving back, and my background and our church's influence stirred my heart to foster, with the potential of adopting, since we wouldn't be able to have any more biological kids.

Adam and I were mourning the recent loss of his dad to cancer and vowed to always take care of his mom. The loss of his dad made both of us especially emotionally vulnerable when the opportunity at our church arose to become foster parents.

GOD CHANGED HIS HEART

*A*dam wasn't initially in agreement, so I prayed for God to open his heart, to make it his desire as much as it was mine. When our church had its first weekend workshop for foster training, we registered. During that time, I received a message that my grandfather William in Kansas was very ill and would not make it. With the recent loss of Adam's dad and now my grandfather, my son's grandparents, it was equally important to have the closure I needed. I decided at the last minute to take our son and see him and my family. Although I wanted to attend the workshop, I knew it was best for me to say goodbye to my grandfather instead. We decided Adam would go to the workshop without me. This was best because I wanted God to move his heart and make it his decision to get involved, not mine. As he learned about the children and the need for love and help, God softened his heart to help these children and made it his vision equally, and so began our journey as foster parents.

LEAST EXPECTED

*A*fter months of classes and a home inspection, we were rejected by our first agency and not allowed to have any placements. We tried another agency, did more classes, and eventually got the call! Our first placement was two great kids, legally free, which meant ready for adoption. They were a perfect match for our family. We were so excited. We were getting a sibling group: a four-year-old boy and a five-year-old girl. As we nested our home, we realized that our car would not be able to accommodate three car seats, so we bought a bigger car. We prepared rooms for them and put bunk beds in my son's room for him to share with the boy.

As we prepared our hearts and home, we asked questions about how to incorporate our daily routines with the kids. Can the boys share rooms, get dressed together, and have bath time together? It was a big stretch to go from one to three kids, and we were trying to adapt to the change in schedule. "Why yes, of course the boys can be treated equally, just as if the children were your own biologically," we were told. After trying to introduce these kids as our own, the children became very comfortable and wanted to reciprocate their love in the only way they knew, unbeknownst to us.

One day we took them camping. I was getting the boys ready for the day and had undressed my son. I turned around and walked a few steps to get a missing piece of clothing. Suddenly I heard my son yell out, "Hey, he's touching my privates." I quickly turned around in shock and calmly separated the boys and dressed my son. I asked the little boy why he did that and told him it was inappropriate. He said, "Because I love him." I was speechless and my heart was crushed.

I took my son outside with Adam and called our agency to report the incident. They then divulged very important information that was not relayed to us at the time of placement. The children had been exposed to sexual abuse, which was why they were taken from their family and the family rights terminated. When they lived with their aunt, people would go into their rooms with masks on and perform heinous acts on them. There was an investigation, but no evidence found, so the case was closed. This information was supposed to be reported initially but wasn't, even when we asked. Now we understand the general rule of fostering—only take children younger than your biological children. Do not disrupt the birth order. I now understood what that meant the hard way.

RIGHT OR WRONG DECISION?

After 32 long days, the children were moved. We cried and prayed for them and for us. We felt it was our duty to adopt and save them, but how could we at my son's expense? My son was sleeping in our room, and daily activities such as cooking were very difficult because the boy would physically invade my son and his sister's space. Once the children were moved, we felt a sense of guilt and relief. Each move for these kids added another layer of trauma. I felt guilty for giving up on them and not being able to fulfill the commitment. I couldn't understand how God could have allowed this situation for these poor babies. I felt helpless for these kids and realized all I could do was pray for them.

The agency blamed us for the behavior, stating our response to the situation caused the boy to act in this manner, and they closed our home. They stated I specifically needed to get counseling and be released by a professional to foster again. They attributed it to my childhood past. It was true, fostering did resurface some of my hidden memories; however, how would my past cause these children to act out in the only way they knew how to reciprocate love? I agreed to seek professional counseling not because of what they said but because my heart was broken for these kids, my child, and myself. This was a small glimpse into the tragedies these children face in the foster realm.

Our license was put on hold, and it left us devastated, confused, and questioning God's plan for us. We joined a couple of support groups for foster parents at our church as we worked through healing and understanding the system. We found out through our support groups the agency was responsible for reporting such information to us initially. The agency could have been reported as well and may have been trying to protect themselves by labeling us as the cause of the boy's behavior. We didn't realize our foster parental rights and were blinded by the desire to help kids and adopt.

A DAY AT THE PARK

We eventually healed and completed the necessary requests to reopen our license and home. Once again, the dream of moving forward with fostering and adopting left a burning desire in our hearts.

Yet another setback arose when I was attacked at our neighborhood park by two pit bulls. We had walked to the park while my son rode his new bike. As he played on the equipment, I watched while two dogs dug out from under a wrought iron fence. The dog's backyard faced the neighborhood playground encircled by another 12-foot fencing. We were trapped as they marked their territory, and I made watchful eye contact with them. I advised my husband it was time to go, but he dismissed my sense of potential danger. We stayed as the dogs became increasingly agitated by neighboring dogs, the sight of runners, and other people outside of the park's enclosure.

A couple driving by stopped to let their small child play at the park. They weren't living in the community but decided to stop for some playtime. Watching the dogs, I stayed on the elevated landing of the playground equipment with my dog, telling the couple that my docile dog would be an easy target for the dogs' aggression. As we went to leave, the dogs ambushed my dog. My husband, the other visiting father, and a young adult with a tennis racket were all beating and kicking the dogs, grabbing them to distract their locked jaws on my dog. Finally, their clenched teeth let go as I picked up my dog and ushered my son toward the gate to leave the park.

Suddenly, there was a hard impact on the back of my legs as I was slammed to the ground. One dog had my back thigh clenched in his teeth as another dog lunged for my neck, and the loud, continuous honking of a truck horn was all I could hear. All I remember was both dogs coming at me from both sides, laying vulnerable and helpless as if prey to the predator, and wondering if my son would be ok. A different lady appeared standing before me, swooped up her son, and ran away. Later, it was discovered she was one of the owners of the dogs and feared for her and her own son's safety, leaving me helpless on the ground at the mercy of the dogs. The men got the dogs to release their grip on my neck and leg. They tried to block us while someone was screaming, "Get in the truck, get in the truck." I put my son, dog, and myself in the truck bed as the dogs' paws curled around the rim of the bed and their feet tried to push up on the tires. The truck backed up and turned down the street for at least a mile before the dogs retreated.

After calling the police and a quick regrouping, my husband took our dog to the vet, and my best friend Dana took me to urgent care. The marks on my neck were a telltale sign, framing my jugular vein, a red outline of what could have been, and the gash on my leg was too deep for stitches. As I sat on that cold steel table, I couldn't help but think about what would have become of my son and my family if I wasn't spared. That day, I owed my husband, the one-time park visitor, and the truck driver for sparing my life. It was discovered after weeks of an unending headache that the injury was much like whiplash, and I sought medical treatment. The physical pain, extreme exhaustion, and the reminder from others, "you are really lucky to be alive," etched deep into an already wounded psyche, led me to seek mental healing and a safe place to process from Rosalinda Orta, a professional counselor in Houston.

VICTIMIZED

*W*e tried to warn the community about the potential danger at the park on social media. I couldn't bear the thought of another person or child being mauled helplessly. Comments such as, "What did you do to entice the dogs" and several suggestions that it was probably my fault for triggering the dogs made us realize that our community was no longer a safe place to live.

Adam didn't want to move and hoped to have the same stability for our family that he did growing up, but he realized the danger. In trying to protect other families, we pleaded a dangerous dog case with the local county court, which was found to be credible. The owners didn't comply with the requirements after court, and the dogs were later euthanized. It broke my heart that innocent animals had to pay the price for the owners' inadequate care and provision for these creatures. However, we couldn't trust the potential loss of life or allow our son to roam the streets freely on his bike or in the playground.

Shortly afterward, we moved from our dream home, leaving our first family memories behind.[19]

> **Friends: Have you ever felt like a victim, where you were the one blind-sided while doing the right thing?**

---

19   If this chapter touched you and you would like more information to help on your own *Quest*, see page 312, **Counseling** and page 315, **WoodsEdge-stream church, prayer.**

Chapter 18
THE MOVE

EMBRACING CHANGE
AS AN ADVENTURE

We purchased a new house, and a very small part of me was happy to leave the most tragic experiences of fostering behind. However, not really knowing if we could pick up the pieces again in fostering left us apprehensive. We decided to build what we thought would be another dream home. We picked the perfect model, trying to envision adding more space for future children. We sold our house and moved in with my mother-in-law for three months during the build. This gave Adam a chance to create a stronger, more personal relationship with his mom and for God to repair my previous hurts of not experiencing a normal mother-daughter relationship during a new season.

His mom would graciously cook dinner, help us with laundry, and made every effort to make sure we were comfortable and had what we needed, which even included talking about work stresses, budget planning, and home preparation—all the things I had never experienced from a mom. My relationship with Adam seemed much easier without the additional burdens of managing a home and raising a family. We almost felt as if we were back in time, falling in love before kids all over again.

His mom helped watch our son while we monitored the home-building process, which truly spared us from a bad decision. During one of our frequent visits to the home, I noticed a crack going across the foundation and mentioned it to Adam. He had fallen for the community, and we were looking forward to a new beginning. The crack was wider than a Texas pine needle, but Adam said it was fine and dismissed it as one of my "worries," ignoring the potential cost of the mistake to our family. I prayed God would show us the path to take and, if it mattered, send someone to give us the word. I didn't want Adam to blame me for backing out of his dream home purchase.

Without hesitation, I contacted the realtor who sold our home. She referred us to a home surveyor and foundation specialist who met us that following Saturday morning. Upon completing his inspection, he looked us square in the eyes and said, "I don't need to tell you what you already know," motioning to the faulty foundation. "I will email you a report to submit to the home builder; see if you can get your deposit back." He walked away, and we were left standing in dismay. What now? We had no home or place to live?

We called our realtor immediately to let her know the news and requested to see a home in a neighborhood we previously dismissed as being too far and too expensive. Adam had seen pictures of the house a few days earlier, so we were both looking at the same house and didn't realize it. It had actually been for sale several months, and just that morning, the price had dropped to match our price range. The timing was all too perfect as we cast our bid on the house that had two other offers pending.

As we waited for our offer to be accepted, we contacted the home builder and emailed them a copy of the faulty foundation report. They confessed. The reinforced rebar had not been stretched before the concrete dried and before framing. Not only would stretching the rebar cause potential damage to the frame but also to the split porous concrete foundation. They acknowledged their fault and agreed to return our deposit. That day we avoided a costly financial mistake that would have resulted in additional unnecessary strain on our marriage and family. I was thankful the truth was revealed.

> Friends: Build your family/home on a solid foundation! One that can withstand the storms of life.

A MOVE TO FOSTER CHILDREN

The new home had to be relicensed so we could foster again. We humbly contacted our agency and requested the block on our license be lifted, and they came to inspect the new home and interviewed us again. Shortly after our meeting, we learned our home was open again!

In less than two weeks, we received our second foster child placement, a two-year-old little boy who arrived late in the evening. He didn't know who we were or what he did to be moved to our home as he mourned and cried tears, longing for his lost family. My husband and I sat on the floor next to his bed, trying to comfort him as best we could late into the morning hours. The number one rule in fostering is no co-sleeping. We understood the rules clearly as we tried to appease his loss and sadness the best way we could.

He came with few belongings that, of course, did not fit, a bag packed in a moment's notice as we tried to assemble clothes to take him to the doctor the following day. He needed a physical and a golden letter of foster parent release to attend school. When the necessary steps were completed to enroll him in daycare, I scrambled back to work. Exhausted and finding no time for the adjustment, we rushed home to prepare the meals and engage in a new nightly routine, expecting little sleep once again.

As we pulled into our driveway, we saw a brightly colored basket of goods at our front door. A "Moses basket," sponsored by the Moses Closet foster care nonprofit agency. I wept, as I was exhausted and emotionally drained from the last 24 hours and trying to fill this child's needs. The basket had the necessities we so needed—a couple of outfits, sippy cups, pacifiers, and an age-appropriate Bible, among other items. There just wasn't enough time to get the needed items, and not even time for sleep. God knew our needs and the babies' needs, and they were provided in that moment.

He lived with us for 40 beautiful days of camping, going to daycare, studying reading, learning the English language, and getting his teeth fixed, and then he was reunited with his family. It was difficult to have him moved from our care. His little arms reached for me, crying "Mamma," as a child protective services (CPS) representative backed up the car and drove away, reuniting him with his family once again. That image won't erase from my mind. Again, we questioned God and his plan.

Friends: Being a foster parent isn't for everyone, but everyone can do something to help foster parents. Bringing a hot meal, a quick run to the store, and watching a biological child while a parent takes a foster child for their doctor and dentist check-ups are all ways one can help. Take classes to provide respite or babysitting support. It will help lighten another's burden and really make a difference.

MOVING CLOSER
TO SCHOOL

*A*dam mapped the location of the house to the pool and the school as he envisioned the kids' future paths for education and pleasure. The school was just across the pond, and each morning, the kids and parents would come out in droves bearing bikes, scooters, and golf carts or just plain walking with the same objective in mind. Our location was so close that it afforded an opportunity I didn't have growing up—as I rode bikes to school with the kids, especially on the first days of school, field days, or a special parent promotion day like donut day.

Thankfully, the company I worked for as a dietitian prided itself on the importance of work/life balance. It supports an employee being able to work and get their job done while honoring time for special events and kids' schedules. I was able to leave for lunch and take my kids lunch or read books to the class. It was important to me to be engaged in my children's lives, have that connection with their teachers, meet their friends, and let them know how valuable they are, making memories that will carry into their adult lives.

A MOVE TOWARD
COMMUNITY

*I*t didn't take long for us to feel at home. It was evident that the community shared our values, and we felt support and encouragement during our fostering journey. We knew God had brought us here and through the adversity we endured during our home-buying journey. It was all for his greater purpose.

It also brought us closer to church. Separated by a pond and a cross street, our family started riding bikes to church. That helped alleviate one more struggle of getting the kids in the car. Our kids looked forward to riding there, resulting in them looking forward to going to church.

We had less time commuting and more time to be engaged in church activities. One time our kids asked, "Why do we always go to church so much?" We asked them, "Do you want mommy and daddy to get along?" They nodded. "Well, we need Jesus, and Jesus teaches us how to treat others and how to communicate with one another. The more we make mistakes, the more we need the church's teachings to keep us on track." We continued to explain it also helps us be better parents. As the kids pondered why we need church, we crossed over the pond's path and headed home on our bikes that day.[20]

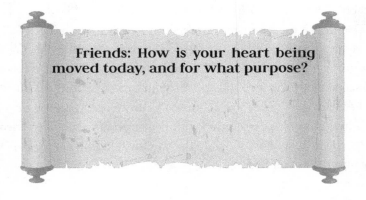

Friends: How is your heart being moved today, and for what purpose?

---

20 If this chapter touched you and you would like more information to help on your own *Quest*, see page 312, **Counseling** and page 313, **Healing Adjustments Chiropractor.**

Chapter 29
AN INTERRACIAL ADOPTION

ENLARGING OUR WORLD,
ENLARGING OUR HEARTS

*W*e remember the day our baby girl was brought home. We had been home less than a week post-vacation and less than a month post-placement when the request for rescue started pouring in. Our caseworker called and said, "We have a sibling pair at the hospital that needs a home, a family tonight."

"OK, really?"

We cautiously asked questions since the child might be quite the opposite of what we expected once the agreement was finalized. We asked the common initial questions: "A boy? A girl? Why are they in foster care?" And of course, age since we knew we couldn't cross birth order. You never truly knew the circumstances until the child was escorted to your door.

"Two boys," she replied," but the only problem is one has a head injury and is just a baby."

"What do you mean?" we asked on speaker phone.

"Well, he will require specialized medical attention and follow-ups, and we don't know the extent of the injuries at this time. The doctors suspect shaken baby syndrome."

The decision left us speechless. How could we say no to these innocent, wounded babies? We knew realistically our marriage, jobs, busy lifestyle, and the needs of our son couldn't survive the demand of helping these children with advanced injuries get well. We received call after call as we asked basic questions for children who had non-basic needs or levels 2, 3, and 4, as their degree of care matched their chances of survival and increased the demand for personal care.

We cried, and our spirits mourned the pain, suffering, and turbulence these babies had succumbed to. Feeling guilty, we promised we would help, all in vain as tiny footprints raced across my mind until the light of dawn appeared when I laid my head to rest.

The next day, weary and guilt-stricken, we both went to work, our minds racing and wondering. Is this a test? Maybe God had a different vision from what we thought it should be.

Once at work, the daily routine fell into place until the phone rang again. Should I answer it? Needing to be strong at work, I watched it ring, reflecting on the previous night's call for help.

As the call concluded, the screen flashed with a voicemail prompt. Picking up the agency's message was, "We have a baby for you. Call us back."

I returned the call, and the caseworker stated, "We have an African American baby less than two years old. She has been sleeping in the CPS office since yesterday, with nowhere to go."

"Oh no, nowhere to go? Let me check with my husband." I hung up the phone, pondering if this could be our baby.

I called Adam immediately and said, "They have a baby. She's been sleeping at the CPS office all night and day. Do you want to foster again?" I asked him.

"Where is she?" he asked.

"At the Office," I replied.

"Everything is full. The foster homes are full, and the hospitals are full. There is no other place for her. The CPS worker has been with her since yesterday at the CPS office," I replied.

It didn't take long for him to respond. "Yes, yes, bring her home. She needs a home!"

I called our caseworker back. She asked again, desperate for this little girl that was removed from her situation by police the night before, pleading her case. "Can you take her?"

We both had agreed. "Yes, yes, we will take her," I replied as excitement and fear welled up inside. I hung up the phone and went to find my boss in the clinic. I explained the situation and asked if I could leave early. Her background was social work, and she understood the situation.

"Yes, Jess. Go. This is the moment you have been waiting and preparing for." she said, giving me her blessing to meet the baby.

Little did we know that early release from work would have been a life-altering, permanently ingrained decision, leaving our family wonderfully imprinted for generations to come. The CPS agent met me at our house, bringing in a car seat and small duffle bag, which, upon review, had clothes too small to wear.

"Where shall I put the sleeping baby?" the agent asked, "in another room?"

"No, no, lay her at my feet so I can watch her," I replied. Thinking I didn't want her to be alarmed when she woke up in another foreign place, adding to her trauma. Page by page, putting ink to paper, I signed the attestation of acceptance, looking up every so often and pondering what brought this precious innocent baby to this place. Suddenly I watched her slowly roll over and lock her innocent yet inquisitive baby-brown eyes with mine. This was our first moment of connection, and our lifelong bond was initiated.

A BABY GIRL AND A
DAD REDEEMED

*A*dam quickly took to the idea of having a daughter and was very protective of her. Any little whimper or sound at night would make him spring up out of bed and check on her. He was all in and took the initiative to help make sure she was safe and comfortable. His help was much appreciated and desired, especially since he could always get back to sleep easier than I could. I could see how much Adam had grown into the father role from our first experience with a newborn, and this only made me love Adam more as I watched him with Abigail and Beau.

Baby Abigail's first court date was three months later, and the CPS agent called to explain the process and situation. Then she boldly asked, "Will you adopt her?"

The caseworker knew more than we did about the situation and was fighting for this baby's rights and future.

"If you can't adopt her, I will plead to have her moved to someone who can."

We had already talked about fostering, with adoption as our primary goal, and had lovingly grown attached to Abigail.

"Yes, we will adopt her!" I responded.

"Ok, great! I will petition on her behalf before the judge," she replied.

After work, we both rushed home to meet with the agent and hear what we thought was the conclusion to Abigail's case. Could it be that easy, all the struggles we had previously endured? Maybe God was turning the table for this baby and us as we awaited the judge's decision. Suddenly the doorbell rang. Adam was holding Abigail in his lap, and I answered the door, welcoming our case worker in. As she turned the corner and Abigail saw her, Abigail responded in an unexpected way. She quickly turned to face Adam and literally began reaching for him, climbing up on him to hold on tight and vying not to be taken by the agent. She was only 18 months old but knew what it meant to be moved. She chose us that day as we all watched in awe with tears welling in our eyes. This baby had made her choice without words, only actions.

THE COURT'S NEW PLAN

The CPS worker stated the judge declined the offer to move toward adoption, and there was an 18-month plan for the family to work to get Abigail back. The room suddenly filled with darkness as a heavy cloud covered our hopefulness of giving this child stability and the permanency we all hoped for.

She was our third and final foster child to date. We had to go through several hurdles over the course of three years to get to that moment. When you foster a child, there are many restrictions. You cannot go anywhere you please and leave the child with anyone, which strains the relationship. Those weekly date nights that the church recommends to maintain a healthy relationship are not possible without support from a licensed person who attends the required curriculum and has a clear background.

Adams' mom was our main support through this process, yet she was not accepting of inter-racial adoption. Her traditional father, though he had previously passed away, was openly opinionated and voiced his beliefs during family dinner gatherings. My mother-in-law never vocalized feelings about us fostering until we were given the opportunity to adopt.

Adam later expressed his reservations about adopting; after all, it was my initial heart's dream to adopt. God spoke to Adam through a song at church, "Spirit Lead Me," sung by the influencer Michael Ketterer. He later stated, "I heard the chorus of others singing, and it reminded me of God's Spirit, leading me to trust in him, and I began to cry. From that moment on, I trusted God to bring us any child that he wanted." However, his mom called to question his decision to move forward. She had concerns related to acceptance of the adopted child and her grandson, trying to protect the children with her ideologies. Adam was unsure whether or not he would have her support in moving forward with the adoption.

His heart was heavy, as well as mine. I didn't want my son to lose his grandma, and I didn't want to lose my mother-in-law's influence. We prayed for the right plan, God's plan, and her heart changed. Our church, our community, my family, and Adams' family celebrated our baby girl four years later when the adoption was finalized.

Adam's mom didn't have any daughters or granddaughters until Abigail joined our family. Each year for Easter Sunday, grandma bought frilly chiffon dresses and hair bows, adorning Abigail with her love, as many people always complimented her on her beauty. Adam could envision God smiling over the display of grandma's love and adoration for Abigail when others commented on her beauty.

During the four-year process, it seemed like everything was against us pursuing adoption. As we completed the steps required by CPS, we always wondered if, at some point, we would lose our daughter, as we had experienced that before. But we remained faithful and prayed for our daughter's case to be concluded, thus granting her the stability she deserved. We were blessed by God when Abigail became a permanent part of our family, and we knew God was saving her for us.[21]

> **Friends: Don't be afraid to stand up for others and pray for them. God will fight the battles and make your path straight. Let Him fight your battles. All we have to do is be humble, follow the right path, and pray for others.**

---

21 If this chapter touched you and you would like more information to help on your own *Quest*, and page 315, **Unwanted Pregnancy and Adoption.**

Chapter 30
WORKING HARD FOR THE MONEY

A GLANCE BACK TO THE
START OF A NEW CAREER

After watching my mom and stepdad's struggle with their finances and lack of stable work or a career, I knew my escape was to learn as much as I could. Education would be the key to opening the gate and escaping the poverty I grew up in. I wanted to change my life and everything I envisioned to create stability and build the family I never had. Building block by block, I clearly navigated through that gate and never looked back. This chapter captures how the career I worked so hard for set the stage for accepting someone into my heart to marry, the idea of having kids, and the impact growing my family had on growing my second career. I also felt it was important to use this platform to inform my friends about the importance of taking care of themselves. Kidney disease is a growing epidemic in part due to the increase of unmanaged, undiagnosed high blood pressure, diabetes, the overuse of "natural" supplements, and poor dietary habits.

DILIGENCE PAYS OFF

*O*always knew being a dietician would never produce an affluent lifestyle, but I was drawn to the field because I liked helping others. My experience with food growing up was modeled by an eating disorder paired with excessive bouts of exercise to correct an eating imbalance. So just like working in the hair industry helped me overcome the childhood pain of being bullied about my own hair and, in return, helping others be beautiful, I wanted to learn more about food to help others eat better and live healthier lives while learning how to eat properly myself.

Breaking through the ceiling of working retail to working in a hospital was a robust move that took lots of courage while swallowing my inadequacies and fear of being found out about how little I knew. At the same time, I hung on to working in the salon on weekends since I wasn't ready to let go of the security of the job and the long-term relationships that were created. The change in careers earned me a lower salary since I was starting over and was the low man on the totem pole. This was another leap of faith with a new house mortgage. Ultimately, working in the hospital would be much more conducive to creating a consistent and reliable schedule and income that would help build a foundation for my family.

No more working nights, holidays, and weekends. It would afford a lifestyle and schedule that would mirror the kids' schedule and allow a parental presence to nurture those relationships. Just to clarify, these were my thoughts following my own childhood experiences and in no way discredits other jobs, schedules, or lifestyles. Each person's brushstrokes and masterpiece will be different and unique to their own gifts, talents, lifestyles, and resources. The main idea is to envision your own family and how to cultivate that in whatever you do.

FINDING THE
RIGHT CAREER

*O*f you want to change your career path, local community colleges offer free skills testing, which is very helpful.

The test helps highlight your strengths and things you like to do and categorizes them into jobs. It identifies the job market demand, salary, and necessary education and skills needed to acquire and qualify for the job or career at hand. For those like me who are not well-versed in the job market and the training requirements the test is completed with the guidance of a school counselor. I also learned that college counselors screen students regarding degrees and career plans to help keep the economy from getting over-saturated with too many people in the same industry.

Take a dietitian, for example. The hospitals and community can only accommodate so many people in the field, so the criteria and testing are quite stringent to manage the demand on society. On the other hand, a truck driver has a very large demand for positions, so the job requirements would bend to fill the need. If you or your child wants to be an astronaut, there may not be much demand in the job market. Don't let a school counselor talk you out of a dream or vision because their school just met their quota and they're trying to deter you from that pathway. I say go for it!

FUTURE PAYMENTS

*O*f you didn't have the opportunity to go to college or had to pay for your own college classes, there are several avenues to take to be successful. For example, many high schools offer classes and training for trade jobs, which include cosmetology, mechanics, welding, and childcare, to list a few. These career paths can be high paying but may not have the insurance, retirement benefits, or a consistent income, unlike working in business or in the medical field. Some high schools even offer college-level classes and credits for students who can excel in their academics. That helps thwart some of the college fees.

If you want to work in the medical field and can get past a fear of needles and blood like I did, there are many starting positions. If you work for a hospital or dialysis company, they may reimburse you for college classes while you work for them. Some job titles may include patient care technician in dialysis, diet technician, food service in a hospital setting, and ultrasound or X-ray technician. Sometimes I wish I had known that information. I could have used the benefit of letting them help me pay for my college education; however, I would never have changed my experiences with wonderful people while cutting hair. As a parent now, I hope I can help my own children have as many life experiences as possible while growing their knowledge and skills. I hope to help guide them to find their strengths and jobs that use those strengths to work in a career they enjoy, thus living a fulfilling life.

GROWING A CAREER

*A*fter working a year as a diet technician—one who manages patients' special diets—and manager of the diet office in a large nonprofit hospital in Houston, it was time to grow my career. I applied for a position in a county clinic teaching special diets to an indigent population.

My husband always laughed as we pondered how I was accepted into the role of teaching diets to a largely Spanish-speaking population when I was never taught Spanish in school. My friends would always say when we traveled abroad, I always found a way to communicate with others without knowing the native language, and this seemed to hold true in my new role. Diet education was taught at a sixth-grade reading level to the patients in either English, Spanish, or Asian language based on the need of the referred patient and may have included interpretation services. In some instances, second- and third-generation families came in to support one another as they desired healthy living. My sense of earlier travels reminded me of the culturally accepted diets I had once consumed as I played out in my mind ways to meet their nutritional needs and preserve their health needs.

Eventually, an opportunity was available to work out of one of the largest trauma hospitals in the Medical Center of Houston associated with the county clinics. A large network of dietitians all worked very closely together in all of the clinics and Houston hospitals as we all learned from each other and worked with families. During this time of growth and building knowledge and connections in my career, I conceived our firstborn son Beau. Our fourth attempt at having a child. The ladies at work all helped welcome him in with a grand party, knowing the difficulty in trying to conceive our child. I felt loved and supported by my own team just as much as our patients felt supported on their journeys, reflected in the large amount of booked return appointments for nutrition counseling at our facilities.

RECONCILING
MOTHERHOOD
AND CAREER

*O*nce our baby was born, I had enough paid time off, including disability, to spend the first three months at home with my baby. My heart was full due to being given the opportunity to bond with our son. The most unusual experience was giving him his first kiss, as I felt like I was invading this foreigner's physical space. The miracle of life helps us understand more about how a supreme being sees us as his own children when we peer into our own children's faces.

When I went back to work, the days seemed longer and the commute farther, and with the added expense of daycare, my heart was stirred to look for a new job closer to home with possibly more income. Our child was getting sicker and sicker from daycare, as all the babies shared the same slobbery toys each day, despite the nightly cleaning regimen, prompting more illness. We suddenly had more time restraints as we consistently cleaned bottles, measured and prefilled with formula, used the supply, and started over again. This continuous cycle of bottle production, changing diapers and soiled outfits, jumbled with a busy work schedule and multiple doctor visits, placed more demands and stress on our seemingly perfect relationship.

OVERLOOKING THE
NEEDLE IN EXCHANGE
FOR FAMILY

The change in our family prompted another job change in a specialized field working with dialysis patients, despite the bond I had created with my fellow peers and patients. I wasn't used to changing jobs as frequently since my eighteen years as a hairdresser, but it was necessary to help relieve some stress on our family and continue to overcome a new degree of fear and intimidation. It was up to me to face my lifelong fear of needles; after all, I wasn't the one performing the needle perforation.

The tour of the clinic had a feeling of familiarity, as it had rows of dialysis chairs and left me with the same sensation of working in the salon. The magnitude of the clinic, with the ability to dialyze up to 300 patients between two days and six shifts, parallel that of the salon that housed up to approximately 29 chairs rotating clients every 30 minutes. It spoke my name as I discussed the potential job role with the hiring manager, swallowing the fear of the unknown and a sense of failure.

At this point, it was all about survival again, survival as a mother, wife, and dietitian, and nothing would hinder me, including fear.

A human resource representative called and said, "The clinic manager and team liked your answers during the interview. The manager would like to extend an offer; you will receive it in your email. Take a look and let us know what you think." His tone came across the phone line raspy and dry, and he hung up. That was it. I was the one chosen out of other candidates for the position. My friend had stated I was the lucky one.

I accepted the offer. After all, it was the increase in salary I was going for to help offset the cost of daycare, and so began my career in dialysis, a specialty in the world of dietetics. The position would require a lot of training and passing a certification exam. I was a nervous wreck. What a leap of faith once again into the unknown, and my whole career and family depended on it. After two strenuous weeks of studying and training, the moment of truth came, the exam. My trainer was so matter-of-fact. Maybe she knew something I didn't. Or maybe she just had faith in me and knew I was ready as she reassured me that seldom do dietitians not pass the exam. In fact, I aced the test despite the deeply rooted fear of failing. As I reflected on the answered prayer and another achievement, I sighed a breath of fresh air.

BALANCING THE SCHEDULE: WORK AND LIFE

This new career direction afforded so many opportunities. Not only did I learn about kidney disease and dialysis—an often confusing and overlooked illness by most doctors, except kidney doctors, of course— but my new job helped me embrace my new family life.

The clinic had up to 300 patients assigned to dialyze at one time. Some came to the clinic multiple times a week, Monday, Wednesday, Friday (MWF) for four hours and one of the three daily shifts, either morning, lunchtime, or afternoon. The other scheduled set of patients followed the same pattern Tuesday, Thursday, and Saturday (TTS). By the state of Texas law, dietitians can only manage a maximum of 125 patients each month unless additional temporary coverage is needed, which means this clinic required more than one dietitian.

The lead dietitian, Sarah, was part of the selection process and chose me as her partner. She taught me many wonderful things about how to build a toolbox of resources and help the patients. Working with her was a wonderful experience as I walked in her shadows of expertise at work and at home. If I had a question about motherhood and my son, who was not yet a year old, I would seek her wisdom. I started to refer to her as Mamacita, and we would chuckle together.

There were many advantages to this new era in addition to the challenge of learning. Work was much closer than driving to south Houston or the medical center, which helped in the early morning chaos of baby duties and transporting to daycare each morning. The schedule was a bit more flexible and not as rigid as the previous schedule starting at 8 a.m. and ending at 5:00 p.m., with the potential to flex the day's schedule as needed to see patients or for pertinent appointments outside of work.

Dialysis patients came in early shifts and the last afternoon shift, so as long as I saw them before they left in the morning and greeted them in the afternoon, the schedule was more fluid. I could leave for a lunch break at various times, which later afforded me the time to meet my son for lunch at school or see one of his many activities. At times I could come to work a bit later and stay later if I read to his class or he had a doctor's appointment. The opportunity to be engaged in his school activities was more available when I began to work one day a week in a new clinic that opened closer to my home.

The company takes pride in its work/life balance motto, almost as if it was a core value. As the dialysis patient population unfortunately grows, so do the clinics, which usually stretch into the communities they serve. A benefit of working in this specialized field, which helped me achieve my family goals, was that it created an environment that focused on work–life balance and flexibility. This helped support my journey through infertility, becoming a licensed foster parent, and finally, in adopting. Are your current career plans and path harnessing or inhabiting a future that will help you build the family you desire?

HEALTHY BENEFITS

ompanies in the field of Dialysis often offer excellent health benefits and place an emphasis on maintenance and encouraging the staff to go to the doctor for their annual checkups, as they know firsthand how important it is. Many preventable conditions lead to kidney disease. First, individuals should always know what their "GFR," or glomerular filtration rate, is. A normal range is above 90, and if it starts to decline and is well-monitored, one may take steps to prevent the decline of the kidneys. A range of less than 60 puts an individual in a state of progressively declining kidney function, which eventually leads to the need for dialysis. Most doctors don't tell patients this until they end up in the emergency room with kidney failure, a GFR of less than 15, a need to dialyze, and a life-changing diagnosis. It's heartbreaking to watch patients being thrown this curveball in life as we help them process, learn, and adapt to the new lifestyle.

What leads to kidney disease? The top causes are uncontrolled blood pressure or hypertension, history of diabetes, genetic kidney disease or kidney abnormalities, exposure to environmental toxins, and in some cases, COVID-19, as there has been an increase since the onset of the virus. Basically, anything the kidneys have to filter over time can cause damage, i.e., unregulated medications, herbs, over-the-counter medications, and popularly used weight loss drugs and substances. Make sure to ask your doctor every year what your GFR number is. Our company understands the importance of this and ensures that its staff has access to preserve their own health in the best way possible.

FAMILY PLANNING

ot only were the health benefits exceptional, but the company also offered adoption and family-planning resources, reimbursements, counseling, etc. We utilized a referral for in-home day-care, which is how we found our lifelong friend and caregiver for our son. She watched him in her home and helped minimize his illnesses. Later, we were able to return the favor in her family's time of need.

STAFFING TRANSITIONS

*D*ietitian positions came and went as other clinics closer to my home had rotations in staffing. I would follow the proper chain of command and share my desire to pursue positions closer to home with my clinic manager, and she would wish me luck. I made several attempts to transfer, but before I could interview or apply for the posted positions, the jobs were filled by those new to the field.

The lead dietitian had, in fact, snagged one of these opportunities, advising me she would be transferring as I sat in her office. My eyes welled up with tears. She knew the heavy demand and workload that came with working in such a big clinic, and now she was leaving. I was speechless and defeated. I loved what I did, but the burnout was real and I would be touted the next stand-alone "Mamacita" for the clinic until the position was filled. Most seasoned dietitians didn't prefer to work in such a big clinic either, leaving the position available for some time.

I learned to cope with the work stresses and denials for transfer by finding refuge in the counselor Rosalinda, whom I met after the dog attack. Her wisdom and advice for coping with work stresses helped me practice breathing techniques and music therapy. So I found it easy to play inspirational Christian music. While performing my charting and work assignments, I would pray and believe the lyrics about how God could move mountains and create a way when none seemed possible.

My position and dedication to the patients and clinic stretched over a period of six years. During the last few years, I also volunteered to work in a brand-new clinic one day a week with hopes of eventually transferring to full time. Once the new clinic was licensed by the state, upper management informed me the clinic hours would be given to another dietitian despite my hard work in helping the team and the clinic pass all of the state's requirements. That was a hard blow, as that clinic was my only chance of being close to home after several thwarted attempts.

When the lead dietitian left, all the patients leaned on my guidance for their monthly labs and diet education, which did not seem to lessen when the new dietitian was hired. This only increased the level of burn-out, and many suggested that my request to transfer was denied because I managed the larger clinic "too well." Finally, at one of our quarterly nutrition meetings, the upper managers encouraged us to challenge our salaries. Many people were not happy with the pay scale increases, and his remedy was that we could do our own research to determine the salary for years of service and expertise that others were getting paid or what is called "market value." If we found our salary was less than the market, we would request a fair market value increase in pay. This was brilliant, so I did my research and found out that the experience and grade of work I was managing were far below the market salary. I wrote a letter directly to these managers. Well, to my dismay, after several requests for approval and follow-up, I received a nominal 0.50 cents per hour increase.

DREAMS REALLY
DO COME TRUE

As I prayed, I started dreaming about driving to the mall, following the same path I had for so many years while cutting hair. I told my friends at work about the dream, and although I was burned out from working in such a large clinic, I just couldn't imagine cutting hair again. Yet the dreams continuously repeated themselves many nights. It was as if I was arguing with God in my sleep, reminding Him about the time, money, and energy invested in my new career. I just couldn't see Him sending me back to the mall to cut hair.

I skimmed the job market, and there was an opportunity for a full-time dietitian at a rehab/nursing home. This was a rare posting since they were usually contracted positions, and thus, I applied!

When I was driving to the interview, it was a déjà vu; no, it was my reoccurring dreams as I saw myself driving the exact path in my dream. God had shown me this was his message of my way out to a new path. I didn't believe it and asked for his reassurance and confirmation when I was offered the salary I initially requested, a fair market value salary, a 22% increase in pay from the dialysis job. All of the signs and confirmations came together in a surreal moment of time as I accepted a new career path once again.

PROVING THE POSITION

Working with elderly patients and those receiving physical therapy while learning about their nutritional needs was quite a different aspect of dietetics. I didn't only learn about their diets but also how to handle the psychological aspects of those with mental decline, such as dementia, Parkinson's, and childlike mannerisms that came with many distractions that kept them from eating. It is often stated we leave the world the way we come in, which is reflected in cyclical periods of advancing age.

Working in the homes of these individuals each day was an adjustment and a change in mindset that stretched over a 24-hour/7 days a week span. The team consisted of 23 managers, all of which rotated on weekends. Over the course of almost two years, the patient population got smaller and staff generally turned over, with most leaving after their first anniversary. In time, the workload got heavier, and the shift stretched into the dusk of night. The increased demands required more time to complete the assessments and fulfill the duties, as the food service department hinged on my licensed credentials as a reminder, hanging in the kitchen.

Increased demands were necessary to prove to corporate management my position was a requirement, and I didn't argue. The increasing responsibilities paired with resistance from management as I advocated for patients and what they needed started to clash with my moral standards. The constant reminder of the virtue I swore on embodied by my signature on the displayed license was a catalyst that prompted yet another job change. As I sojourned the job market, a previous dietitian I had helped in our last common workplace reached out. The company she had started was hiring a dietitian, and she asked if I was interested.

She said, "The clinic is in another town surrounding Houston, and they haven't had their own Dietitian for a while. I know it's far for you, but they will really appreciate you and the skills you bring to the clinic."

As I pondered the position, I thought if I was willing to drive and interview for other jobs in downtown Houston, then driving 49 miles to the country would probably be an easier feat. Once again, the job opportunity was an answer to a prayer, so I applied and was offered the job. I worked with an amazing team and the top-ranked clinic in the entire Houston region. Once I left the nursing home, I found out that four people were hired in order to complete the tasks I used to complete.

TODAY IN DIALYSIS

*O*have the privilege of working in the specialty of dialysis and am very happy and grateful for my company and the clinics I provide dietetic services to. The home clinic assigned to me is actually less than ten miles from my house. I had watched it being built and prayed that someday I could be so blessed to be that close to home. Looking back, I know God was growing my experience and teaching me how to handle difficult conversations while finding my value in the workplace. Sometimes things may not look like we think they should, even in our jobs, but God is always creating a path that has only our name on it, and what He has for us is for us. I can excel in my current job because of what I learned through my other work experiences, as they only made me wiser and more resilient and were the most effective use of my skills. Sometimes things get hard because God is moving us to change, to grow us into another season as He molds us into what He wants us to be. Without the resistance in my other jobs, I would not have left and would not have found the work/life balance, benefits, and salary that God had for my family. I would not have had the opportunity to work with and learn from so many wonderful people.[22]

> **Friends: I have always said if you love what you are doing and helping others career-wise, the money will always follow. In other words, money should not be the focus, but doing what you love and impacting lives should be.**

---

22 If this chapter touched you and you would like more information to help on your own *Quest*, see page 313, **KSBJ Contemporary Christian Music, Streaming, Prayer.**

Chapter 31
GRANDMA: KNOWING
WHERE I CAME FROM

GRANDMA NAMED OLIVE

My grandma Olive recently passed away, and we buried her on 9/11, my birthday. Maybe in a sense, it was her way of saying she would always be with me. I had 49 robust years with her. God must have known how much I needed her as I did my weekly check-ins and talked about the weather in Kansas and Houston, her weekly tea parties and doctor visits, the kids, my job, and my relationships. She always seemed to help me make sense of the senseless. She always knew the past and the things I overcame, so when something else would happen to trigger a previous wound, she was a voice of reason. She helped me understand the past so I could do better, striving each day for the person I hoped to be. She was the only one who always had my back. She was the motherly love and role model I didn't have growing up, the closest thing to "mom" wrapped up in an everlasting love of grandma, poured into the annual reception of cookies and Czech kolaches she baked each holiday for me.

Grandma was funny. She was able to watch my son grow up through his first decade of life. My daughter had enough visits to remember climbing up and sitting on her lap and the stuffed singing turkey we played each Thanksgiving holiday that drove her crazy as the kids giggled and danced.

When Beau was young, he had temper tantrums as any boy would. Grandma would always say my girls never acted like that. I would say, "Grandma, you're absolutely right! Your kids never acted that way because you took them everywhere on the farm and they watched you do all your chores. They watched you cut heads off chickens. Of course, they never acted that way!" She smiled, and we laughed. She was the last extension of my eldest family lineage, someone who loved me dearly, and I miss her deeply.

Losing a loved one is like losing a part of yourself, almost like erasing the past as if it never happened, leaving only memories behind. Fortunately, I have enough of those memories created and stored away, my own private memories with grandma and my family, and she will always live on. One of the last memories was watching her taste the Czech Kolaches the kids and I had made on our last visit.

MY LAST WORDS
TO GRANDMA

*O*always told Grandma I would write a book about my life, and it seemed I recited those chapters each week as I spoke with her.

During grandma's last breath on the phone, I stated, "Grandma, I can't call you anymore, but when I think of you or feel sad or want to share, I will write to talk to you. I promise."

Grandma replied in her ever so soft, shallow breaths, "Ok, I know you will, honey. I love you."

She softly relayed her affirmations with a sense of closure and an acceptance that we would both be ok. It was as if God was showing me in my spirit that it was time to let go of the past and look forward to what God had for me. It was time to heal and continue to move forward to a new horizon. This is what spawned the creation of this story in this season as I continue to move forward in writing and sharing with you and with grandma.

LOOKING BACK AND
LOSING GRANDMA GG

I got the call that Grandma GG wasn't doing well and I needed to come quickly to Oregon to say my last goodbyes. We had just gone to visit in the summer when my son was four years old. Grandma had moved to live with her youngest daughter after her second husband, my grandfather, had passed away.

As I sat at my grandmother's bedside playing songs of worship, I thanked her once again for all the things she had done and the impact she had in changing my life and destiny. I saw some tears stream down her cheeks as she lay speechless and motionless, as if I could feel her say she was sorry. She was sorry she couldn't do more. She didn't have control over our relationship. Her youngest daughter dictated how my grandmother did things. I could see the influence.

Years later while working in the nursing home, it made sense when I had a heart-to-heart discussion with one of the managers. She said that elderly people were afraid of their own kids now. Adult children would take control of their finances and lives, and the elderly had little influence on managing their own lives. I reflected back to the many times grandma would say she was coming to town and I would volunteer to get her at the airport and take her to dinner and then to her daughter Delilah's house. Grandma would always answer sternly, "Oh, I don't know Jessica!"

Everything had to meet Delilah's approval, as she was the gatekeeper to grandma's schedule. If I got lucky, I would get a dinner invite during that week's visit and that was about it. I could see in the tears grandma wished for so much more in our relationship but couldn't give it. Grandma wasn't to blame, and I could feel her love for me expressed in her tears in those last minutes of her life. Moments later, as the harpist played her favorite song of deliverance of being lost and now found, she slowly slipped away to meet our maker.

MY MOM'S GRANDMA

When my grandmother passed away in Kansas, I inherited a box of pictures and letters. One letter in particular was from my mom to her grandmother, who passed away on a trip to Hawaii at a young age. My mother was 16 at the time and reflected on how much her grandma meant to her and how she treasured the relationship. One thing my mother wrote in the letter was as follows:

You always made the best rolls, Kolaches, and buns. People were always calling on you to make them for different functions, public and private. You were going to show me how, but there wasn't time for that either. I'm going to learn how though; I know that mine will never compare with yours, but if someday I am so blessed as to have children and grandchildren, I hope that they can remember me by my baking.

My mother's mom fled the relationship for unknown reasons and moved to Texas, leaving my mom with her dad and younger siblings in Kansas. My mom was the oldest daughter and did not cope well with the separation, as she had to cook and take care of her siblings when her dad worked. It was clear my mom loved and cherished her grandma as much as I did mine. Her grandmother helped fill the void of not having her mother's love and presence.

In the box, I also found a copy of my mother's report card with her dad's, my grandfather, signature. My mother skipped school and had failing grades. Reflecting back on these relics that symbolized that era of my mother's life showed that my mom was deeply saddened by the disruption in her parents' marriage and the loss of her grandmother.

It was evident she was not making good choices despite her own yearning for family. The choices she made outlined in my story clearly reflect that, and now my mother is left divorced and penniless, with possibly little to no retirement and no family connection as she once desired. As you see, my mother is reaping the consequences of the poor choices she made while she was young. Those choices follow us for a lifetime and follow our children's children for their lifetime as we repeat the same patterns.

It saddens me to think she had two paths—one of which was a man who loved her very much and one of temptation. She chose the path of temptation and threw away the potential for a better life, and now she is living out the effects of those choices. It saddens me to think of the loss. We all have a choice, a choice to recognize the weaknesses of our forefathers and a choice to work hard and make things better, believing for a better future and breaking the chains for future generations. We all have a choice to make through awareness and understanding. I chose to break the chains.

Friends: Always be mindful. Your choices today will pave the steps of your future. We have a choice between good and evil, choosing light over darkness.

Chapter 32
CONFESSIONS AND
RESTORATION IN MARRIAGE

CHOOSING A NEW ROAD

The lack of communication and miscommunication between my husband and me created division in our relationship. During several years of Bible studies, we realized how important meaningful discussions were in order for our relationship to thrive. When we were approached by our Bible study leaders and asked to be part of a pilot group to study ReEngage, we felt honored to participate and wanted to take advantage of the opportunity to grow our own marriage and help others.

ReEngage is a biblically based program that brings one closer to God and closer to your spouse, as it focuses on strengthening marriages. It is two parts, teaching individuals to focus on themselves or stay in their own circle and then focuses on simple truths to strengthen the relationship of the couple.

I had no idea what to expect, only that we kept studying other marriage books and the Bible to learn how to follow what Jesus did and how to treat others. This Bible study was different and uncovered the unexpected. I had no idea there was an underlying, deeply rooted sin causing some of the misfires of communication and the culture of our own relationship.

After attending the pilot class, we were fully initiated to lead a small group, one of about six other couples, which constituted the leader's group for the program. As we led each group, it seemed another layer of hurt, discovery, or confession caused us to draw closer to God and each other.

During our second session, I noticed that our relationship wasn't in the right place. My heart was heavy, and I almost felt as if we needed the class more than some of the couples we were leading. I couldn't quite understand what was creating the division in our relationship and felt inadequate in leading others. I continued to pray and ask for God's guidance, as my heart was heavy and guilt-laden. We were co-leading with a couple we had been in Bible studies with for the last three seasons, so it was as if the dissensions in our own marriage were blanketed, riding in their marriage coattails of blessings.

We agreed to lead our own group for a third session. This time was different as a couple who came from another church shared their marriage testimony and then began leading with all of the other leader groups. They had several years' experience working with multiple marriage couples, sharing many stories of redemption, including their own story. I was awe-struck by how God redeemed their marriage and used them to help others.

A PRAYER CALENDAR
THAT CHANGES THINGS

I remember the day one of our fellow small group leaders gave me a prayer calendar from *www.inspiredtoaction.com*, encouraging me to pray for my husband. Our relationship was at one of its lowest points, and I was so hurt and angry and felt like I was living a life full of lies. I accepted her invitation and calendar to pray despite what my feelings and mind were telling me. I asked God to help me pray and restore our relationship. The calendar contained 30 days of words such as Faith, Future, Self-Image, Obedience, Deliverance, Speech, Walk, etc. and a scripture defining each word to pray and meditate on for that specific day. Praying the word and subsequent Bible verse spoke life into my spouse's life.

For example:
- Day 1 "Truth" – And you will know the truth, and the truth will set you free. John 8:32 (ESV).
- Day 2 "Husband" – Husbands love your wives as Christ loved the church and gave himself up for her. Ephesians 5:25 (ESV).

If you desire God's traits for your own husband, you may also make your own prayer calendar. As I prayed each day, begrudgingly trusting the process, I started to see my husband change and confess to the things I was praying for and things I wasn't expecting, as lies were uncovered. He was transforming before my eyes and acknowledging his part in how he had hurt me and wasn't living up to God's plan for his life.

During the week we studied the chapter on emotional intimacy, the kids were home with grandma instead of at the childcare program at church. He asked if we could talk afterward. I agreed. It was common to talk about how our studies influenced us or the group as we would unpack and share our thoughts. One key point discussed in this chapter was "safeguarding your marriage."

He confessed, "I haven't always been faithful to you."

I said, "What?"

Tears welled up in my eyes, and all the broken marriages my mom had created flashed before my eyes as I envisioned a life of lies and imagined the worst. I listened as another voice calmly said, "Listen, don't speak; you have been praying for this."

He said, "I get distracted by pop-up pictures of girls on my phone and have lustful thoughts."

"Whew," I sighed.

I was relieved! I knew men were visually distracted and that ads and Siri could seemingly read our minds, flashing our weaknesses across the phone screen in a moment. I also knew what the Bible said about removing your eye that causes you to sin, as it is better to lose your eye than your soul. This means a lustful thought in our hearts can enter through what we see. He said he wanted me to be his accountability partner to make sure he stayed true to our marriage. I was awestruck as I heard my prayers being recited back to me in confession as I pondered Adam's request.

A flashback took me to a memory as we were driving on the highway to a wedding in Galveston. We were talking and laughing when I noticed an adult billboard. I mentioned how young the girl looked, dressed scantily in exchange for the wrong type of attention. I quietly processed what got that young girl to that place in her life. The next thing we knew, cop lights were on behind us, signaling us to pull over.

As the cop approached us, he said, "Son, did you know you were speeding?"

Adam replied, "No, sir."

The cop asked for his identification and walked back to his car. Adam then stated he was distracted by looking at the board and didn't even realize he was speeding.

Looking back, I should have recognized there was more to that image that met our eyes that day as he confessed his weakness before me and asked me to carry his burden. I advised him to get help in the church, to find someone trained in that sort of thing. I could help by praying for him, I assured him. I knew I couldn't help him. We had already argued when he got defensive when I asked simple questions. I couldn't imagine the increased level of blame or defensiveness that would arise if I asked him what he was looking at on his phone or took his phone to review his history. He assured me he would release this weakness to God and work on it. I dismissed the problem as if it would disappear on its own.

THE NEXT ROUND

Our church continued to lead the ReEngage Bible study, and each August, like clockwork, we would complete the survey and promise to return as leaders. At home, we would study and prepare our sessions each week. We reviewed how we could support the unique needs of our group and agreed on what was safe to reveal about our own marriage and hardships beforehand. During the course, each leader shared their marriage testimonies with the entire group of married couples. You may visit *https://www.woodsedge.org/reengage/* to learn more about ReEngage and the testimonies of what God did in each leader's marriage.

As the season progressed, we found ourselves reviewing the emotional intimacy chapter again. As usual, my heart stirred. Had he made any changes since the last season? I prayed, "God, I need to know. How do I ask for the truth? I knew my husband's demeanor hadn't changed since last season. It was evident that he wasn't always kind, and I often felt he treated me in a demeaning way. So I bravely asked, "What have you done since last season to safeguard our marriage?"

I asked firmly, not sure if I was ready to handle the truth. It was Sunday night, and we both had our busy work schedules and the ReEngage Bible study the following evening. Silence and a pause filled the air as I swallowed and held my breath. Would I be able to handle his revealing comment? Adam said that he had the same problem of being disloyal in our marriage, as he couldn't get past the pop-up images and videos that seemed to find their way to him on his phone and haunt his mind. It was an ongoing problem stemming from the magazines he saw as a young boy.

Initially, he tried to blame me, as he often did. "But you didn't help me when I asked," he reflected.

After another confrontation, I said, "You need help! I've been working on overcoming my own past problems, and you clearly haven't!" I stated in anguish.

I was deeply wounded. He triggered my childhood and a previous offense. He broke my trust in him, and in my mind, everything we did with the church was a fake presentation, taking me back to my parents' false religion. I couldn't believe the same pattern was playing out in my own life after every effort was made to always move forward. Everything seemed to be a constant push and pull. How he would belittle me and discount my opinions and views made more sense. I cried out to God for one of the first times in my life. My mind wanted to tell me to run, run as far as I could and not look back. Once again, it was as if God said, "I got this; trust me!

At this time, I needed safe boundaries for me and the kids. As long as Adam was seeking help and working through his addiction, I was able to trust God's plan. In his humility, Adam admitted to hurting me deeply and continued to reassure me he would change.

GETTING HELP

After a moment's reflection, I said, "You need help. Contact our group leader and make your confession known; seek his advice on the matter. He agreed and contacted him the next day before the group met, putting his pride aside, repenting his sin, and being ready to submit a motion for us to step down as leaders. After Adam had a conversation with our leader, he submitted a token of forgiveness and laid out a path for him to get help through the church. We agreed to lead our group that night, not wanting to let anyone down at the last minute.

Adam quickly found a men's Bible study support group at the church named Band of Brothers, and they were studying a book called *The Freedom Fight*, written by Ted Shimer. As he shared what he was researching, he found out how common this problem actually was and the effect it has on marriages. According to *The Freedom Fight*, the largest pornography website in the world had 42 billion visits in 2019. The United States is the largest consumer of content, with 50% of adult men watching weekly and 25% daily. A 1980s study by Dr. Zillman showed there is a direct correlation between how much pornography is watched and how much a man sees the value of a woman. Adam wasn't alone in this struggle and found comfort in his brotherly support while finding forgiveness and grace through humility.

Another truth Adam realized for himself was reflecting back to what magnified this bad habit—the anonymity and ease of access to the internet through his phone. We had always laughed because he carried a flip phone for many years, well after most people had a smartphone. Only in the last seven years did Adam get a smartphone, which may have contributed to feeding the habit.

We sought marriage counseling at the church, which helped us walk through the hurts and establish our relationship more with God instead of depending on each other to find our worth and satisfaction. We started to learn more about practicing daily habits that draw us closer to God, such as reading the daily Bible verse on the Bible App each day, praying together intentionally, and doing family devotionals and family time at dinner on most evenings. Adam had a new appreciation for family, and I had a new appreciation for the man God was creating him to be.

Adam was growing in God's truth as he was freed from his sins by His blood, and now he finally truly understands what God said in Romans 12:2: "Be not conformed to this world but be transformed by the renewing of your mind." He lives in the light now and has no desire to go back to his old ways. We now have more intimacy as a result of his transformation.

FINDING COMMUNITY
IN REENGAGE

We were so fortunate to be a part of ReEngage, and it has been an honor to work with the leadership couple who started this ministry. Attending ReEngage has helped Adam and me learn more about cultivating a positive marriage, family, and relationships. It has helped us hold a level of accountability and is a constant reminder of seeking God to help lead others in a positive way. As one of our couples commented in the conclusion to one of our sessions, "Thank you for being a living example of continually growing in marriage. You encouraged us to keep working at it because it's worth it!"

LIFELONG HEALING

*A*dam is also working on building other positive habits to help his cup stay full. In addition to seeking God first and attending his Bible study group, he is working on increasing his exercise level to help build positive feelings and endorphins that create a new level of excitement. He has strengthened his bond with godly men from his various Bible study groups, with whom he goes to baseball games and participates in sports such as frisbee golf. He also builds other positive, life-changing habits.

I have sought advice from my counselor, addressing my trust issues and the triggers of trauma from my past that resurfaced during this stressful time. I am sharing my story in hopes of helping other families that may be struggling with this in their own lives. I hope that God can rescue your family as he did mine.[23]

> **Friends: If you are hiding a secret in your marriage, pray and seek God. Follow his timely lead in confession and in asking for forgiveness. It will free your spirit and allow you to advance in your relationship.**

23 If this chapter touched you and you would like more information to help on your own *Quest*, see page 312, **Family Support** and page 315, **WoodsEdge-stream church, prayer.**

Chapter 33
WASTING AWAY

FACING NEW CHALLENGES

*W*e saw the change in Beau but wanted to believe it was a surge of growth. He was eating, drinking, and using the bathroom constantly at an abnormal frequency. Being a dietitian, I saw the early signs a year earlier that may have indicated a food dye allergy or insensitivity to sugar. I disputed with his primary doctor and asked for blood work when he was ten.

It was easily dismissed with a basic panel and, at the time, a normal fasting blood glucose level. During the end of the year as school was winding down for the holidays, Beau had progressed to the regional spelling bee competition representing his elementary school.

As we sat with him to study columns of words, I observed an abnormal cycle of eating, drinking, bathroom breaks, and fluctuating emotions. He had his annual doctor checkup, so I figured I would protest with the doctor to do blood work again; however, we didn't make it that long.

On Monday morning, the weekend after his Marshmello birthday celebration, I went to wake him up for school. He was sleeping, lying on the couch shirtless and blanketless. I couldn't believe what I was seeing. His temples were concave and sunken in, his cheeks squeezed, and his lips turned up as if he was drinking from a straw. His shoulder bones were protruding as if a small shirt stretched over the corners of a hanger, bone by bone of each rib cage revealing itself as if each one was waiting to be counted, knees protruding, pencil-thin legs all bent in a fetal position. How could I have missed this? How did he get so thin and waste away before my eyes? As a dietitian, I knew better, as these were the traits I looked for in my malnourished population. How did this happen before my very own eyes?

I sent him to school that day, went to work, and borrowed a glucometer. I knew I needed to check his blood sugars. He called me as he was leaving school, barely having the energy to peddle his bike home. I could hear the teachers' and kids' voices. "Are you feeling ok?"

"Go home and drink some water and get some rest." The voices echoed in the background.

I left work early and raced to meet him, asking him not to eat until we could check his sugar. As he waited, he fell asleep on the couch. I took the pen and, pop, stuck his finger with the needle, nervously anticipating the truth in that little blood sample. Finally, the glucometer made a sounding alarm, 563! I wept frantically. I knew it would be high, but not like this. My child's fate and future flashed before me. A normal glucose level was 70-180 mg/dl. My husband loaded him in the car as he whimpered," I am bleeding; I am bleeding" when he woke up and saw the remnants of a finger stick. Adam whisked him away, driving somewhere, anywhere, that would take a child at 5 p.m.

I called Adam's mother. I wasn't thinking straight, but I knew I had to be present for the diagnosis. I couldn't leave our daughter, so she picked us up and took us to the hospital, stopping on the way for a burrito bowl and burritos. It was going to be a long night, and I knew from experience the hospital's kitchen would be closed.

It was a long two days at the children's hospital. All the rooms were full except the ICU. During our first night, we slept on the floor and on a little half-reclining chair as we awaited the dawn of a new day, a new life. They had opened the hospital just a few days prior since COVID-19, allowing two parents to be present. I knew what to expect, but I was the brains in the matter. My husband was the student, learning firsthand what Type 1 diabetes was, which requires insulin to eat and live, meal planning, and carb counting to dose the insulin. Thankfully, Adam took the lead on figuring out all the meds and equipment, as I always get lost in names and titles. It all ran together in my head, probably much like the carb counting was for Adam. Beau was all ears as he learned and recited back to the nurses and his class his new destiny.

Our family went home that night, changed for what didn't seem to be the better. We stopped at the store on the way home, trying to figure it all out in what seemed a moment's notice. We read labels and tried meal planning enough to get through the rest of the week. I won't lie; it was another hit on the family as we debated who would take on the new meal planning and the making of all the meals, as time-consuming as it was.

I became the provider at work and home as Adam remorsefully reminded me of my position. He seemed to withdraw initially. Ethan often cried at night, mourning the loss of his independence and the need for someone to prepare his insulin and help prepare breakfast, lunch, and dinner.

The nights were even harder when his blood sugar monitoring system would beep and alert us that his blood sugar had dropped to dangerously low or high numbers that required an intervention. I felt guilty for missing his first night's low blood sugar alert of 67 that night. Thankfully by God's grace, the number rebounded by itself. It was like having a newborn all over again, leaving feelings of being overwhelmed, exhausted, and fearful of what the future held.

Our church group, ReEngage, was praying for us, as we were supposed to present our testimony on the church's stage that night. All the prayers were much needed and felt in every way as God worked out every situation for the best. The stress was insurmountable as we turned to the church. We were already on a waiting list for counseling due to just coming through the difficult season with Adam's repentance and seeking help for ourselves and our marriage.

The counselors helped us work together to tackle the obstacle at hand. We were covered by blankets of prayers and felt God's covering as we slowly worked past the previous triggers from the stress of Beau's childhood illnesses.

AWAITING TEXAS LIONS CAMP

The Texas Lions Camp offers a free camp every summer to kids with disabilities and now includes families. We were told of the resource while in the hospital and were placed on a waiting list to attend.

During Beau's baptism and letter of dedication, a lady stepped forward and suggested the camp, stating her sister had volunteered there. When we relayed we were on a waiting list, she replied, "I will pray with y'all and believe in an invitation to attend."

We patiently waited. Each month I touched base with the camp manager and organizer of the event. She would say the camp was full, but it wasn't a no, just "not yet." Two weeks before the camp, we received a call that they had a spot for us as long as we could submit the daily family temperature screening. We were elated and knew it was an answer to prayer.

The Lion Camp's new experience of taking families this year was brilliant, meeting the needs of limited staff while bringing families together in a fun and carefree environment. The impact they provide in releasing stress and drawing parents and children together in a way that promotes unity is priceless. My son would like to return each year and eventually work there. It was a much-needed break and reprieve during the new onset of this disease. It helped my son and our family process and accept our new normal while engaging with others and not feeling alienated from the external beeping reminders of being different. I would highly suggest the Lions Camp as a resource for families with children who have disabilities. Here is their link to find a location near you:

AMERICAN DIABETES ASSOCIATION AND SIBLINGS

The second resource that we used was the American Diabetes Association (ADA), a non-profit organization that seeks to educate the public about diabetes. Camps are available in most states across the nation. Here is the link to find a camp near you:

https://www. diabetes. org/get-involved/community/camp/find-a-camp

My son and daughter were both able to attend, and he got to meet more kids close to his age with diabetes while learning more about the disease and how to manage it. My daughter got a doll symbolizing a baby with diabetes and is learning about the disease by treating it. She has to give it the correct dosages, manage carb counting with paper cut-out food, and give pretend insulin shots. This helped take her concern and attention off of her brother, allowing him to process his own disease.

Both camps are run almost completely by volunteers, with many adults who once attended as kids. We were so grateful and would like to thank the volunteers for the hard work they do for these kids. We were so grateful to participate in both events as we navigated through the process of this new life with a disability.

NO CARBS CRUISIN'

Finally, when we returned to our normal lives, we went on our Alaskan cruise, twice delayed due to COVID-19. We packed doubles, triples, and quadruples of insulin; alcohol wipes; and alternate diabetes supplies, expecting the worst-case scenario as we set out in faith for the Alaskan frontier. We tried to do our homework ahead of time, applying our carb-counting skills to his units of insulin injections, but it was seemingly impossible to complete the task at hand.

At dinner on the ship, our waiter kindly passed us a menu with an array of delectable cuisine, void of the portions and carb counting necessary for children whose lives depend on such remedies. We asked the managers about the nutritional content of the food. They advised, "Diabetics can control what they eat, while people with allergies can die." This suggested a limitation of sugar or portion control would fix the problem, while only allergy-sensitive foods are listed.

Sadly, this particular response from the cruise industry's misrepresentation and comprehension of type one diabetes commonly mirrors that of society, as they put our fragile kids' lives at risk with each meal. Cruise lines may be walking a fine line of safety with insulin-dependent children/people who suddenly present with confusion and blood sugar in the 300s (normal is 70-180 bg/dl) and may need immediate medical attention to prevent a coma after a simple meal. I hope someday the cruise industry may consider hiring a dietitian to identify portion control and carb counting on the menus. I hope the cruise industry takes a stand to keep these kids/people safe and help them overcome their fears of managing their blood sugars. I hope the kids and parents find refuge in cruising as a means of escape, without adding more trauma. The kids may share their childhood experiences with their own families and generations to come, as each generation passes another in tradition and travel.[24]

> **Friends: Watch your kids and loved ones. If you notice the same abnormally excessive patterns of eating, drinking, bathroom breaks, and weight loss, don't wait to take them for a checkup. Hemoglobin A1C levels should be <7%, so make sure the doctor checks this annually for yourself and those who depend on you.**

24 If this chapter touched you and you would like more information to help on your own *Quest*, see page 313, **JDRF.org-Juvenile Diabetes.**

Chapter 34
HELPING OTHERS CULTIVATE FAMILY

GENERATIONAL CAMPING

My grandparents had an RV and were campers, and I always hoped to go camping when I got older. That was one of my escapes, and once I convinced Adam to camp, that became one of our escapes when things were hard. The white noise of the AC humming at night always put everything to rest and carried me into a deep sleep throughout the night. In fact, we love camping so much that I always try to share it with others. We often take the kids' friends, single moms with their kids in tow, and other family friends. We love to share the great outdoors and help others revel in God's creation while taking time to see and smell the flowers.

BUILDING STRONG FAMILY
TIES WITH RV RENTALS

*S*ince God used camping to bring us closer to Him and I wanted to share it with others, we tried renting our RV during COVID-19. I wish I had time to tell you about all the stories. But it had a significant impact on those who were able to do things with family they couldn't do because of the lockdown. They shared the camping experience and brought their families closer together.

We helped families go to reunions out of state and see family they hadn't seen in years, attend funerals and say goodbye to their loved ones, participate in an annual Jewish celebration with extended family, take their immunity-compromised daughter for her quarterly medical appointments and shots out of state, attend an annual dog fundraiser and dog race, see their sister get married and not miss work because of quarantine coming back from out of state, celebrate Mom's birthday, and move away to college, among many other celebrations. We left a notebook with a letter to all our guests, letting them know how much we hoped God would use our vessel to bless their family experience, and we asked for a letter in return.

LETTER OF LOVE
AND SIMPLICITY

*O*ne young boy celebrated his birthday outside, camping, fishing, riding bikes, and making campfires with his dad. He left a letter behind without his parents' knowledge. He stated how much he enjoyed camping and being outside with the simplicity of life, playing among nature, taking time in the peacefulness and slower pace to celebrate his mom's birthday as he and his dad set a table for a queen, with only the birds' music as a backdrop. He then stated that his family usually flies somewhere and takes big trips, but this trip trumped all of them and was now his favorite by all measures.

I shared the letter with his mom as a buried treasure revealed, and she was unaware of the prize. She acknowledged their family trips were what she considered big trips. They were always very busy ones, and this one was different. She stated they didn't realize how much of an impact the simplicity of being outside camping had influenced and served their family. They vowed to take more time for family by camping again someday.

It was evident God heard all my prayers for our fellow families and friends as He kept them safe and drew them near to him. He had always done the same for me as I found Him in the quietness of nature, in the Garden of Eden.

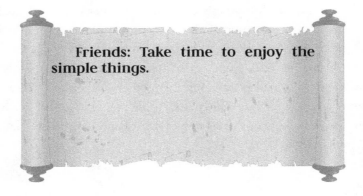

Friends: Take time to enjoy the simple things.

Chapter 35
FORGIVENESS AND
THANKFULNESS

GRANTING FORGIVENESS
TO OTHERS

My counselor, Rosalinda, has always encouraged me to write a book and share my story. As we have worked through healing and understanding, she shared one of her visions with me. She teaches techniques to help people move toward healing and wholeness. One of her visions was a no-send forgiveness letter, which I have outlined below with her permission, of course.

I would like to include my own no-send forgiveness letter as part of my proclamation for those who have hurt me. In this way, I can liberate them and set them free from the hurts I have carried in my life. I hope my proclamation of forgiveness will not only be a release for those who have hurt me but also for myself. I hope it may be an example that you may follow to find your own release, healing, and pathway to God's blessings, as you, too, may be set free from the past.

Keep in mind this is a practical letter to grant forgiveness to those you are unable to talk to for various reasons.

"WORDS GOD GAVE ME FOR NO SEND LETTER" BY ROSALINDA ORTA MA, NCC, LPC-S

Express – convey a thought or feeling in words (definition from Oxford language)

Release – the act of setting free or letting go (Definition from Miriam–Webster. com)

Surrender – to give oneself over to something (Definition from Miriam–Webster. com)

Let Go – allow someone or something to escape or go free (Definition from Oxford language)

Give and Receive Forgiveness

——— > Receive the Blessing

JESSICA'S FORGIVENESS LETTER

EXPRESS

I would like to forgive my mother for the hurts she caused, either through physical, emotional, spiritual, or religious abuse, including those of manipulation, and by carelessly allowing others to hurt me. I realize my mom had her own pain and insecurities that she never resolved in her own life, impacting her ability to protect and defend me. Her mother, my GG, lost her mom in her adolescence, married young, and did the best she could.

I forgive my mother's husbands number two and three for the harm they caused my mind, body, and soul.

I forgive my aunt Delilah. I am sorry I had to come live with you and invade your space. I can only imagine being raised as an only child for many of your early years and then having a young, troubled niece move in. That must have been hard. I forgive you for the quarreling and fighting and dissension between us. I was really hopeful our relationship could have been like our younger pen pal years, as I would cherish having the older sister I always wanted.

I forgive my grandparents in Kansas for not reporting my parents and seeking help to set me free from the oppression I was living in. There were few options in a small town, and reporting them would have removed my grandparents from my life.

I forgive my grandparents in Texas who asked me to move out young, as they did what they could to take care of their daughter (Delilah), my aunt, and my new cousin. I forgive stepdad #3's snake parents for not intervening with their son and addressing his behavior and treatment of an innocent little girl.

I forgive each child in school who made fun of me, my hair, clothes, and body shape or bullied me, especially for instances relating to status and societal class.

I'm also forgiving those who said I would or could never do something, i.e., become a cosmetologist.

I forgive those who hurt my friend in junior high, who participated in a dare because he wanted to fit in and be accepted. I pray for his soul to have peace,

I forgive those who took advantage of my innocence in my teen and younger years.

I forgive my first boyfriend, who physically hurt me, as he had his own childhood pain from his parents' broken relationship that he never worked through. I pray for his soul to have peace.

I forgive my friend Dana for parting ways in Europe and leaving me, as I felt abandoned and isolated, all of which were exasperated by my own childhood traumas.

I forgive my boyfriend and his mother, who wished harm on me. I pray God will reveal his magic to them and rescue them from darkness.

I forgive my husband for not always seeing eye to eye on things or raising kids in the way I think we should, as God helps us to identify our differences and use those as our strengths together, not weaknesses. I also forgive you for not always being honest in our relationship.

Finally, I forgive myself for not always Being God-like and not always making good choices. I forgive myself for not always creating safe boundaries to protect others and myself. I forgive myself for not always being the daughter, granddaughter, wife, mother, and friend that God created me to be.

RELEASE

For each named and unnamed, God knows all who were used in my life to help mold me into who I am now. I pray for each person's soul and their own hurts that they harbor in their hearts and lives. I pray for each person's hurt to be released to you in heaven, as they, too, may find healing and redemption from you. For those who have left this earth, I pray each soul finds rest in the presence and comfort of your light. May this story be a reflection of exoneration and redemption in each person's own lives, with only peace and love abounding

SURRENDER

Lord God, I surrender my body, mind, and life a living sacrifice to you and the plan you have for my life. I surrender each person and the hurts as stated above to you as you redeem each one to be used as part of your purpose and plan for their life. I pray that each hurt may be used to help others and not be made in vain as I give them all back to you.

LET GO

*D*ear God, I pray each named and unnamed person may go forth into their own lives and live the purpose that you may have for them. I pray that you guide them to find their own path and be fruitful in a positive way, as they, too, may overcome and let go of their own past.

GIVE AND RECEIVE FORGIVENESS

*D*ear God, for all those named and unnamed, please grant each one forgiveness and the willingness to overlook their own offenses in their lives. Help them to grant mercy and grace to those who have crossed boundaries and caused harm and grant mercy and grace to themselves for their own mistakes. Dear God, allow me to receive your forgiveness for my own sins and faults. Please draw my attention to those so I can be more like you through your granted forgiveness and correction.

RECEIVE BLESSINGS

*D*ear God, please allow those named and unnamed to receive the blessings you have for them in their own lives. Please allow not only myself but also my husband and kids to receive your blessings for generations to come as you wrap us in your almighty love.

"It's Time for Us to Do Something" by Matthew West

LETTER OF THANKFULNESS

*D*ear God, thank you for all that you have done in my life. Thank you for every obstacle and barrier, as you taught me how to navigate past those experiences.

I am thankful for each person who heard your beckoning call and mentored and believed in me. Those who led by an example that was not afforded by my own family of origin. I will forever be grateful for each of you that played that role.

I am thankful for the person you have made me today, although I am still the vessel being created in the hands of the sculptor. I am still the masterpiece in the hand of the artist, oh God, as you continue to reshape and redefine my life into something beautiful.

Friends: Please feel free to use this prayer of forgiveness as an example for your own healing and setting others free, including yourself.

Chapter 36
THE BLESSING FOR GENERATIONS TO COME

A HOPE AND A PROMISE

We feel called to help others. The stronger our relationship becomes, the more we can do God's work and fulfill his purpose in our lives. The more work and healing God does in breaking generational strongholds, the more we can help our own kids leave a lasting legacy. God has helped me create a family I never had before, for our kids and for their kids and generations to come. And just maybe through adoption, we can help our daughter break strongholds and change her future, the dysfunction of her forefathers that brought her to the system.

FRIENDLY REMINDERS

Mothers, fathers, and grandparents, do your best work each day and know that it is not in vain. Today will be the fruit of tomorrow for your kids and their kids and generations to come. Understand your past and make changes to make each generation better, leaving a legacy stronger than the one before you.

Grandparents, you may not see it, but know that your work is not in vain. It may not look pretty or like what you hoped for, but know it's not in vain, as I am a living example of this and I want to encourage you in strength and love!

Mothers, love your babies more than your mom did. If you don't know how, seek the church or mentors to learn, as I am doing.

Fathers, provide yourself as a living sacrifice to your wife and kids. I promise it will be worth it, and someday you will reap the benefits as you see your legacy return the blessing.

FRUITS OF OUR LABOR

I am so pleased to see some of the fruit of my own labor with my own kids. Am I perfect? No! Is our family perfect? No! But I hope God looks down on me and knows that I am still growing, trying, and learning to do better for generations to come.

I recently discovered a poem my eleven-year-old son wrote in school. With his permission, I wanted to include it. It might influence you in a positive way, as it brought tears to my own eyes.

BEAU'S POEM CALLED
PERSEVERING 5/25/22

I feel like I use this very special word a lot in my life.

I also like using it because it helps me achieve a lot of things.

For example, I play the guitar, and even if I keep messing up, I keep on doing it over and over again until I get it right, and then it sounds amazing and I finally succeed.

I also do Boy Scouts, and when I got Type 1 Diabetes, I thought I could never succeed.

But just a couple weeks back, I reframed my thinking and persevered, so that now I am halfway done with completing the Scout rank!

THE ETERNAL GIFT

One Sunday at church, our family was walking past the outside baptism, charmed by loud clapping and rejoicing as my six-year-old daughter asked, "What is Baptism?"

We explained baptism is a sense of rebirth symbolizing being cleansed of our sins, helping us remember Jesus' death and resurrection. She said, "Oh, I want to get baptized!"

She was at the next baptism celebration, and here is her dedication letter as shared with the church:

"Our daughter witnessed baptism, watching other young children get baptized. As she asked about what baptism was and meant, she declared she wanted to get baptized. Abigail had said her salvation prayer with both of us and has been raised in the church, loves God and Jesus while lovingly calling Him her Father. We are so proud of her decision to declare her love for Jesus in his rebirth with all of you.

But Jesus said, "Let the little children come to me and do not hinder them, for to such belongs the kingdom of Heaven," as He laid his hands on them and walked away. (Mathew 19:14-15)

"We pray many blessings over her life as she continues to seek and find her Father.

Love, Mommy and Daddy"

LAST WORDS OF
ENCOURAGEMENT

*L*oved ones, it will all be worth it. Don't give up, keep working at it with your whole heart, and know that it was worth the journey. Our own brushstrokes aren't painted in vain but will also paint your own beautiful masterpiece for generations to come!

Blessed are the poor in spirit, for theirs is the kingdom of heaven.

Blessed are those who mourn, for they shall be comforted.

Blessed are the meek, for they shall inherit the earth.

Blessed are those who hunger and thirst for righteousness, for they shall be satisfied.

Blessed are the merciful, for they shall find mercy.

Blessed are the pure in heart, for they shall be called sons of God.

Blessed are those who are persecuted for righteousness' sake, for theirs is the kingdom of heaven.

Blessed are you when others revile you and persecute you and utter all kinds of evil against you falsely on my account. Rejoice and be glad, for your reward is great in heaven, for so they persecuted the prophets who were before you. Matthew 5:3-12 (ESV)[25]

> **Friends: Be Strong and Courageous as you continue to seek to understand and do the work of breaking your own chains to the past for your generation, your children's generations, and their children's generations to come.**

25   If this chapter touched you and you would like more information to help on your own *Quest,* see page 314, **Music for the Soul Lessons** and page 315, **WoodsEdge-stream church, prayer.**

Chapter 37
CALL TO ACTION

20 TIPS TO PRACTICE

*I*t was important for me to share my story to help others. To let others who may have had similar experiences see how they can overcome trauma, neglect, and insecurities and succeed in their own personal life's goals with God's help. It is also a reminder to all that if you can help someone else, be the person that others were for me. Be that person that helped me become the person I am today.

These are some main ideas that helped create the person I am today, and I wanted to conclude with some easy takeaways from my testimony.

1. Find Faith and Pray! Prayer changes things.
2. Learn to read and strive to learn; teach your kids to read.
3. Seek mentors and wise counsel. Find those who are successful in their own lives, i.e., a goal of finding a family or families that modeled the family I desired. Welcome constructive criticism.
4. Don't be afraid to dream; set big goals and work hard.
5. Travel. Focus on simple things, nature, and the beauty around you. Seek to learn about other families and their cultures.

6. Don't be afraid to talk about your experiences, good and bad. It is healing and helps you understand them better. If you are able to, speak to a professional counselor or someone you trust.

7. Exercise, or be active, and try to focus on eating healthy foods. Research shows exercise can be like medicine to our minds and may help treat depression and sadness.

8. Accept your body. Don't try to depend on weight loss gimmicks like pills, drinks, and unrealistic cycles of diet plans. If it came in a pill and worked, everybody would be thin.

9. Journal about the experiences that impact you deeply.

10. Don't let others define you, especially through social media.

11. Forgive. This will release you from much pain and help you receive your blessings.

12. Everything happens for a reason, and those experiences can actually help you grow as a person if you allow them to.

13. Help others; give back with your time and resources.

14. Don't set yourself up for disappointment by having unspoken expectations left unfulfilled by others.

15. Learn to create safe boundaries to protect yourself and your family.

16. Practice being appreciative and grateful each day.

17. Be empathetic. Seek to understand others.

18. We all have a purpose. Finding and living out your purpose will be healing and most rewarding.

19. Don't accept no for an answer unless you have exhausted all resources and avenues. And even in doing so, the no will more likely become a yes!

20. Count your miracles. The events that happen to us and influence us deeply may actually be miracles in disguise.

PURPOSED FOR
HIS FUTURE

*J*essica: In summary, through all my hard times and losses, it was as if I could hear God saying in my heart, "But I have a purpose for you."

For I know the plans I have for you, declares the Lord. Plans to prosper you and not harm you, plans to give you hope and a future, declares the Lord.

Jeremiah 29:11 (NIV)

As I continuously pray to God daily, reveal yourself and the plans you have for me and let my life not be in vain. This story is about how my faith brought me through difficult times and what I desire to share to help others. It is about the quest for the family I never had growing up!

*A*dam: Through the ups and downs, my wife and I have come to realize that we can trust God with our marriage. The Lord is righteous in all his ways and faithful in all He does. Psalm 145:17 (NIV)

I look forward to walking with Jessica and seeing how God uses us through this story to help others.

WHO AM I? WHO ARE WE?

*L*ooking back and moving forward, my past does not define me. Our past does not define us. It is only part of the journey if we allow it to stretch us and grow us. I am not defined by the things that happened to me. I am defined as a child of God. My Father is in the heavens and was brought to this earth to save me. He walks with me, He talks with me, He carries me through good and bad, growing me as He reveals his wisdom and plans for my life. Your Father is waiting for you to walk with him, speak with him, and seek his wise counsel during this life's journey.

Just as your past does not define you, remember to love others and not make judgments on their past or mishaps. Remember to pray for others, releasing them to God. Just as you would want others to grant you grace, live by the same grace God has given you. Seek God's grace. You don't have to stay in the darkness of your past-hiding. You can step into the light, be exposed, and be redeemed.

FAMILY ALL AROUND US

One may say, but I don't have a family, or my family does not look like the one you share in your story. Not everyone is destined to be married, and no one has a perfect family or marriage. Family may not be inclusive of genealogy and genetic ancestors. Family may have many different and implausible appearances, unique to its own. One thing we know for sure is we are all human, tied together in our father's likeness. We all have kindred hearts drawn to each other, drawn to community, as we were not made to be alone. Community can be found through neighbors, home groups, Bible study groups, and even the body of the church as we journey in the seasons of life together. As we live and walk side by side, closely knit to others as if one family in community, we can embrace one another's joys, sorrow, tears, and achievements while lifting others up. In doing so, we can make this world a better place as we move closer to our reward, our castle in Heaven, and become heirs to the Most High King. I can only imagine what that day will be like.

GO FORTH AND GIFT IT!

If you enjoyed reading this story and felt that it helped you in any way, please feel free to gift it to someone who may benefit from it. Gift it to someone who may share the same struggles and may not be able to purchase it for themselves. Gift it to a child who is aging out of the government system with no parents. Gift it to someone who questions why they were born and if it really matters, soon to be lost in despair. Gift it to someone who always asks, "Why me, Lord?" Gift it to a single mom, domestic abuse survivor, widow, or grandparents who are doing their best to raise their kids on their own. Gift it to someone whose marriage needs to be restored. Gift it to a man, husband, father, or brother who has suffered from abuse and or experiences it through the lady in his life. Gift it to someone who may be looking for their own purpose and wants to help others but aren't sure where to start, helping them mentor and provide guidance.

Why gift it? Because it matters. They matter. We all matter. Make sure to sign and date it so others will know they are loved and matter as you go forth and gift it!

For we are God's handiwork, created in Christ Jesus to do good works, which God prepared in advance for us to do (Ephesians 2:10 NIV).

The Reward

Heirs to the King

Prayer of Reformation
for Kindred Hearts

Cherished Brothers and Sisters,

First of all, I want to take this opportunity to thank each of you for reading my story and sharing it with others. I want to pray with you and for you.

Dear Abba, Father God,

You know this person standing before you; please hear my prayer for them as you begin a work in their lives. Please meet with them in this moment and let them see you, revealing your love for them. Remove the veil from their eyes and allow them to see you in a more intimate way as you bring healing and blessing into their lives and the lives of those around them. No matter the hurt and level of despair, Lord, bring help in a time of need. Reveal yourself through dreams and visions, walking them into the purpose and plans you have for their lives.

Our Protector, provide a blanket of protection over their lives and their loved ones as they move forward in fulfilling the purpose you have destined for their lives.

Our Counselor, speak to them as they seek you, provide guidance, and make reason when there is none. Speak through them as they go forth and help others, sharing their own stories. Help them to find their voice as He did for me.

Our Saviour, as you hold our souls in your loving arms, help us to trust you no matter the outcome.

Our Provider, as you meet our spiritual and physical needs. We humbly ask you to bless this person, giving them and their families favor for generations to come.

If you have never met with Jesus in a personal way but feel his beckoning for you at this moment in time . . . if you feel Jesus is calling you, speaking directly to your heart, please feel free to reach up to Him and repent of the way you have lived your life, humbly reciting the error of your ways and asking Him to forgive you. Humbly ask Jesus to reside in your heart as your Saviour, Father, Redeemer, and Counselor, inviting Him to stay with you forever as you reciprocate his love and respond to his call.

Meditate on this:
And we know that in all things God works for the good of those who love Him, who have been called according to his purpose.
Romans 8:28 NIV

In Jesus' Name, the Author of My Story

With Grace and Love,

Jessica Clancy

Appendices

ACKNOWLEDGMENTS

*O*n loving memory of my grandparents, as I don't know where I would be without your guidance and love.

This is for my church elders and body of the church, friends, managers, clients, and teachers, as there are too many names to list. I am so grateful for those who impacted my life, stepping in and serving as mentors and helping to guide me on the right path. I will forever be grateful, as you served the role of family for me when I needed you most. I truly wouldn't be the person I am today without your love and the confidence you gave me to move forward. You always believed in me when I couldn't believe in myself. Your prayers were heard and coveted.

To the babysitting family in Zion, Illinois, for giving the gift of life and a blanket of protection to weather the storm. If you are reading this, I want to say thank you from the bottom of my heart. I hope I can meet you someday to extend my thanks in a hug, as I have often thought of your gift and how God used you in that moment of time.

To Tod, Lorri, Ron, and Peggy, who both mirrored patriarchal roles in my life when I needed it most.

To my family now, as I took time to write this book, reliving many of the past hurts and feelings as they were brought back to the surface and shared again. For the sacrifice of time in hopes of planting seeds to help others.

To my Mother-in-law, who has been more of a mom to me, helping us in many ways and providing family support I never had.

To my first editor, Wendy, who believed in my story and motivated me to keep writing.

To all my friends, including Lorri, Nedra, Patty Cake, my camping enthusiast; Cat, my coworker; Dana and Shawn, my best friends, who read my first raw chapters and encouraged me to keep writing

To my hairdresser, Abel, at Haircuts by Abel, who told me to keep my eyes on Jesus and remember it's God's story, not mine, and led me to the castle: Mike Neumann at Newman's castle, who gave me rights to use it for my cover.

For Carlos, my photographer at UnoCinco.com: # 713-259-6381 and email *unocincoxv@gmail.com* or *carlos@unocinco.com*.

To my friend Charlene, who helped me brainstorm my chapter summaries to narrate my book on social media.

To AshleyRmarketing for creating my beautiful website and having patience with my repetitive questions as I tried to figure out the IT world

Thank you to my publishing company, Equip Press, which believed in my story as much as I did and agreed to publish it.

Special thanks to my artist and friend who created my chapter summaries and YouTube page, as he made my book come alive with animation, music, and feeling. Suman Dutta, Animator and Cartoonist from Kolkata, India

Otherwise known as "Croods" on Fiverr.

Please like and follow him on Instagram, Facebook, and YouTube to see his work

ABOUT THE AUTHOR

Jessica Clancy is a native Texan who began working professionally at the age of 17 as a cosmetologist. She worked for 18 years while completing her BS in Nutrition at the University of Houston. She worked on Oxford Street in London through BUNAC, British Universities of North America Club in 1996, and traveled to 17 European countries.

She completed her MA in Nutrition with a business minor from Sam Houston State University in 2002, studying business in Pueblo, Mexico. Jessica and Adam were licensed foster parents for five years. Jessica has been a registered dietitian since 2008. She cherishes church, family time, traveling, and camping.

Website: JessicaClancyPerseveres.com
Instagram: Jessica Clancy Perseveres
Facebook: Jessica Clancy Perseveres
Email: *JessicaClancyPerseveres@gmail.com*
YouTube: Jessica Clancy Perseveres or @jessicaclancy9795

To inquire about booking a speaking engagement, podcast, Zoom, or any other special event, please make your request at one of the social media sites listed above. If any part of my book helped you, please comment on my website so I may share your victories with others as well.

INDEX OF RESOURCES
AND NUMBERS

BULLYING:
Stopbullying.Gov

BUNAC
Work Abroad and Travel in Canada, the UK, the US, Australia, and New Zealand
Available:
UK 0333-014-8484
US 1-332-330-3222
Australia 61-3-9119-5252
New Zealand 64-9-883-2525
https://bunac.org/contact#

COUNSELING:
Kingdom Dwelling Christian Counseling
In-office and video sessions available
Contact: *https://kingdomdwellingcc.com/contact*
Phone # 281-826-9777
https://www.therapyportal.com/p/kdcc/

FOOD ASSISTANCE:
Meals on Wheels: delivers warm meals to citizens who can no longer cook for themselves *https://www.mealsonwheelsamerica.org/*
Feeding America *https://www.feedingamerica.org/*
Feeding Children
Phone number 1-800-627-4556
https://partners.feedthechildren.org/Home/ContactUs

FAMILY SUPPORT:
Focus on the Family

8605 Explorer Drive Colorado Springs, CO 80920-1051
Help@focusonthefamily.com
1-800-A-FAMILY (232-6459)
https://www.focusonthefamily.com/

HEALING ADJUSTMENTS CHIROPRACTOR:
North Houston Spine and Sports Medicine
Dr. Timothy Runnels
5643 Treaschwig Rd
Spring, Texas 77373
info@northhoustonspine.com
#281-443-1287

HOUSING, FOOD, FAMILY SUPPORT:
https://www.catholiccharitiesusa.org/find-help/

JDRF.ORG
Global Organization that provides research and funding for Type 1 Diabetes
If you know someone affected by Type 1 Diabetes and need support or would like to sponsor this organization, contact them at:
1-800-533-CURE (2873)
info@jdrf.org
https://www.jdrf.org/contact-us/k

KSBJ CONTEMPORARY CHRISTIAN MUSIC, STREAMING, AND PRAYER:
KSBJ 89.3 God listens (Houston)
https://player.streamguys.com/ksbj/sgplayer/player.php

KSBJ PRAYER AND CARE LINE, 24 HOURS A DAY
281-652-5555
Text 893893

89.3KSBJ On air now; listen live

Free music streaming

LIVING PROOF MINISTRIES:
Beth Moore's women's ministry through which she has written several best-selling Bible studies and books
1-888-700-1999
https://www.lproof.org/contact

MUSIC FOR THE SOUL:
Feel free to contact Nina Cook for private musical training and healing through music. She specializes in Vocals, Guitar, and Piano lessons
Lessons available by zoom or in person (Houston, Texas)
Contact info:
Email: *rainne12@gmail.com*
Instagram: nina_vocals

NATIONAL DOMESTIC VIOLENCE HOTLINE HOURS: 24/7
Languages: English, Spanish, and 200+ through interpretation service
800-799-7233
SMS: Text START to 88788
Chat: *https://chat.thehotline.us/v2/index.html?dkey=783ea42e-3aa0-42f4-9899-ad886e4995b4&skill=g1b*

PREGNANCY PREVENTION:
https://www.plannedparenthood.org/learn/birth-control

SAFE HORIZON.ORG
Being stalked and need help? Need a safe place?
24 hours a day 1-866-689-HELP (4357)

AND INTERNET SECURITY – IS SOMEONE MONITORING YOU?
800-799-SAFE (7233)

SUICIDE HOTLINE 988
Feeling hopeless, call 1-800-273-8255 (English)
Desesperanzado? 1-888-628-9454 (Espanol)
Deaf/Hard of Hearing 1-800-799-4889
mailto:Help@focusonthefamily.com

UNWANTED PREGNANCY AND ADOPTION
Phone number:1-800-ADOPTION
https://www.americanadoptions.com/pregnant/
cps-involvement-placing-child-for-adoption
https://www.depelchin.org/ (Texas)

WOODSEDGE COMMUNITY CHURCH:
Watch the latest Service at woodsedge.org
281-364-0415
Info@woodsedge.org
https://www.woodsedge.org/

TO HEAR JESSICA AND ADAM'S MARRIAGE TESTIMONY, VISIT
https://m.soundcloud.com/woodsedgecommunitychurch/reengage-mar-
riage-story-adam-jessica-9-12-22?in=woodsedgecommunitychurch%2F-
sets%2Fre-engage-fall-2022

NEED PRAYER?
Our church would love to pray with you. Simply make your request known and submit it via the following prayer link:
https://woodsedge.formstack.com/forms/prayer_request

When you watch the WoodsEdge church service online, there is a live host ready to answer any questions or concerns (CST)

These resources serve as a starting point in finding help. I cannot speak directly to what they can or cannot do. I have heard and seen people benefiting from them, and I hope they can help you as well.

INDEX OF CHARACTERS

PARENTS AND SIBLINGS:

- Jo – biological mom: Meaning fun-loving, free spirit
- Clancy – dad by marriage birthright name
- #2 stepdad – mean man
- #3 stepdad – brute or snake: Meaning wild or savage, also identified as snake, charmer, king
- Grace – neighbor who moved from North Carolina to Kansas and lived with us
- Bethany – Grace's daughter, my friend and classmate
- Warrick "ski" – Biological dad whom I found in my 30s
- Stepmom married to Warrick and two sons/my brothers

GRANDPARENTS:

- GG – grandma in Texas
- Frank – grandpa in Texas
- Delilah – daughter to GG and Frank. Aunt who was three years older in age and two years by school grade
- Olive – grandma by marriage in Kansas, peacemaker William – grandpa in Kansas

NEIGHBORS TO GRANDPARENTS, FIRST HOUSE:

- Elizabeth – oath or fullness of God
- Noah – Peaceful rest

NEIGHBORS TO GRANDPARENTS, SECOND HOUSE:

- Lydia – a standing pool
- Abraham – Father to multitudes

SCHOOL FRIENDS

- Abbey – One of three band friends who had a boyfriend in football
- Brianna – band friend who had a scooter
- Cate – band friend who had lively parents
- Dina – friend who had a single mom
- Linda – friend who had divorced parents
- Valencia – friend from high school. Went dancing together and were roommates. Name means strength and vigor. AKA annual festival held in Spain
- Dana – Cosmetology/High school/Lifelong friend, traveled Europe together. Lifelong friends
- Deane – aunt's friend in high school who attended cosmetology

SALON FRIENDS/COWORKER:

- Sheila – Salon/best friend, very straightforward, became my workout buddy and met at high school cosmetology
- Tabitha – Salon/best friend who was very artistic and helped

with decorating my apartment and my wedding
- Rona – Salon friend who invited me to visit her church, New Jerusalem Whole Truth Church in Humble, Texas

CAMBODIAN/BRITISH/ GREEK/AUSTRIAN FRIENDS:

- Sharon – Cambodian workout friend who shared her family's culture with me
- Wanda – my British client's mom who invited us to her home in Chelmsford, England
- Andy – Greek friend of my client who allowed Dana and me to stay at his flat in Athens
- Greg – my client who invited us to stay with his friend and family in Thessaloniki, Greece
- Alex –Austrian friend I met in Houston at the youth hostel and stayed with at his flat

ADDITIONAL CHARACTERS:

- Bermuda landlord – who was protective of us when mom dated Brute
- Ramona – apartment neighbor during my lonely adult years in Houston. Meaning wise savior or protector
- Jerry – bodybuilder from gym
- Charles – first boyfriend with apartment
- Dan – second boyfriend, soccer player
- Walker – third boyfriend whom I have known since I was 18 years old. Dated off and on
- Brad – temporary roommate who didn't pay his portion of the rent
- Denise – friend who invited me to church, on a mission trip, and to live with her

- Rosalinda – counselor who advised me to write a book, confirming a previous prophesy
- Sharon – dietitian friend who mentored me in my first job working with end-stage renal dialysis

MY FAMILY

- Adam – met in singles Bible study, Married
- Beau – our biological son
- Abigail – our adopted daughter

INDEX OF MIRACLES

Think about your own lives and count the perils and hardships God rescued you from. Maybe, just maybe, those moments of despair, either in the past or currently, are your own miracles. When feeling despair, look back and count all those times and experiences God rescued you from. Write them down one by one, and remember how valuable you are and what He has done. I have 37 examples of miracles here in each chapter. Although many of them may seem dire, I count them as my miracles, as God increased my faith in Him and gave me strength to keep putting one foot in front of the other and persevere.

Printed in the USA
CPSIA information can be obtained
at www.ICGtesting.com
LVHW041747260823
756387LV00003B/591